"A vivid portrait of personal and profess[...] gifts made his purposeful life in the law m[...] represented, and Vermont"

—Jeff Amestoy, former Vermont Attorney General and Chief Justice of the Vermont Supreme Court and author of *Slavish Shore: The Odyssey of Richard Henry Dana Jr.*

"Over the past half-century, Kim Cheney has been known in Vermont as one of the smartest and most influential lawyers in the state. Now we know from his autobiography that he is also one of the wisest. He has written a fascinating and introspective memoir of his public life (with humble and poignant glimpses into his private life. As a private practitioner his heart and mind were always focused on necessary reform of our laws and improvement of the public weal. Most notable are Cheney's accounts of corruption within the state's police forces and his efforts to clean it up."

—Bernie Lambek, lawyer in Montpelier, Vermont and author of *Uncivil Liberties: A Novel*

"Kim Cheney's memoir is an engaging story and familiar and illuminating. Personal and poignant, the memoir reveals how a child of relative comfort and privilege grows up to dedicate his life to public service and the pursuit of justice. With occasional humorous anecdotes and insights, Cheney captures the nuance and human complexities of the law. His story is also, importantly, one that will appeal to young people of any calling, seeking a career by taking on new challenges with no idea how to do a job, working hard to learn it, and then doing it very well, This is a great read for anyone interested in the evolution of the legal community in Vermont."

—Robert Sand, former Windsor County State's Attorney, Founding Director, Vermont Law School Center for Justice Reform

"If Atticus Finch had written a memoir of his complete life as a country lawyer, I believe it would have read much like Kim Cheney's. Kim's book is an honest account, sometimes painfully honest, of his personal and professional life. But as one traverses the different stages of his life, you cannot help but recall and reflect on similar stages in your own life; a blessing in disguise. It is a well written, good read. It is a good story about a good man."

—M. Jerome Diamond, former Windham County State's Attorney and Vermont Attorney General

"The early 1970s were rough on Vermont's criminal justice system. Central to that era was the long criminal career of Paul Lawrence, the bad cop who, while working as an undercover narcotics agent for state and local police, framed more than 100 young Vermonters on drug charges. Lawrence's depredations managed to contaminate the whole justice system — state police and several prosecutors and judges — and his crimes and the resulting turmoil put Vermont on front pages across the land.

But he also offers a striking assessment of what became known as the "Paul Lawrence Affair." Lawrence's crimes (the bad cop who, while working as an undercover narcotics agent for state and local police, framed more than 100 young Vermonters on drug charges) were committed long ago, but Cheney's book is an important reminder of how things can go wrong The author is as tough on himself as he is on other players who were far more involved in that affair. That's a quality that is rare and praiseworthy in the literature of public life."

—Hamilton E. Davis, author
Mocking Justice: America's Biggest Drug Scandal

"Memoirs of important Vermonters are rare, but what there is rarely fails to prick our imaginations and appreciation for the lives they led. Kim Cheney's *A Lawyer's Life to Live* is an intimate account of this former Vermont Attorney General's life and career in the law. It illuminates a period of our history that is just over the horizon of memory with wit and candor, including a new perspective on the Paul Lawrence scandal of the mid-1970s where a rogue law enforcement officer falsified drug arrests in dozens of cases. There should be a law that requires retired officials to write their stories to preserve them. Kim Cheney's book now joins the memoirs of Deane Davis, Peter Langrock, and Lucius Chittenden in the pantheon of classic works on the history of Vermont and its laws."

—Paul Gilles, author of
The Law Of The Hills: A Judicial History of Vermont

"As I read Kim's memoir I found an engaging first-hand account of the history of Vermont's local government and law enforcement. In my career as a teacher, I encountered many young people wondering who they would be and how they could make a difference in the world. Middle school and high school students might enjoy reading how one Vermont lawyer could begin a position with no experience and make a difference for others. This book may inspire some young people to expand their thinking and consider a career in the law."

—Tina Muncy, former Vermont teacher and school principal

"Kim Cheney's memoir traces his journey from becoming a lawyer in Vermont to becoming a one-term Attorney General in 1972. He includes observations of both his successes and failures in his personal and public life. The book can be of interest to those who wish to learnmore about the important Vermont cases which made headlines in the 70's. It adds an interesting perspective to the history of that time."

— Madeleine M. Kunin, former Governor and author,
Coming of Age: My Journey to the Eighties

A LAWYER'S LIFE TO LIVE

A LAWYER'S LIFE TO LIVE

KIMBERLY B. CHENEY

Rootstock Publishing

Published by Rootstock Publishing
an imprint of Multicultural Media, Inc.
27 Main Street, Suite 6
Montpelier, VT 05602 USA

www.rootstockpublishing.com

info@rootstockpublishing.com

Interior and Cover design by Eddie Vincent ENC Graphic Services
(ed.vincent@encirclepub.com)

Printed in the USA

ACKNOWLEDGMENTS

In 2016, as I reached my intended retirement age of eighty and contemplated what was to come, I was fortunate to meet occasionally for lunch with fellow lawyer Bernie Lambek. I respected his legal skills and came to admire his breadth of vision about the ever-changing scope of life, that I was now facing. When he told me he was writing a murder mystery with illuminations about the practice of law I thought, *Great idea—I should do that too*. Having no idea how to write a book, I enrolled in Maggie Thompson's creative writing class at the Montpelier Senior Center. Her encouragement, as well as that of the other would-be writers, propelled me forward.

Local historian, Brian Linder, provided invaluable assistance, supplying me with numerous press accounts of the murders that occurred while I was state's attorney. Local history writer Paul Heller and I used Brian's collection to write a first draft, which we sent to the Vermont Historical Society for feedback. My good friends, Arthur Edelstein, reporter for the *Times Argus*, and Paul Gillies, lawyer and author of legal articles, read my fictionalized draft and recognized that my stories would be better told in memoir form. I agreed, and started over.

I sent my next attempt to Hamilton E. Davis, whose book *Mocking Justice: America's Biggest Drug Scandal* (Crown Publishers, 1978) excellently described events that occurred, to my chagrin, while I was Vermont's attorney general. Davis complimented me on a promising draft and suggested Dirk Van Susteren, respected reporter of Vermont politics for several newspapers, who made a fine coach and editor, helping to bring the story to life. Dirk, whose father was a judge, drew out the human interest aspects of my story with deeply personal and searching conversations and suggestions, which led to great improvements in my book. Dirk's questions, exhaustive but not rude, helped me, to more fully understand my life and how these events shaped it.

Bernie Lambek was kind enough to read and compliment me on my second draft. My wife, Barbara Smith, also read that draft and provided helpful suggestions and encouragement. Michael Sherman, former director of the Vermont Historical Society, edited the manuscript, corrected historical errors, and was helpful in clarifying opaque passages. Courtney B. Jenkins, self-described "word nerd" and proprietor of Soaring Arrow Editing, did a careful and skillful copyedit to produce the final result. Stephen McArthur, Co-Founder of Rootstock Publishing, brought creativity and encouragement to the book, helping to create an engaging narrative. All who assisted have been a vital part of the process of recording my life, for which I am grateful.

TABLE OF CONTENTS

INTRODUCTION

"Far and away the best prize that
life has to offer is the chance to
work hard at work worth doing."
Theodore Roosevelt, 1910

It's a summer morning in June, 2017. I am sitting in a booth at the Coffee Corner at the intersection of State and Main in Montpelier, Vermont, waiting patiently for my thirty-nine-year-old son Benjamin, the child of my second marriage, to arrive for breakfast. By eight o'clock the day has burst into blinding sunshine. Usually the picture window facing the city's main intersection offers a view to the center of my universe—the community where I've spent two-thirds of my life—but today the view is obscured both by people waiting to be seated and those already seated at the table in front of the window. I'm early to meet Ben, and since I can't see out, I begin looking inward, rummaging around into past preoccupations both occupational and intimate, as old men such as myself are inclined to do. Darkness obscures much of what I hope to see, but there are flashes of clarity.

I am 12. I am climbing Mt. Marcy which, at 5,000 feet, is the highest of the Adirondack mountains in New York. I am probably with my father. It has been a long hike, the trail uneven, and I am tired—until I finally reach the bare rock dome of the summit and quickly scale to it's very peak. I am transfixed by the beauty of surrounding mountain tops, some lit by the sun, others still shrouded in fog; and then I see in all directions, a carpet of trees below, the wonderful and mysterious wilderness.

In my mind I visit other mountains I've climbed in New York and throughout New England, and quickly relive a number of hikes. The physical

1

beauty of the Northeast is one reason I'm here today—but hardly the only reason.

I switch mental scenes and am now at sea. I am twenty-four, a U.S. Naval officer in peacetime, serving as deck officer on a small landing ship bound for South Korea. I stand deck watches, sometimes alone, in all kinds of weather. One night, heading across the East China Sea to the Korean naval base at Chinhae, we encounter a strong headwind. Being a landing ship, the forward draft is much less than that aft, and the helmsman struggles to stay on course as the wind catches the bow. Standing orders when a course change is required are that I call the captain, who is asleep in his cabin, but we begin to lose it and there's no time for that. No matter how hard I put the rudder hard left and the vessel into the wind, the ship does not respond. No other ships are seen in the area, either by radar or visually. "Well, screw it," I think to myself. "We're going 'round."

I order full-right rudder. The ship careens through the wind and waves in a sharp turn. When we are exactly one hundred eighty degrees off course, I order the rudder amidships. The momentum of the ship swings it slowly into the wind and back to our course. This happens twice. I tell the captain about it when he comes on deck early in the morning. He has no criticism, saying there was not much else that could have been done. This is an adventure. I love it. I love being in charge and making decisions.

In my mind I fast-forward, thinking about my beginning as a lawyer. Law school is almost as exciting as climbing a mountain or being at sea. The intellectual rigor requires learning a whole new language and understanding how and why great (and not so great) minds have formed the rules we live by. This is an adventure of the mind—how a civilized system resolves conflict by applying reason instead of sometimes lethal force is a fascinating study. I graduate and take a job with a New Haven, Connecticut, law firm. But I soon find it tedious and seek escape from the intellectual and cultural dreariness of the 1950s and early '60s. Missing mountains, I come to Vermont in 1967, along with scores of other urban refugees.

Back in the present, there's still no sign of Ben. I'm on my second or third cup of coffee, the breakfast crowd is starting to clear out, and, for some reason, Bob Dylan's *The Times They Are a Changin'* comes to mind. It is a song of my consciousness. I'd fantasized that life could always be changing, that in Vermont I could blend traditional work with an untraditional lifestyle— at least one more vital than drudgery.

But I also thoroughly agree with Theodore Roosevelt's insight, that working hard at work worth doing is one of the great pleasures of life. In Vermont I am constantly looking for new work worth doing. I've had several jobs for which I had no training but met with success. In Connecticut I considered myself a Democrat, but in Vermont my friends and many leaders I know are progressive Republicans. I ran as a Republican for Washington County state's attorney and was elected, which thrust me into unfamiliar criminal justice issues relating but not limited to: murder and other violent crimes, punishment, prison conditions, working with state and local police, and trying cases. I struggled to learn to be an effective trial lawyer. I was also required to make judgments about how to manage the "drug war," and to cope with the rapid cultural changes and social unrest arising in the wake of the Vietnam War.

There were setbacks. I was elected state attorney general, but my tenure and political career was cut short at one term, thanks in part to President Richard Nixon's criminal cover-up in the Watergate scandal, which tarnished scores of fellow Republican incumbents seeking reelection. In Vermont at the time, there was also a huge police scandal known as the Paul Lawrence Affair, in which an undercover cop by that name, who was hired by several communities in the state, framed dozens of young people—all of whom were eventually pardoned by the governor—with bogus drug buys. I had nothing to do with Lawrence's hiring, but the local state's attorney had a conflict of interest requiring that I assign an assistant attorney general to fill in for prosecuting some of the Lawrence case. I became suspicious of Lawrence, and asked the state police to hire a "narc" to see if he was legitimate. The commissioner said he would, but didn't. Lawrence was caught by the Burlington Police, but my efforts to nail him remained unknown to the public. The Lawrence affair may have had a significant effect on my bid for re-election as attorney general.

The loss of that election was painful. To soothe the misery and recalibrate, I decided to get away for a spell. I left on a train for the West Coast with only a backpack of clothes and books. I visited one of my brothers, a college professor, and his family in Seattle, then another brother who was a builder in San Francisco, living a countercultural lifestyle in that countercultural city. At a party, I smoked (and inhaled) dope for the first time. After a few weeks on rails and by bus, including a side trip to visit Texas where my forebears were from, I returned to Vermont and opened a law practice. For the next forty years, I practiced criminal law, personal injury and family law, and served on various governmental boards.

Ben is still not here, so more shards of experience, either joyful or painful, enter my mind. I think of my marriages and relationships with regrets, but then think of my children and the happiness that has come with having kids. I think of Ben's childhood. I think of myself growing up in a wealthy community in Connecticut, and how people with all the breaks still struggle to meet expectations. I think about how, throughout this short life, there have been plenty of opportunities to become better acquainted with myself, and at eighty-two, I know this is a never-ending process.

A private lawyer's job is just another form of politics. The practice of law is fundamentally that of advocating values inherent in a problem, in a way that will benefit a client. I've had views of life from multiple vantage points, some of which infused understanding of what I did in my youth. This memoir is principally about events in my political life. I realize that, compared to the conflicts of many other places, Vermont is a simple, almost archaic world, but it is nevertheless rife with conflict.

Ben finally arrives, and with a quick step passes the patrons standing at the register. He slides into the booth across from me, shows a broad smile, and greets me with evident pleasure. He's wearing his usual semi-clean work clothes, shedding sawdust from the shop where he builds all kinds of things, including furniture and cabinets. I long ago gave up my lawyer's three-piece suit. I always hated it. Today I'm wearing khaki pants and a polo shirt.

"Hello Pops," Ben says, using his favorite salutation. Noticing my pensive face, he asks, "What are you thinking?"

"Stick around," I say. "I'll tell you about it. No, maybe I'll write it down for you, but how about some eggs and coffee first? This will be another adventure in 'work worth doing,' at least for me, and you can read all about it."

The view to the street now clears. Except for the cars, the corner of State and Main looks much as it probably has for the last century: three-story brick buildings with cornices and rhythmic windows, housing stores, eateries, and upstairs offices for lobbyists, lawyers, accountants, and non-profit groups. If I stood up I could see many of the buildings that housed offices I'd worked in for the past almost-fifty years. After coffee and eggs, Ben and I say our goodbyes. As I step out onto the corner of State and Main, I meditate on this place I chose as my home for good part of my life, and to consider how it has helped mold my life as a person and a lawyer.

CHAPTER 1

"Listen to the silence and you will hear wolves howling at the moon, but the sound is really souls lost in their self-absorption, unable to voice their own loneliness for fear of being heard and condemned."

Kimberly B. Cheney, 2019

A WALK BACK IN TIME

I leave the Coffee Corner to walk home, about a mile away. With hands in my pockets, I dodge the few other walkers who escaped their cars to visit the bookstore or nearby pharmacy. It is quiet, no roar of traffic in Montpelier, the smallest state capital in the U.S. There are no horns bleating for attention or other unpleasant urban distractions. The weekly farmers' market is setting up just off State Street, near the statehouse. I pass the four-story granite City Hall, with its hundred-foot-tall clock tower, built in 1909 at the exuberant start of a new century and still in use. My thoughts, near the short steps of City Hall, drift to a press account of a city council meeting held soon after my arrival from Connecticut in 1967. The article detailed how the public and other councilors chastised a counselor for voting to award a contract to buy a city truck from his own firm without a bid. Wow, I'd thought, if people get excited about that, this sure is a different place than the down-country cities I was used to!

Montpelier is supported economically by two major entities, both of which have contributed mightily to the small city's security, as well as its character. The National Life Insurance Company, a Fortune-500 company, houses its

5

well-paid employees in a sprawling edifice atop a hill. The other entity is the State of Vermont, with numerous employees at the statehouse, supreme court, Department of Transportation, and myriad other office buildings that constitute the Capitol District.

My mind wanders into a reverie about place, change, and living in a small town—all punctuated by more specific fleeting thoughts of what I have been doing since I arrived as a thirty-two-year-old in 1967, seemingly a century ago. The city (as it is called, though it has fewer than 8,000 residents) is situated at the confluence of three rivers—the Winooski, the North Branch, and the Dog—creating the beginning of the only level route going from east to west across Vermont. Otherwise, any roads would have had to cross over the Green Mountains. It is for that reason, as well as its central location, that Montpelier was made the state capital. Twenty-three small towns, situated around the city on spokes of rivers and streams, comprise Washington County, one of fourteen counties in the state. The landscape is peaceful, but, as anyone would expect, the tranquility is punctuated from time to time by controversy.

After passing City Hall I come to a twentieth-century building housing a pharmacy, a Chinese take-out restaurant, and a tattoo parlor. Across the street is the building where I had my office as state's attorney in 1969. In about 150 yards, I turn left onto Barre Street. The monumental form of St. Augustine Church rises ahead. Dedicated in 1903, three years before City Hall, its spire made the church the tallest structure in town. Almost 2,500 people were estimated to have attended the three masses held on Easter when the church was dedicated.

The church may have been a welcome landmark, but the city fathers didn't seem all that keen to have the city clock tower play second fiddle to a steeple. The city embraced a plan that had City Hall's tower stretching six feet higher than St. Augustine's spire, asserting civil authority over ecclesiastical.

I am not in a hurry. In fact, time is on my side this Saturday. I am free to think about all kinds of things, like how I landed in this small city, the years spent here in public service, time spent poring through law books, my family, and the very mystery of being alive. I think about when I first came to Montpelier, and the Catholic presence on Barre Street expressed the power of the Catholic Church. To one side of St. Augustine was a parish house, and on the other, a home for the monsignor, a revered figure, plus two large schools bustling with parochial activity. Now only the parish house and church remain as they were. The house adjacent to the church is presently a lawyer's office, and the school buildings, which once housed kindergarten through high school, have morphed into an art gallery and the city's senior center. There have been rumors that St. Augustine needed maintenance beyond the financial reach of the dwindling parish, mandating a sale or collapse.

Some enterprises start with high hopes, lofty ideals, and excitement but wind up with a slow-dragging struggle to maintain an initial promise. I ask myself, what will I do with my remaining time; what have I done with my life? I slow to a shuffle with these thoughts, bothering no one but myself.

I consider the city again. Some decayed monuments have metamorphosed into objects of hope and renewed success. One building at the top of the hill, now part of the Vermont College of Fine Arts, had been a Civil War hospital where the maimed, dying, and struggling to live had been cared for. Another massive masonry building of cruciform style with four stories and a tower, College Hall, was built in 1872 to provide classrooms for secular education, and is now on the National Register of Historic sites. It has been persistent as a site for higher education, adjoining its own beautiful green, a metaphor for transition from calamity, religious fervor, and education to one proclaiming the centrality of art in a digital world.

On the roads leading into the city from the west, and along Main Street heading north, there are showcase homes of extractive granite and wood industries built by wealthy entrepreneurs, as well as sheep farms and other former homes of agriculture. Many, well preserved, now house offices for lawyers, therapists, and lobbyists in a way that enhances the city's charm.

The Vermont Statehouse is the centerpiece. The present building, the third structure built on the site, was first occupied in 1859. It is a massive neoclassical and Greek Revival with granite foundations and walls, topped by a golden dome. Ceres, the goddess of agriculture in the form of a wonderfully carved wooden figure, looks out from atop the gold dome, greeting people arriving at the capitol from the interstate.

The capitol itself, more than any other building, was my introduction to how a free people work out their lives. There I learned the rudiments of political dialogue, and experienced the success of writing legislation on public-school reform in such a manner that it would be enacted, all while getting to know influential people and why they were so. To me, at the time, the people with whom I worked were breathing new life and bringing important change to the field of education.

As I continue walking, my mind inexplicably fills with pictures of places far from these streets, of a time far from this day. As I consider what brought me here, images of childhood flash through my head.

I imagine myself sixty years ago, with my parents and three brothers on a trip to my grandfather Howell Cheney's house for Thanksgiving dinner, in Manchester, Connecticut. We boys wore clean presentable clothes and were given a parental inspection before departing in the family's Plymouth sedan. We would leave our suburban house on Foxcroft Road, a quiet street in West Hartford, for the drive to Manchester for an adventure into a bygone world— my father's past. As we drove, my elder brother Eric and I would roughhouse, inviting my father's shouts of "Boys! Boys! Be quiet! Stop that." Mother would try to calm us all down by directing attention to some passing attraction.

In Manchester, we drove up the half-mile driveway to Gramp's red brick house near the top of the hill, on fine gravel that led through the Great Lawn, a sweeping well-maintained golf-course-like lawn of many acres. Along the way were six or seven mansions that once held Gramp's cousins' families who managed Cheney Brothers Silks, a company that manufactured and sold beautiful silks around the world. Cheney Brothers owned and operated 175 buildings on 275 acres, bringing riches to the family. Earlier on these drives we saw the company mills, power plant, railroad shipping line, and community center that had been established for the workers and their neighbors. Many of these structures were visible from Gramp's house.

On arrival were be greeted by aunts, uncles, and cousins. These reunions were happy, replete with bursts of laughter and teasing, and always began with Gramp welcoming us enthusiastically with hugs. His wife, Anne Kimberly Bunce, died years before and he didn't remarry, so he was the chief welcomer. Cocktails and wine were served to two dozen adult family members at a large dining room table laid with china and linen. Card tables were set for the children. Gramp, who was short with wispy white hair and an expansive waist, looked almost round. He stood at the head of the table in front of the picture window offering views of the Great Lawn, and would hold forth, gesturing and bantering with carving knife in hand. As he spoke, servants carried in the turkey, potatoes, other vegetables, and cranberry sauces. Gramp would say a grace and do the carving. Undoubtedly, the adults in the room felt they were in the presence of a great man. I saw only a friendly old fellow, much in charge.

The fun would continue after dinner, as we kids chased each other about the house, running through the kitchen, up the backstairs, down the corridor with all the bedrooms, sometimes ducking up another stairway to the servants' quarters, and then, laughing and hooting, we would race down the front stairs to the living room where the adults had gathered. Often, we would chuck our Sunday clothes and head for the Great Lawn for touch football, encouraged by my father. This, we came to understand, had been my father's world growing up.

On these holidays, we would visit the Cheney Cemetery, a sylvan grove where the simple headstones of deceased Cheneys and their families, going back to the eighteenth century, were meticulously cared for. As a child, this cemetery meant little. As I aged and experienced the joy and pain of life, it provided a comfort to know I would join others in a long line of loving ancestors. My parents are buried there, with space for four more headstones—one for each of their children.

Father told stories about growing up in Gramp's house, known as "The Place." He told stories about Cheney Brothers Silks, the Cheneys' big families, their rituals, successes and failures. I learned even more as I researched the past. At one time, Cheney Brothers employed more than 5,000 people from across Europe: Germans, Italians, Swedish, French, Polish, and Lithuanian. The company built the Manchester Library, established several parks, a fire department, water system, and several schools. Since Cheney Brothers employed many women as seamstresses, Howell established a program granting them paid time off for company-sponsored basic education courses. (His interest in promoting women's education resulted in him serving on the board of Mt. Holyoke College.) He also established housing for workers, and provided health care benefits and pensions. As early as 1919, Howell wrote a paper urging universal health care for workers, another sign of his progressive thinking.

Sadly for the family and others, the business began collapsing in the 1930s, teetering as a result of general drop in demand during the Great Depression; labor troubles elsewhere, which required solidarity and caused slowdowns by Cheney Brothers' employees; and the firm's failure to diversify and compete with companies making synthetic threads, such as nylon. Father told me when I was a child that Cheney Brothers had gone bankrupt. I didn't know what that meant, except that "The Place" with the lawn and the mansions was a kind of monument to an important past that had died.

But Cheney Brothers remained in my father's personality and worldview. He enjoyed a large family, and though easily irritated to the point of rage, he showed a basic tolerance for individual foibles. He was informal; we called him "Pappy" or "Frozen Head," because he loved wearing a T-shirt with that logo. I can't now remember where that name came from, but he happily answered to it. He loved involving his boys in multiple activities. One trait I inherited was his inclination to tell and retell jokes as the spirit moved him, whether timely

The Big House
photo of painting by Ruth Pope, of Middlesex, VT

or relevant or not. He was an outdoors enthusiast, passionate about hiking and visiting Gramp's house in the Adirondacks, in Keene Valley, New York, known as The Big House.

My father also had a strong sense of right and wrong, which he imparted to his kids. He insisted that I and my brothers follow the family code: work hard and be productive; help where you can; do unto others as you would have them do unto you; be honest; don't assume you are superior to anyone because of their religion, occupation, or race; and don't take advantage of someone who doesn't have your advantages in life. His favorite words of scorn when any breach of decorum occurred among his children: "Cheneys just don't do that!" That admonition followed me through life. I never needed the Christian concept of sin to govern my moral compass.

Father went to Yale for college and law school. He was draft deferred in World War II on account of chronic ulcers, and found work at a Hartford Law firm while many men of his generation left familiar surroundings for war. He eventually opened his own law firm, a solo practice, and after a number of years quit law to become a life insurance salesman.

Religion played a role in my childhood, yet didn't dominate. Eric and I sang in the Episcopal choir, which was tolerable, but I did not enjoy dressing up and acting like an angel on Sundays. In time I began to have serious doubts about the value of religious devotion.

As I sat in the front row of the church nave on Sundays, dressed in my red robe and white surplice, I saw my parents' friends come to the communion rail with faces suggesting holy thoughts. Then later, every Sunday, I would

10

see them at after-church cocktail parties at our house or elsewhere. There would be laughter and conviviality, and what I considered empty talk, and everyone would seem to forget the Lord. I judged the grownups to be hypocrites.

My mother's experience as a child was much different, as was her style and emotional makeup. Mother was an only child—worse, a fatherless and motherless one, with no extended family.

She was slim, short, and regarded as beautiful. Her father, apparently a warm and doting man whom she deeply loved, died of tuberculosis when she was twelve and away at boarding school in Connecticut. Her mother, having inherited money on the cruel condition that she not remarry, opted for a lonely life of travel and, though she had the opportunity, visited her daughter infrequently. Mother told of being raised by cruel nannies, one of whom would force her into a tub of cold water if she misbehaved. After graduating from high school she earned a BA with honors from Bryn Mawr college. After marrying and bearing four sons, she earned a master's degree in archeology from Trinity College in Hartford, fulfilling a lifelong dream.

Her intellectual prowess did not interfere with her being warm, attentive, and maternal. She read to Eric and me, singly or together, almost every night, and paid close attention to our education. Contrary to my boyish interest in sports, she insisted I take piano lessons until it was clear they were a hopeless endeavor. She attempted to raise my cultural standards by having Eric and me attend Miss Mary Alice's dancing school, where I at least learned to hold a girl while learning basic dance steps (and to wear clean white gloves in the process). This feminization was engagingly supplemented by weekly vocabulary quizzes she gave me, based on *Reader's Digest* condensed books. She even attempted basic sex education, a subject Father totally ignored, giving us books about animal breeding.

Mother was athletic. She played golf with Father, had me caddy for her and hit a few shots from time to time. She joined Eric, me, and Father on overnight hikes in the Adirondacks. Though we had good times on these trips, she did complain of the "tyranny of food," finding it more onerous to plan meals and cook over a wood fire than in a pristine kitchen, as she did most evenings at home. Peter, six years younger than me, and Nathaniel ten years,

11

were not so fortunate, as she descended into alcohol. I perceived that she loved being part of the large Cheney family, but was sad about losing connection with her Swenson relatives, as though her name change at marriage was a divorce from them.

She, too, came from wealth. Her family were Swedes who immigrated in 1848, and settled in Texas. Her grandfather, Svante Magnus Swenson, who at one time owned the second largest cattle ranch in Texas, moved to New York and by 1880 had come to dominate Wall Street finance. Both Svante and her father left her with a considerable inheritance sufficient to pay for all her children and grandchildren's college and graduate educations.

While raising four rambunctious boys, she found time for one creative endeavor after another; she became an excellent amateur photographer, developed a passion for archeology, and became a scholar of St. Paul's life and various early Christian schisms. Her slide shows depicting St. Paul's travels were presented to several organizations in the area. She was especially interested in the Nestorian Schism, which was based on the belief that Jesus had not been born of a virgin. I felt her interest in religion appeared motivated more by scholarship than faith.

She also expressed an artistic side, making papier-mâché puppets, a stage, and lighting, which she used in personally-scripted community puppet shows for children. She supported my father's family code, and added to it a demand that her youngsters use their intellect and excel in education.

During World War II, although she was fortunate enough to retain an occasional live-in nanny, mother started a day care program at the aircraft manufacturing plant, Pratt and Whitney, so women could work. I found it ironic that she hired someone to look after her children so she could manage a day care program for working women. What made sense as I reflected on this endeavor was that, because the culture denied her the opportunity to have a profession other than "housewife," a title she hated, she wanted to help women achieve better status. In time she began drinking too much and became an alcoholic, I believe, largely in response to the limitations imposed on women by society. She needed and deserved a career. Her eventual recovery, for which we were all grateful, was mediated by becoming a fully committed participant in Alcoholics Anonymous, where she found support and companionship. As she recovered, she also found an outpouring of love from her husband and sons as she came to terms with what her life had become.

She died at age ninety-two, after suffering from dementia. As her mind clouded, she became wonderfully happy. When I visited her in the last few years of her life, she would recount the joy of living in exotic places with stimulating male company, enjoying world travels and pursuing her chosen career in archeology of the holy land. From what I knew of her life, none of this was true. Instead, as I grew up in suburban Connecticut, mother wistfully spoke of all the things she had wanted to do in her life but never did.

The story of the St. Augustine Church in Montpelier illustrating the diminishing force of the Catholic Church, as well as the story of Cheney Brothers Silks in Manchester, are metaphors for life itself. It is the essence of Shelley's poem *Ozymandias*, where the weary traveler in the desert comes upon a set of broken stones—all that remains of a once-grand empire—on which are engraved, "Look at my Works, ye Mighty, and despair!"

As my meandering thoughts came to an end, so did my steps. They took me home, where I sat with Mombasa, a big black-and-white mutt, successor to Hector, my first Vermont dog. As the memories of my parents drifted from my consciousness, I began thinking of writing down my story, and wondered if it had meaning to anyone but myself—still an open question.

CHAPTER 2

"We naturally associate democracy, to be sure, with freedom of action, but freedom of action without freed capacity of thought behind it is only chaos."

John Dewey, 1952

EDUCATION

There were no females in any of the schools I attended, from kindergarten through graduating from Yale, and there weren't any people of color in my formal education, until Yale College. My nine years in the Naval Reserve, with four years of active duty (many at sea), after college were similarly discriminatory, but still an extremely valuable education. A few women and people of color were in my Yale law school classes after I finished my Navy duty. The lack of diversity in my education was a deficit in my trip through life that required constant remediation.

The other peculiarity of my school years, from

My Brothers and I and our Father about 1985

14

sixth grade through law school, was that I never watched television with the exception of news broadcasts. Television was either unavailable or I just didn't have time for it, nor did I have friends for whom television was part of life. I found entertainment in books or movies. I never saw the *Ed Sullivan Show*, or *Dick Van Dyke*, and attained near-total lack of understanding or knowledge of popular culture. To this day, I find myself puzzled by references to popular television shows from the 1950s or '60s, and regard this as a positive rather than negative feature of my youth.

My segregated and discriminatory education was a family pattern; both my parents attended same-sex boarding schools and colleges. I doubt they gave any thought to change for me. The sole purpose of education, in their view, was to equip me with the knowledge, intellectual tools, and toughness of mind necessary to succeed in a male-dominated world. In that, it was successful.

Father took an active hand in my education, insisting I learn not only in a boarding school for predominantly wealthy kids, but also in a different world. He arranged summer jobs for me with less fortunate people. One summer I worked as an orderly at Hartford's public McCook Hospital. I helped patients use bedpans, cleaned up vomit, made beds, assisted patients in and out of bed, and sewed deceased people into special sheets for transport to the morgue. I saw how others lived, or didn't.

Another summer, both Eric and I were directed to jobs in the tobacco fields in East Hartford. At the time, Connecticut had a thriving business producing shade-grown tobacco, the leaves of which were used as cigar wrappers. Acres of fields were covered with white cloth supported by wooden poles about five feet high. The spaces between poles were called "bents." The shade actually produced hotter temperatures, improving both the size and rapid growth of the plants. We worked alongside migrant Jamaicans in the shaded fields, doing hot, dirty work. In early summer, the 'suckers' (small leaves) were picked off the plants so the plants would grow tall, with large leaves. This involved sitting on burlap bags, dragging ourselves along each row to pick off the suckers. "Suckering" was piece work, paid by the "bent." Toward the end of summer the plants were tall enough for us to walk along the rows, picking the large leaves and laying them carefully in baskets. Pickers were paid by the basket. Although the work was easier and more lucrative, because you could stand up and move quickly, it nonetheless inspired me to pursue an education to avoid a life of such work. At the same time, I gained empathy, to some degree, for people less fortunate than myself.

A critical and life-long educational experience included summers at my grandfather's house in the Adirondacks, with its view of Mount Dix, plus two summers in a boys' camp in the Adirondacks in the late 1940s. The summer camp was run by one of my grade school teachers, James Goodwin, who insisted on a vigorous schedule of physical activity. I learned to hike farther than I could imagine, carry a pack that seemed too heavy, paddle a canoe beyond exhaustion, cope with insects, sleep on the ground, and enjoy it all. I read a collection of my grandfather's letters that were circulated within the family, wherein he related trips made over the same mountains, walking twenty-five miles a day or more, which intimidated me, as I became exhausted after ten and only once did fifteen. I would be forever enthralled by the beauty of the Adirondacks' far-off mountains, rushing brooks, sunlight flashing off lakes, and the welcoming trees. The experience of hiking along well-worn trials and "herd paths" formed by hikers bushwhacking up trailless peaks formed my values: if something wasn't useful in the woods, it wouldn't be useful anywhere else. Thus, I have a lifetime aversion to neckties, pressed shirts, and shined shoes—though, truth be told, I've found it necessary over the years to compromise occasionally. I became a deist. I was captivated by the mountains, as taken by the "glittering" of those mountain scenes as Robert Herrick was by his lover's clothes, as expressed in his poem, *Upon Julia's Clothes*:

> Whenas in silks my Julia goes,
> Then, then (methinks) how sweetly flows
> That liquefaction of her clothes.
>
> Next, when I cast mine eyes, and see
> That brave vibration each way free,
> O how that glittering taketh me!

My deism was fostered by an unanticipated consequence of the religious education at St. Paul's School. The curriculum required students to go to chapel every day and twice on Sundays, where I and fellow students listened to priests, clad in customary costumes, lead endless prayers, which to me consisted of unintelligible jargon. There were also mandatory "sacred studies" classes espousing Protestant Christian doctrine. These experiences led me to cast off the religion of my parents, which seemed relevant only on certain days, like Christmas and Easter, and only took place in large stone buildings, like Christ Church or St. Augustine's in Montpelier. The beauty of nature, to me, was more compelling. St. Paul's School vaccinated me against religion, and imbued in me a love of nature.

College at Yale

At Yale I was an English major, acquiring knowledge of nineteenth-century poetry which I mostly ignored thereafter. Study of such literature, though, did help me become a lawyer. I became accustomed to seeing words on the page that made little sense, and through hard work extracting a meaning. Being an English major did have the virtue of requiring a lot of writing and coaching in analyzing critical essays.

Other studies offered exposure to many new subjects, among my favorites being a Classical Civilization course covering the ancient Greek culture that introduced democracy to humankind. Today I find the familiar jealousy and bickering of the Greek gods everywhere in our society, perhaps most prominently on the internet where contemporary harpies flourish.

I took a year of Russian language with a course that had one serious drawback. It met at 8:30 every morning, six days a week. Having earned my foreign language credit in high school French, I dropped the course after the first year and have regretted that bit of youthful laziness ever since. I'm sure it would have opened up some interesting career serving the American Empire.

I also took several art history courses: European, Asian, and American. One was taught by Vincent Scully, whose famous art history survey course included photographs of famous buildings or paintings accompanied by recordings of music of the era under consideration, all brought to life by Scully's mesmerizing presentation. His lectures were so powerful, students from the divinity school often attended, to learn how to give a sermon. Courses in history, political science, and linguistics exposed me to novel thinking. So did reading fiction. I loved Thomas Hardy's portrayal of the inequity of English life, and Sinclair Lewis's novels emphasizing the banality of American corporate life. The book that influenced my future career choices most was Sloan Wilson's *The Man in the Gray Flannel Suit*, which depicted the regimentation and dullness of life in corporate America after World War II. I decided I never wanted to work for a large impersonal corporation, and was successful at that.

Like many other students of the time, I was especially influenced by a trip to Europe. In 1955 I crossed the Atlantic on a cruise ship to London, to participate in a volunteer youth program named after Gilbert Winant, America's World War II ambassador to Great Britain. Winant conceived the arrangement that American kids, who had not been savaged by the Nazi bombing of their homes, come to London to bring hope and vitality to British organizations dedicated to reviving demoralized youth. On that program I met Barbara Suter, a senior at Mt. Holyoke College who was also a volunteer. I lived with a British family and participated in the activities of the Stamford Hill Boys and Girls Club, hoping to inject new ideas and positive visions of the future, but more importantly learning about an entirely different culture. British kids welcomed me. They were glad to be with a "Yank" as a representative of a country that had helped preserve theirs. I was humbled by the presence of resilience in the face of a cataclysmic past.

At the close of summer, I and my cousin, Ben Moore, who was my college roommate, hitchhiked through Europe with two young women, all of us having been in the volunteer program. We arranged to stay each night at a youth hostel in our destination city, and after reuniting after a day of separate rides, would celebrate by reading *Winnie the Pooh* episodes to each other. As hitchhikers through Europe, we hung American flags on our backpacks and never failed to get a prompt ride and often a free meal. The Yale liberal education combined with travel with interesting and adventurous companions helped me see the enticing depth of human experience.

After graduation from Yale, in June of 1957, I went to Washington, D.C., to find a job. I wound up as a copy boy with the *Washington Post*, running errands for reporters and editors. I visited Barbara, who was with her parents in New Jersey, a few times. She was pretty and thoughtful. She played guitar and sang popular folk songs beautifully. We had sex. It was before the pill, and I have no memory of what, if any, precautions we took. All I remember is that our early experiences together—instead of being loving and intimate—were, for me at least, rather frightening. I worried that I was taking advantage of a woman and was concerned about pregnancy. Our encounters eventually grew more frequent, and we began to care about each other, though there was no commitment or request for one.

Navy Service

Much as I enjoyed Washington and *The Post*—with its deadlines, rumpled reporters, newsroom banter, Herb Block cartoons, and stories covering cops, Congress, and seemingly everything between—I decided journalism wasn't for me. Naively, I didn't want merely to report on events, but to be an active participant in them. One night, around 3:00 a.m., as I arrived at my apartment building after work, I heard a commotion outside. The Cairo Hotel across the street was on fire, with flames at the window and people fleeing into the street. I thought of calling in the story to the paper, thinking it might make the morning editions, but in my naive belief that reporters weren't actors, I decided not to. I knew then that I didn't want to be a journalist. More motivating was the impending military draft. Rather than take my chances with the Selective Service and the Army, I applied for and was accepted, in June of 1958, at the U.S. Navy's officers candidate school in Newport, Rhode Island. The curriculum included military customs, close-order drill, coastal piloting, celestial navigation, gunnery, and hours of watching *Victory At Sea* films of the Navy in action in World War II. With that war only twelve years in the past, the films had immediacy. I was excited and proud to become part of such a distinguished and heroic organization. I would be part of "Pax Americana," with its mission to bring peace and democracy to a shattered world.

The years encompassing my Navy career was the best of times and the worst of times. The best times were being at sea aboard a ship. The worst was when I got married. I loved life aboard ship. Gone, then, are the familiarities of living on land. Day after day the weather is not merely a phenomenon dictating what you wear and potentially interfering with planned activity; it defines your existence. At sea the ship is your home, and your welfare depends on the weather and the people you live and work with. It is a shared, mostly cooperative, experience. Responsibility increases with rank. Competence is demanded of all. The more rank you have, the more people depend on your technical competence and judgment. Effectiveness requires hard work. In the Navy, I gained understanding about leadership, command, and bureaucracy.

My first assignment as an Ensign in the Naval Reserve was to attend cryptography school in Newport (which reminded me a bit of eighteenth- and nineteenth-century poetry). I learned how to protect and use codes on a machine that would turn gibberish into readable documents. When crypto school ended, I was entitled to a leave. I hoped to use the time to continue my acquaintance with Barb. We made plans to meet in West Hartford, at my parents' house. They seemed to approve of our budding relationship. But this reunion was not to be.

I was ordered to leave Newport within twenty-four hours of my arrival, for duty at the Naval Communication Station in Pearl Harbor, Hawaii. A crisis had arisen between China and Formosa that required an acceleration of U.S. Naval activity. A Navy personnel officer handed me tickets for a series of civilian flights to Honolulu. Frantic telephone calls to Barb went unanswered. I left messages between changes of flights across the country, but I was not able to talk to her until I got to Pearl Harbor. Though I missed Barbara, I was excited to be at the historic Pearl Harbor communications station where the Japanese naval code was broken, leading to the battle of Midway six months after the attack on Pearl Harbor. At Midway, four of the Japanese aircraft carriers, most of the pilots, and all the planes that had participated in the Pearl Harbor raid were destroyed. I was given the responsibility of being part of communications between the Pacific Fleet and higher command in Washington. It was my first job that required my entire attention—I certainly didn't want to garble any important messages. In addition to concerns about a possible Chinese invasion of Formosa, the U.S. was monitoring Communist forces in Vietnam that were getting an upper hand against the French.

I served at Pearl Harbor for about six months. The station was in an underground building with a strictly controlled entrance. Ship, aircraft, and personnel movements urgently needed encrypted command communications. That was our business. I was ordered from there to San Diego to serve as an operations officer on the *USS Dunn County* (LST 742), a Landing Ship Tank, also known as a "long, slow target." The photo is of me in November, 1958. I find it hard to believe I was once so young, and harder still that I gave orders others had to follow. I obtained a leave of about five days, three of which I spent with Barbara on the East Coast before reporting for duty in San Diego. I did not see her again until almost a year later. For that year, she embarked on an education program in England and Europe while I was either aboard a ship in the Western Pacific or stationed in San Diego.

Dunn County, powered by two diesel engines, was capable of speeds up to twelve knots, but generally cruised at about nine. The *Dunn County* was one of many LSTs that survived World War II. In many ways, they were the ships that won the war, landing tanks and heavy armor up on beaches to support invasions. They had none of the drama or élan of swift destroyers, heavy cruisers, or aircraft carriers, but they were serviceable, expendable crafts. The *Dunn County* had returned to San Diego from a trip to the Bering Sea, where its mission had been to conduct electronic surveillance of Russian communications while remaining electronically dark—that is, without the use of radios or technologically modern navigational devices. Consequently, the navigator was one of the best celestial navigators in the Navy. Chief Petty Officer Steamis could get a celestial star site fix faster than anyone else. In theory, the operations officer is in charge of communications, including radio, radar, visual signals, and crypto. No one could do that without well-trained technical enlisted men who did the real work.

The *Dunn County* was assigned to cruise across the Pacific to Japan, Korea, and Okinawa, essentially to show those countries that the U.S. Navy was still present, and to train young sailors like me to get there and back following orders. The captain was Lt. James Lacy, who I estimated to be about thirty years old. Including the captain and executive officer (the XO was also a lieutenant), there were six officers and 150 enlisted men on board. I quickly came to admire and trust Captain Lacy. His service on destroyers had taught him ship handling and other skills of command. The *Dunn County* had prepared for this cruise

by making several short trips up the coast of California and back before being deployed to Japan. I had never been to sea and was both excited and intimidated by the prospect of being an officer at sea. I had much to learn about how a ship at sea is managed. The Captain and the XO did not stand watches, so the four other officers rotated in four-hour shifts. The deck officer is responsible for maintaining the ship's course, avoiding collisions, monitoring communications, and generally, the ship's safe navigation. The duty requires knowledge of coastal navigation, both day and night. At times, for example the 0400 to 0800 watch, I'd be the only officer on board awake.

Leaving port, even in peacetime, is not a simple matter. Joseph Conrad wrote, in *Mirror of the Sea*, the best description of what a "departure" of a ship for an ocean voyage really means. It is not just leaving on a trip, as you would on land. On land you get yourself into some sort of a conveyance and sit passively or drive until you reach your destination. Nothing prevents you from stopping. Nothing prevents you from detouring to some unplanned designation. And weather is mostly not critical. A ship's departure, either by throwing off all lines from the pier or hauling anchor, is a purposeful act entailing a process of leaving a familiar environment for an entirely new one. As Conrad writes:

> ". . . Departure, if not the last sight of land, is, perhaps, the last professional recognition of the land on the part of a sailor. It is the technical, as distinguished from the sentimental, "good-bye." . . . It is a matter personal to the man . . . [T] he seaman takes his Departure by means of cross-bearings which fix the place of the first tiny pencil-cross on the white expanse of the track-chart, where the ship's position at noon shall be marked by just such another tiny pencil cross for every day of her passage."

A departure is also a matter of routine. Every day on the *Dunn County* was the same for the four trained watch officers, except for the rotation of watches—four hours on, four hours off. And if you had the morning watch you would leave the deck at 0800 (8:00 a.m.) and do your necessary day's work until 1400 (2:00 p.m.), before taking the 1600-to-midnite watch. Every day we had the same duties to fulfill and there was no need to conjure up a purpose for being alive that day. We simply did what we were trained to do. We were busy, suffering from lack of sleep characteristic of life at sea.

We left San Diego for Japan, via Hawaii. Chief Steamis did the navigating. Our final destination was Sasebo on the south coast of Kyushu, Japan's southernmost island. There were no electronic systems, radio beacons, or satellite GPS positions to rely on. Instead, Steamis navigated by the stars, putting our position every few hours on the chart in the Combat Information Center below the bridge. At the beginning of each watch I would check our location on the chart and enter it in the log. I had no ability or responsibility to verify where we were. After about ten days out of Honolulu, with 2,000 miles to go with nothing to see but ocean, Steamis called the officers on deck to celebrate what he considered the peak of his navigating career. He pointed to what appeared to be rock rising out of the ocean. "There it is," he said. "It's Lot's Wife! I know exactly where we are. I have a visual fix, a celestial fix, and a faint loran fix. We're exactly where I had us plotted on the chart."

"Lot's Wife," named after Lot's unfortunate spouse in the Bible who turned to salt after looking back on Sodom, is two acres of volcanic rock situated miles and miles from any other land that juts more than ten feet straight out of the Pacific Ocean, approximately 450 miles off the south island of Japan. It was comforting, as a young man travelling for the first time in such an alien environment, to have a man at the top of his profession tell you exactly, beyond doubt, where you were. In later years I looked back fondly at that moment, for our arrival at Lot's Wife would serve metaphorically for my own occasional efforts to check where exactly I was in life.

We arrived at Sasebo, did some needed maintenance, then made a cruise to South Korea and later to the island of Okinawa, the site of one of the bloodiest and most famous battles of World War II. Soon after anchoring in Okinawa, where the ship was scheduled to stay for several days, we learned of an approaching typhoon. The ship was ordered back to sea to head for and circumnavigate Taiwan to gain some protection from the wind and tremendous waves. The *Dunn County* avoided the worst of the weather, but going downwind we still experienced waves longer than the ship. We surfed down the face of these gigantic swells; the vessel would bury its bow in the trough with a thump before being picked up by another monster for another sleigh ride down.

After the storm, we headed for Tokyo. This voyage provided a high point for me. I, as the sole deck officer awake, had the 0400 to 0800 watch on a course taking the ship from sea up crowded Tokyo Bay to the City. In the dark I viewed the small green dots on the radar, and with binoculars could occasionally see the running lights of other ships or boats, judging their courses and speeds to avoid any possible collision. As daylight broke and the cook appeared with a fresh cup of coffee, the other vessels gradually appeared and my anxiety burned away with the sun as I enjoyed a beautiful cruise so far from home. My sense of history stirred as I recalled my great grandfather's collected letters describing a similar trip. He had steamed up Tokyo bay with Admiral Matthew C. Perry in his black gunships almost one hundred years earlier, in 1854. Frank Woodbridge Cheney was a trade representative going to "open" Japan to U.S. trade of silks with Cheney Brothers.

Our "West Pac" cruise at an end, the *Dunn County* returned nonstop via the great circle route to San Diego. Although uncertain, we expected the ship to be scrapped, its useful life over. After several weeks, I was promoted to lieutenant junior grade with the satisfaction of having served on a long voyage, a confidence builder. We took short trips along the coast, none longer than five days, and I was able to spend more time ashore, much of it—perhaps too much—socializing.

At a party I met several local teachers, including Mary Jane (not her real name), with whom I began an intimate relationship. Barbara remained on my mind, and although we had not made a commitment to one another, I still felt a strong tug. I was determined to end this budding relationship with Mary Jane, but confusion and loneliness on my part, and entreaties on her part, delayed the breakup.

Unfortunately for the two of us, Mary Jane became pregnant. My world exploded. I not only felt deeply guilty for breaching the family code of honorable behavior, I knew I had seriously jeopardized Mary Jane's well-being and future. I became deeply depressed. Should we marry? Was abortion an option? Abortion was illegal in the U.S., but could we go to Mexico? Would that be dishonorable and medically risky? After a period of emotional and situational turmoil, Mary Jane and I decided on adoption through an agency. Mary Jane gave birth to a girl, who I thought about with sorrow and concern. With the *Dunn County* to be scrapped, I had earned leave and went home to West Hartford awaiting my next assignment, and to admit my transgressions to my parents and Barbara. I remained deeply distressed by my obvious betrayal and my failure to meet parental expectations. Mother, in an attempt to ease the swirl of emotions, called Barbara and me together and urged that we marry. She gave me a family ring to give Barbara, which I did. My leave was short, and I soon returned to San Diego.

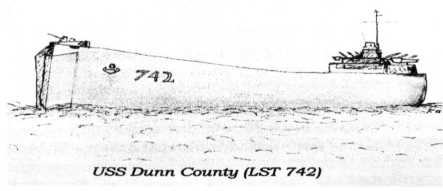

USS Dunn County (LST 742)

sketch by Kim Cheney

To my good fortune, my orders were to go to Chinhae, South Korea, to be the mine warfare advisor as part of the U.S. Military Advisory Group to the Korean Navy. I had one year left in my four-year active duty commitment. I had no training or experience in mine warfare, but I was glad to go. My relief at leaving home, Barbara, and Mary Jane for an assignment halfway across the world was liberating. It would give me an opportunity to see more of a distant part of the world, and I hoped to escape the messes I had left behind. I packed my gear and caught the flight to Chinhae, a small town on the south coast of Korea, west of Pusan, in June, 1959. It was a stunningly beautiful place.

At that time, the U.S. Navy was supporting development of the South Korean Navy. Korean officers were required to learn English and American doctrine and protocol through joint exercises with the U.S. Navy. My assignment was to go to sea every other week to monitor Korean mine-sweeping exercises at various places along the coast. This was not heavy lifting. I enjoyed being at sea. I was the only American officer in the flotilla of South Korean ships on the exercise, had no watches to stand, and was treated as an honored guest. I settled in to an enjoyable assignment.

Wedding Photo day prior to honeymoon trip

This period of emotional calm was shattered when I began to get impassioned letters from Barb suggesting we marry. She'd completed her European studies and was contemplating an uncertain future. She loved me despite everything, she said. Barb proposed that we marry in Tokyo, and said she would join me in Chinhae thereafter. Waves of guilt and shame concerning Mary Jane's pregnancy returned. Mother's well-meaning but terrible advice convinced me this mistake could be remedied if I married Barb. The Navy didn't object. We married in Tokyo on September 22, 1960.

But it was hardly a blissful occasion. On our first honeymoon morning, in a Japanese resort, Barb had a shocking announcement of her own. She had just discovered she was pregnant. The child certainly couldn't be mine, because we'd had no sexual relations for more than a year. Now it was her turn to express guilt and shame. It was a standoff of betrayal between two reckless and inexperienced young people. So, given the circumstances, we somehow tried to wall off our sorrow, smother our remorse with hope, and set off to finish my naval service in Chinhae. I vowed to forgive and move on with life.

Back in Chinhae, I moved out of the officer's quarters on base and we rented a house belonging to a high-ranking South Korean naval officer, then serving in Seoul. The house had no running water. A child of a family living nearby spent an hour or so every day collecting water in a gourd and saving it in a barrel for us; from there it flowed from a spigot about six inches off the ground. Our house had electricity only on Mondays, Wednesdays, and Fridays from 4 to 8 p.m. On other nights we used Coleman lanterns. There was no stove, but the navy shipyard fashioned one for us, which was nothing more than a sheet of steel elevated about six inches on corner posts with a kerosene burner, fashioned from tubes built from empty beer cans, in which a lantern wick was led to the kerosene, like a lantern. The wick could be raised or lowered for heat, and cooking pots and pans could be moved to different places on the steel plate to vary cooking temperature. It was a common Korean makeshift appliance, and it worked fine.

The house had no furnace, but the Navy provided a space heater and fuel. There was no toilet, aside from a small chamber with a seat above a steel container with an opening to the street, which enabled the "honey wagon" to empty it using a hose and pump. Local kids enjoyed throwing rocks at the steel street-side cover, making a highly satisfactory noise and hopefully scaring the foreign users of the facility. This was hardly the Ritz, but I declared our indoor outhouse and the rest of our quarters to be far more comfortable than some of the shelters where I'd camped in the Adirondacks.

Somehow, we found things to do. When not at sea, I gave evening English language instruction to South Korean officers of the fleet of minesweeping boats. There were other navy wives on the base nearby, and Barbara found ways to connect with them. If not for the unusual circumstances, this might have been a wonderful time of relationship-building experience. As things turned out, in May of 1961, Barb flew to San Diego to give birth to her baby, who was released for adoption through the agency Mary Jane and I had used. It was not the best way to start a marriage.

While in port in Chinhae, or at sea, I often found time to read. Since the point of my Navy service seemed to be countering Russian belligerence, I began reading all I could about the Russian Revolution. I read biographies of Stalin, Lenin, and Trotsky, such classics as *Ten Days that Shook the World* by John Reed, and all of Sholokhov's *And Quiet Flows the Don*, the Nobel Prize-winning quartet of novels depicting Russian events leading to the Revolution, the civil war that followed, the slaughter of Russians in World War I, and the emergence of the Communist state.

I rationalized that reading about Russia was learning about the enemy, but really these books were of general interest, stories of drama, leadership, treachery, cataclysm, idealism, and political knowhow and cunning. These were stories of how determined men seek power. I noted and was impressed by the fact that most of the leaders of the Revolution had been young men imprisoned by the Czarist regime who had been given books and time to think and conspire, becoming steeped in revolutionary dialectic. Behind bars, they were able to develop their oratory skills, giving speeches to prisoners like themselves.

To digress from chronology for a moment: my Russian studies were completed in the summer of 1966. My parents knew of my interest in Russia, so they invited Barbara and me to take a trip to Moscow, St. Petersburg, and Kiev, giving me the chance to practice my Russian language skills and share experiences with other foreign visitors to the U.S.S.R. In Moscow one day I used my rudimentary Russian to give directions to a Muscovite confused by the subway. He was thankful for the directions, which he thought were clear enough, but for all I know he might still be lost, riding the rails to Vladivostok. In Kiev I went to the hotel dining room for breakfast where I saw a group of Black guys from Zaire at a table. They offered to let me join them, and I chatted with them in French as best I could. I remember one of them saying Zaire sends half its students to America and the other half to Russia. "Those like us who are in Russia think America must be the best country in the world, and those who go to America think Russia must be the best," he said. "So, you see, we try not to choose sides."

In June, 1961, when my enlistment in the Navy was about to expire, I was ordered from Chinhae, Korea, to San Francisco to process my release. Barb and I reconnected there and decided to drive home. We chose to go through Canada to see some beautiful scenery and hoped that views of the outside world would smother our inner chaos. We bought a car with folding rear seats to sleep in, a tent, and some primitive camping gear, and headed to see my brother Eric in Seattle, then on to Banff National Park and Lake Louise, a spectacular turquoise glacier-fed lake surrounded by high peaks. The beauty was refreshing. Then we traveled on to Calgary, Medicine Hat, Regina, and Winnipeg, through the plains and eventually arriving at Ship Bottom, New Jersey, where Barb's parents had a summer home on the beach. It was a trip dedicated to being in motion, with a clear destination, external views, elementary bodily needs for sleep and food, and avoidance of talk about what had brought us together or apart.

In Ship Bottom I took a job tending bar at a local pub and wondered what to do next. Leaving the Navy was much like graduating from college. What do I do now? I asked myself. I had no significant civilian skills and no job prospects. I thought of Washington D.C., and the *Washington Post*. Maybe I could find a job there. In late June, I went to the Senate and House office buildings, made cold calls, and looked at random for a legislative job. I had a primitive resume and no introductions, but I did have my first civilian suit, complete with necktie, that I hadn't worn in four years. I was often able to at least talk with office managers. The first question I was asked in any congressional office was, "Where did you go to law school?" followed by, "We don't have any openings right now." I got the message.

Law School

In 1960, I took the Law School Aptitude Test (LSAT) in Seoul, Korea, with no study or preparation. I thought my grade was okay (89 percent), so after returning to the Jersey Shore and tending bar for the rest of the summer, with my father's help I applied and was accepted to the University of Connecticut Law School in Hartford. Barb and I moved that fall to West Hartford where we found a small apartment. I was confident enough but felt my time in the Navy had given me a delayed start in both law studies and a career. Most of my classmates were four or five years younger than, which for some reason inspired me to work harder, studying ten to twelve hours a day or longer, six days a week. Barb found things to do, principally managing the household, cooking, cleaning, and all that it takes to make a decent life. She also investigated possible future education for herself. I didn't interact much with her and we avoided conversations about pregnancies, adoptions, sorrow, and loss. I focused on finding an occupation, and Barb fully supported that effort, for which I was thankful. I seldom had uncommitted time with her, except for a few hours on Sundays, which I declared "a law-free day."

First-year law requires learning an entirely new vocabulary, like learning a foreign language written in English. Any law-related reading required that I have a law dictionary at hand, but I still struggled to understand much of what was on some of the pages. First-year law study amounts to a crash course in the concepts of contract formation and enforcement, property description and ownership, the penalties and enforcement associated with regulating human interactions not amounting to a crime, and the court procedures for resolving civil disputes. Despite the challenges, I was excited to be a burrowing creature feasting on law books. I had little time for friends. I pushed myself and finished that year ranked first in the class.

At the urging of one former college classmate, who was at Yale Law in New Haven, I decided to apply to transfer there, and was accepted to begin in September, 1962. Barb and I moved to a New Haven apartment and she entered the University of Connecticut School of Social Work, working toward a masters in social work degree that required a commute back and forth to Hartford. Second-year studies for me at Yale allowed some choice of subjects constrained only by the necessity to someday pass the bar exam, so I took a course in tax law.

Though I had been an undergraduate at Yale, I was intimidated by the law school. I learned the average LSAT score for students there was 98 percent. During the first weeks of the tax course I was almost in tears. The other students discussed accounting in words and concepts I failed to understand. Fortunately, I had the good sense to approach the professor, and when I told him I didn't know what most of the students were talking about, he replied: "Don't worry, Mr. Cheney, they don't either. Stick it out and you will see." I did, and the professor was right.

One of my most interesting classes was Fred Rodell's constitutional law class. His book, *Nine Men,* was an argument that biographies of Supreme Court justices explained more about what would be the outcome of cases than any consideration of legal concepts or meticulous analysis of a particular case. "Don't read law, read biography!" was his point. So instead of writing on some arcane or pressing legal issue, I wrote a biographical piece on New York Judge Benjamin Cardozo. Ever since, I've been a fan of biography, and somewhat skeptical about any thinking that constitutional law (or any law) is static or independent of human prejudices or a judge's personal concerns.

Yale Law School at the time was innovative and offered a number of courses exploring laws as they impacted other disciplines. Because Barb was getting a master's degree in social work, I took a course in law and psychiatry taught by Joseph Goldstein. He and Anna Freud, the daughter of Sigmund, were writing a book entitled *Beyond the Best Interest of the Child*, based on the theory that children would be better off if a parent were dead than if they were part of a contentious custody fight through divorce. I wrote a paper that found its way to a Connecticut committee interested in what legal standards should be applied if the state were to take a child from a parent. My paper was published in the June 1966 edition of *Children*, a U.S. government journal for professions serving children. My all-time favorite course was taught by Professor Charles Reich, author of *The Greening of America*, who led a seminar on late nineteenth-century gold rushes. He argued that the real value of gold was not that it was a beautiful artifact and of intrinsic value for that reason, but rather that governments simply decided on its worth and bought it to back up their paper money.

Reich's focus was on the fact that in North America, after the white population killed off the indigenous population by war or disease, vast expanses of land were left in the public domain. If gold were discovered on this public land, who was positioned to take it? As it turns out, almost anyone with the encouragement or tacit approval of the government. So a gold rush was a laboratory example of how capitalism with government collaboration allocates something of value in the public domain. Reich, at the time, compared government involvement in the gold rush to the later allocation of the electromagnetic spectrum for radio and television (this was before the internet, or he would have added that to the mix). The air through which these were transmitted was in the public domain, and could only be valuable if the government regulated the spectrum and auctioned off the right to use it to the highest bidder.

Reich's course led me to see that process at work in many contexts of government-encouraged or sponsored activities: for example, land use regulation, highway construction, and water rights. Yale students were expected to see the larger picture involved in any study of law in a capitalist society.

In the early 1960s, students and faculty at Yale were also heavily engaged in the civil rights movement. Songs of change and love were in the air, and students were enthusiastically looking for ways to combat racism and foster civil liberties. Eleanor Holmes Norton, then a student classmate and now the congressional representative for Washington, D.C., started a program called the "The Dixwell Legal Rights Association," named after a neighborhood with predominantly African American representation. The plan was for classmates and students to knock on doors on Dixwell Avenue to ask residents if they had been screwed (using more technical language) by landlords, lenders, etc., and see if they had legitimate complaints to file in small-claims court. Indeed, many of them did. An uproar ensued from the power structure, but the program made some changes. I look back on my solicitations with self-congratulation, and on my association with Eleanor with pride. Yale was an exciting place to be. The school's fundamental proposition was that students would have a better opportunity to make a better world if they understood how things worked. I bought into that. And my effort in that regard was to look for another job in Washington, D.C.—the seat of power—during the summer after my second year.

Joy of Alison being with us.

Meanwhile, Barbara and I had a child of our own. Whether wise or not, we'd decided it would be best to counter the sorrow and challenges resulting from our early months of marriage by having a child we could keep. Our first child, Alison, was born in June, 1963, and came with us to Washington when I accepted a job with a prominent law firm. We were fortunate in that the law firm helped us find a comfortable place to live. Among other things, Washington was alive with praise, fear, anxiety, and hope as the August date for Dr. Martin Luther King Jr.'s heavily promoted March on Washington for civil rights approached. Barb and I decided to attend the march despite a chorus of voices telling us not to, including earnest warnings of fear of a race riot from white employees at the law firm. I snuggled Alison into a Japanese-style baby carrier, strapped her to my back, and joined the crowd surging up Pennsylvania Avenue toward the Lincoln Memorial to hear King deliver his now-famous *I Have a Dream* speech. It was one of the most significant

events in modern American history and I am grateful to this day that I was witness to it.

I graduated near the top of my class in 1964, missing by a less than a percentage point qualifying for the *Order of the Coif*, an honor akin to *Phi Beta Kappa* that is achieved by students who ranked in the top 10 percent of their law school class. A year later, I had my first real job in my chosen profession, and Barbara and I were caring for our second child, new-born Margreta. One week, Alison grew crankier and fussier. We couldn't figure out what was wrong. One afternoon I held her in my arms trying to comfort her, but she started crying and was uncontrollable. I was angry because she was disrupting my home time and was tempted to throw her down, but regained control and put her gently down just as Barb came into the room. She grabbed Alison, cried "She's dying!" and rushed her to the hospital. Alison was found to have an intussusception, a condition in which one segment of intestine folds over another, pops out, and folds over again creating pain and inability to digest food. Alison had an emergency operation by a surgeon who had already been on his feet for twelve hours that day. Barb had been right. She and the surgeon saved Alison's life and I learned something important: mothers always think about what's best for the child, while sometimes fathers think about what's best for them when a child creates turmoil. Mothers are truly amazing. Despite our best efforts, our marriage remained more collaborative than tender and intimate, but our love for our children bonded us.

CHAPTER 3

"A lawyer without history or literature is a mechanic,
a mere working mason; if he possesses some knowledge
of these, he may venture to call himself an architect."

Sir Walter Scott, 1815

LAW PRACTICE TO VERMONT

Soon after law school, I found a job with an established New Haven firm. I had little idea what lawyers actually did, but since I'd been extensively trained to be one I figured a traditional law firm in a good-size city would be a good career start. I set aside my study of Russian literature and history and started reading about lawyers. Like many young lawyers at the time, I was drawn to the image of Atticus Finch in *To Kill a Mockingbird*, a lawyer who stood tall against ignorance and racism, defending a rape charge in a Southern courtroom. I returned to reading biography. I read all I could about and by Clarence Darrow. Darrow's career representing despised people, from Richard Loeb and Nathan Leopold to John Scopes, while pointing out that so much of society itself was despicable, was inspiring. He was the kind of legal architect Sir Walter Scott identified. I absorbed into my consciousness Darrow's statement, "As long as the world shall last there will be wrongs, and if no man objected and no man rebelled, those wrongs would last forever."

Barb and I bought a house near East Rock Park in New Haven as we settled down to work; I at the law firm and she, having earned a master's degree at the University of Connecticut School of Social Work, as a mental health counselor. To do what we could for racial justice, we decided to host a young Black woman from Mississippi, Wyneva J., who was enrolled in a one-year Yale program for young people who showed promise but lacked educational opportunities. The program offered intensive study in a variety of subjects and was designed to permit entry into an excellent college. During her stay, we spent hours talking about her experiences growing up as the daughter of a prominent minister whose mission was to build harmony between the races. A thoughtful young woman, she helped me understand many of the political, economic, and educational challenges faced by Black Americans, especially the crushing impact of white supremacy. Her presence was a welcome education. She went on to Wellesley College and later became a lawyer.

I regretted that my job as a young attorney did not offer immediate opportunity to right social wrongs. I was not a Finch or a Darrow. I spent my time doing legal research and writing memoranda for the partners; I seldom even interacted with clients. Occasionally I took on court-assigned criminal defense cases to learn how that part of the law worked. One was as laughable as it was memorable: the law firm assigned me the case involving members of *Ducks Unlimited,* an organization dedicated to environmental and hunting practices to protect ducks. My clients said they had been wrongfully accused of shooting ducks out of season in New Haven Harbor. The U.S. attorney, on behalf of a federal game warden, brought criminal charges against them. The warden said he heard shots coming from my client's boat in the harbor, thought he saw ducks fall, and sped off to intercept their boat but couldn't find any carcasses, even passing a line under the boat to see if he could find a hidden bag in a futile search for evidence. My clients insisted the warden was mistaken. A little sleuthing on my part, asking other hunters and talking with the warden, led to the possibility that my clients used a common practice to avoid detection. The scheme was to shoot the ducks, retrieve the carcasses, put them in a canvas bag, then throw them overboard attached to a buoy that was timed to surface after a reasonable interval. The bag could then be retrieved when the coast was clear. I questioned my clients closely about this possibility, pointing out the warden was certain to claim they were both liars and hypocrites, which might lead to a severe penalty if convicted. I advised, and they accepted, a guilty plea. I served justice, the courts, and, just as importantly, my clients by making sure they didn't perjure themselves. The virtue of cross-examining your own client was a helpful learning experience.

One case I actually tried taught me another lesson, although at the time I wasn't sure what it was. It was a divorce case, and the first for which I was solely responsible. My client was a woman. At the time, the law required a finding of fault to obtain a divorce, forcing the lawyer and client to present evidence of misconduct by the opposite spouse to get a divorce and perhaps a better financial settlement. My client, whom I will call Mrs. Jones, testified approximately as follows: "My husband drives me nuts. Most nights he dresses in a tight costume and runs around the house cleaning things, wiping the tables, vacuuming, polishing things. He won't talk—he's obsessed. I need out." She gave further details about the frequency and vigor of these scenes. When she finished, and before the opposing lawyer could cross-examine, the judge jumped in and took over the questioning.

> He asked, "And Mrs. Jones, did he wear a cape?"
> "Why yes, Your Honor. How did you know?"
> "And did he wear a white T-shirt and white pants?"
> "Why yes, Your Honor. How did you know?"
> "And he was bald, as we see him today?"
> "Why yes, Your Honor. How did you know?"
> "And did he sometimes wear a gold earring?"
> "Why yes, Your Honor. How did you know?"
> "Thank you, Mrs. Jones, that will be all."

The husband's lawyer didn't ask a thing. I was dumbfounded. She had never mentioned Mr. Jones's costumes. When we finished for the day I asked her if it was true, she nodded affirmatively. But I don't know to this day if it was true or she just thought it best to shut up and agree with the judge because he seemed to be on her side. Soon thereafter the judge issued a ruling favorable to her. About a month later, I was in chambers again with the same judge on a different case. I asked him how on earth he knew Mr. Jones so well. I told him both my client and I were stunned by his questions. How did he know so much about the defendant? The judge broke into laughter. "I just guessed!" he said. "From her testimony I thought he must have been the Mr. Clean I see on all those TV ads."

I was shocked and surprised to find a judge candidly admitting that he manufactured humor out of my client's unhappy marriage. I also realized my client was quite possibly complicit in the joke. This behavior did not coincide with the lofty ideals of law and justice I had imbibed in law school, and left me both puzzled and discouraged. As I gained more experience, I understood that a judge, confronted on a regular basis with the intensity, tedium, and anger that divorce cases often generate, would find a way to compensate for such drudgery. Law, it turns out, is an intensely human process. In this case, perhaps the judge's questioning was also a statement against the inane requirement that couples wanting to end their marriage must first find "fault" in their spouse, possibly enhancing minor irritants instead of merely recognizing they had made a bad choice for themselves, thus figuring out the financial consequences to both arising out of that choice.

Like many who practice law, I was drawn to civic affairs and politics. While in law school I was part of a group called Save the Park, which formed to stop construction of a highway connection to I-91 through New Haven's East Rock Park, a beautiful, wooded 425 acres of hiking trails, ballfields, and places to picnic. Our house was nearby, so I had a personal stake in the outcome. That aside, the project would have destroyed a remarkable place for what I regarded as an illegitimate purpose: placating drivers who were in a hurry. Many Save the Park members were Yale faculty—bright, passionate, articulate, but also busy with their own careers. So I decided to get involved and soon became head of the organization. I saw the undisturbed park as an urban refuge, an extension of the wonderful mountains and lakes that I had hiked and canoed in the Adirondacks. It was my first venture into public policy, and also my first taste of fame, as this effort to save the park attracted the interest of local press and lawmakers.

I realized I need allies to win this one, so I obtained a list of all the plans to construct roads through parks that were on file at the state Department of Highways. I then put the list into a press release asking concerned people in the affected towns to contact me and their legislators to stop the construction. I soon had the whole state in an uproar. There were protests, letters-to-the-editors campaigns, and petitions to local select boards. I energized a Hartford group in protesting a connector road planned through the statehouse grounds within yards of the historic statehouse itself. Groups from across the state lobbied their legislators. At the request of a citizens group in Meriden, I filed a lawsuit against the Connecticut Highway Department seeking to prevent the taking of a park, on the basis that land dedicated to one public use couldn't be taken by another public agency for an incompatible use. The protest efforts produced a major legislative victory. State lawmakers enacted a law preventing the taking of park land for an incompatible purpose unless the taking was approved by the local governing body. Predictably, New Haven's Board of Aldermen refused to approve the East Rock connector. It then went on to appoint me to the city's planning commission. This victory helped preserve the integrity of numerous other parks throughout the state.

I was involved in one other noteworthy controversy during this period, and this one, though unsettling, set my life on a new path. This case involved New Haven's beach near the harbor, which was open to anyone who wanted to use it, regardless of race or residence. This was in contrast with policies in many shore towns along Long Island Sound, which limited use of beachfront parks to residents. I was asked by a coalition of New Haven citizens and residents from some affected towns to sue the offending Connecticut towns to allow non-residents to use these beach parks. The managing partner of my law firm and I determined the firm did not have a conflict of interest, since it didn't represent any of those towns, and I was given the go-ahead. Yet, as publicity grew, some of the firm's partners became concerned.

One Saturday morning my managing partner came to my office and told me I would have to drop the suit. "We have a conflict," he explained. "Yeah—but," I protested, "we both checked our client lists and determined we don't represent any of those towns, and you understood that, and you approved taking on the case." He left without ordering me to drop the case, and I was somewhat relieved, but the next Saturday he again entered my office. "Sorry," he said, "but this conflict is not your typical conflict of interest. You see, we have many clients who live in those towns, and they like their beaches the way they are; if we continue down this route, they will find another firm. Drop it!" He concluded the conversation and left no room for argument.

Okay, I thought, the firm is the boss. I'll drop the case. But I did not go to law school to cater to the whims of the affluent, many of whom did not want people of color on "their" beaches. There must be another, more fulfilling job somewhere. I wanted something to give my life meaning. Thirty-four years later, the Connecticut Supreme Court accepted my position, holding that the principal I asserted was correct. Times change, laws change.[1]

Meanwhile, my marriage was not working. Maybe a change of scenery would help Barbara and me find happiness. Coincidentally and fortuitously,

1. Laydon V. Greenwich 257 Conn. 318 (2001) The ordinance prohibiting non-residents from using the town beach violates a state common-law doctrine pursuant to which municipal parks are deemed to be held in trust for the benefit of the general public and not solely for the use of residents of the municipality.

while trying to find my life's calling, we had a visit from my former college classmate and friend, Jonathan Brownell, who at the time was the Vermont deputy attorney general. Barb and I, along with Jonathan and his wife, had been on a hiking party in western Connecticut several months earlier. On that trip I discussed with Jonathan my dissatisfaction with law practice, so when he came to visit, he mentioned a job as counsel to the Vermont Department of Education in Montpelier. The job would entail updating education laws to improve schools. I was interested, and Barb, too, was enthusiastic.

Soon after Jonathan's visit, I drove north to Montpelier for an interview and to see what Vermont was like. It was a bitter-cold twenty-two-below February day. A snowstorm had come through the prior evening, but the sky was clear, there was no wind, and brilliant sunlight reflected off the new snow, sending shards of light into the air, off the trees and snow covered hills. It was the most gorgeous winter day I had known. I drove on freshly plowed roads with no traffic—a wondrous thing in itself—staggered by the beauty of the place. The intense cold seemed not only to create space fixed in time, but also to sanitize the evil in the world.

Vermont called, and we answered.

CHAPTER 4

*"When you are asked if you can do a job, tell 'em,
'Certainly I can!' Then get busy and find out
how to do it."*

Theodore Roosevelt, c. 1910

DEPARTMENT OF EDUCATION ATTORNEY

When I took the assistant attorney general job, I had no idea what I would be doing or with whom I would do it. Like many other immigrants to Vermont in the 1960s, I was fleeing what I felt was down-county cultural sclerosis. The government and corporate America were impeding our youthful efforts toward freedom and self-expression. Thousands of disaffected young people—urban refugees and Vietnam War veterans and foes—were coming to Vermont to experiment with new lifestyles. Many came with no job prospects. But land was cheap.

I had been hired to be the Vermont Education Department's first full-time lawyer. I was told the attorney general and education commissioner thought such a person would help remove legal impediments to improving education, paving the way for new schools around the state. These projects were considered necessary because of population growth, school consolidations, and demands for better education. When I interviewed for the job, no one suggested how these outcomes were to be achieved. Well, I thought, I can do it—who could be more qualified than a graduate of a top law school, honed by service as officer on a ship that steamed halfway around the world, unencumbered by prejudice, or, for that matter, experience?

I reported to the commissioner of the Department of Education but was subject to supervision by Attorney General James Oakes and my friend Deputy Attorney General Jonathan Brownell. There were a few other assistant attorneys general who worked in other agencies and departments dealing with such matters as highways, corrections, social welfare, and criminal justice. Oakes and Brownell, both Republicans, and Governor Philip Hoff, Vermont's first Democratic governor since before the Civil War, were members of the American Civil Liberties Union, which I considered a sign of openness to new ideas. Vermont's leaders from both parties generally supported programs to help people economically while tolerating individual differences and preserving personal freedoms.

When I reported for duty in the spring of 1967, Education Commissioner Richard Gibboney didn't know what to do with me. The department occupied almost all of the second floor in the state office building across from the statehouse. I had no real idea what the people working there actually did, and was given vague directions by Brownell to review statutes relating to education and to propose change where needed—but that was the only direction I was given. Apparently, I would have to define my own job.

From conversations with Oakes and others, I was aware that the prevailing political mood of decision makers was to bring Vermont out of its deeply conservative past. Before court-ordered legislative reapportionment in 1965, each of Vermont's 250 towns, and therefore each school district, had one representative in the legislature, the result being that the General Assembly had a distinctly conservative base. Many small rural towns were unwilling to spend money on education, or little else, other than roads. The result was that policy initiatives deemed too liberal and too expensive faced major roadblocks in the overpopulated, discriminatorily selected House of Representatives. The reapportioned 1965 legislature, with 150 House members, represented proportionally by the more liberal larger towns and cities, wanted change. So did a majority of the population, as evidenced by the election of Democrat Philip Hoff as governor in 1963.

By the mid '60s, parents of school-aged kids were beginning to realize that their children were growing up in a seemingly backward state. They knew their kids would need the smarts and skills to function in a wider and ever-changing world, even—or especially—if they stayed home on the farm (there were plenty of farms then). Agriculture, like other enterprises, required increasing technical and scientific know-how to be profitable. The educational administrative structure of school superintendents, principals, and planners thought an impediment to improving education was the fact that since 1812 (and up until 2015, when mandatory consolidation was ordered and approved by the supreme court and passed in 2020), each of the state's towns (with few exceptions) was a school district with its own school board and governance. In a state with a population of only 423,000 people, education was of varying quality, management was cumbersome, and the entire effort was more expensive than required. Education was financed entirely by property taxes levied per district. The system had been tolerated by a political class that insisted on direct local control over who taught, what they would be paid, how the schools would be run, and maintaining a personal relationship with those who controlled those functions. Systems for measuring student achievement were, as always, a subject of controversy. Above all, people were concerned about their property taxes.

I had no previous experience with elementary or secondary public schools (indeed, hadn't even attended any since sixth grade), finance, state government, school systems, or town management, so felt I had no bias for any point of view. I would have to learn and sort out various policy options on my own. On the other hand, I had two skills that turned out to be useful. My years in the Navy reserve had introduced me to the necessity of having a clearly articulated system of governance where the roles of people in the chain of command were understood, and where people worked together to make a large bureaucratic system respond to a stated mission. Then, after three years of law school and three years of private practice, I had a total of six years of training in analyzing arguments for or against particular results, often requiring clearly written statements for or against various policies.

Commissioner Gibboney welcomed me, introduced me to the key managers, and showed me my office in a corner as far from the commissioner's office as architecture would permit. I had a desk, a chair, and a telephone, and set out to learn how I might be useful. I walked the halls and visited informally with department managers, inquiring about their functions and problems. I attended meetings of the State Board of Education and listened to people who had kids in school describe their experiences. I asked myself, If "there oughta be a law," as I was repeatedly being told, what in general should it do? I heard complaints about progress in building new schools being thwarted by lawsuits, schools costing too much, and the state needing to support education with a broad-based tax to supplement property tax income. I also heard lots of griping that school decision makers—members of the State Board of Education, the state commissioner of education, local school superintendents, principals, and the voters themselves—too often worked at cross-purposes and never seemed to agree on direction. Teacher qualifications and curricula were also on peoples' minds, but it appeared that education governance was what needed to be thought through.

Like any new lawyer, I was sure the answers would be found through research in the State Law Library. I spent a few days there reading other states' laws, and quickly learned that each state had its own unique legal structure for governing and funding education, so it would be impossible to pull out some model legislation as a guide. I realized my task in Vermont would be to figure out who should make what decisions, especially about how money should be spent and where it would come from. I also realized I would have to talk to many more people about their concerns in order to answer these questions.

I focused first on finance. Property taxes at the time were almost the sole source of operating funds for schools. Not only were taxes rising, but the ability of school districts to raise money was inherently unfair. Simply put, taxes were lowest in some communities, known as "gold towns," where kids were fewest and property values were highest. In short, these towns could afford to have better schools. There was money available from the state for the less-well-funded communities, but only for school construction and repair, not operations. This situation generated demand for at least part of local operating costs to be borne by broader-based statewide taxes. I discussed this and other matters with Commissioner Gibboney, who was almost as ignorant as I was about systems for state aid to education. Together we decided to go to the U.S. Department of Education for a briefing on the subject of state aid. We spent the better part of a day with a competent education economist in Washington who schooled us on various merits and demerits of plans in existence in other states. This session gave me the ability to understand the contours of conversations on the subject going on at home.

A key official in these conversations was the state tax commissioner, Gerald S. Witherspoon, who headed the Hoff Administration's efforts to devise a state aid-to-education formula. I was included in those discussions from time to time, so was aware of administrative thinking, but was not directly involved in legislative schemes. Some policy makers jocularly referred to the evolving plan as the "Robin Hood Bill," as it would raise tax money from property-rich "gold towns" to support the poorer districts—with a sweetener of giving all districts money raised from broad-based state taxes. Such a law was passed in 1969, known as the "Miller Formula," named after the consultant who drafted it, but I had little to do with drafting or the political management of the bill.

Daily controversies over state funding for school construction or improvements were a promising context for my learning about education management. Funds for projects were administered by the Department of Education in the person of Rupert Spencer, who had the power to approve, disapprove, or modify all applications for state aid subject to the concurrence of the state board. Because Spencer traveled around the state discussing new schools and how to pay for them, I quickly figured he would likely be at the center of most education-related arguments, and was therefore a person I should know. I knocked quietly on his door. Rupert, a gregarious fellow in his late 50s or early 60s, waved me in with a "Hello! You must be the new guy!" He sat me down to tell me about the projects on which he was working. Spencer had been in charge for a long time, had a secretary but no staff, and was delighted to have someone who would listen without judgment and appreciate his expertise. He was talkative and carried on his description of projects with a combination of understated Vermont humor and sharp insight. He knew the problems and the personalities he would have to overcome to get a project going, and parceled out millions of dollars in state construction aid, often scaling projects down to make money available for others. He loved his work and was proud of helping others avoid costly mistakes. Spencer invited me to accompany him to a meeting in a town where a costly school addition project had been proposed. The existing school was old, deteriorating, and needed repairs and expansion to serve a growing school-age population. This was just the type of first-hand experience I needed. I had the advantage of being a new employee in a new job, with no boss or accumulated demands on my time and no predetermined schedule—I accepted the invitation.

Spencer often traveled alone, frequently to nighttime meetings, but this was to be a daytime meeting and he was happy to have company. He filled me in on the project and various factions and personalities involved. At the meeting I did not speak. Instead, I listened carefully to what was being said by proponents and opponents of the plan. Mostly, they discussed expenses, but these arguments about costs were camouflaged by questions of educational policy, such as how much space was needed for a particular school function or how elaborate or spartan the plan should be, or why a certain space was necessary for a certain function. Economics pragmatically resolved most of these arguments originally premised on views of how to educate kids. Lurking in the background of these discussions was the fact that if a bond issue considered too much by too many people were approved, a lawsuit to upset it would probably follow.

In this context, meeting participants often commented on various procedural steps, real or imagined, that had been omitted in violation of law. As I travelled and went to meetings, I concluded that many of these arguments were based on uncertainty of what the law actually required, and many, of course, were bluffs. After meetings, Spencer would frequently discuss with me the politics of each project and the personalities as he saw them. Where some would see him as the classic faceless bureaucrat bringing rolls of red tape, I admired him for the skillful work he did. In addition to following Spencer around, I went to any other meeting where there was a public discussion of education issues in order to hear as many arguments about education as I could.

Meanwhile, State Senator Bill Doyle, also a professor at Johnson State College, approached the Education Department with a plan to tour the state and find out what people thought about school consolidation. In 1957, Maine passed the Sinclair Act to consolidate its school districts. Ten years later the effects of that law were being seen. The law resulted in the number of schools dropping by 40 percent and the number of school boards declining by 50 percent, while existing schools doubled in size. The Sinclair Act, which was supposed to reduce costs and improve education, had begun stimulating thinking in Vermont. Whether it did that or not was hotly debated.

Commissioner Gibboney encouraged Senator Doyle and suggested I join him in the project. Soon, Doyle and I were on the road, spending a good part of the summer of 1967 going to Vermont towns, talking with school administrators and school board members about their opinions on Vermont consolidation plans. The issue, again, was money, but concern also was voiced about loss of local control as school districts became larger. It was rare to hear debate concerning how or what children actually learned. Despite all the talk that summer, I remained agnostic about the wisdom of consolidation. Senator Doyle and I wrote a report which, like many that followed over the next fifty years, has been lost (at least I was unable to find it in the state archives) or ignored. But those visits across the state that summer were important to me, as I learned what I thought I needed to know.

It wasn't long after my tour with Senator Doyle that Commissioner Gibboney was fired by the State Board of Education. I don't recall the reasons, but have a vague recollection it had much to do with politics. The search was on for a new commissioner, but I wasn't concerned. I assumed that because I was an assistant attorney general my tenure depended on Oakes, and that there was a consensus among decision makers that some new education laws were needed and I was going to do the drafting.

In early 1968, Harvey B. Scribner was appointed commissioner. He was an inspiration to me. Scribner was born in 1914, grew up on an island in Maine, and after his schooling went to work doing odd jobs on Matinicus Isle. He became restless, went to a mainland teacher training school, and obtained a teaching job. He then pursued more education, graduated from Farmington State Teachers College in 1946, which allowed him to become a chief school administrator in Dedham, Massachusetts, in 1954. While there, he continued his education, earning a master's in education from the University of Maine, and PhD from Boston University in 1960.

Scribner became superintendent of schools in Teaneck, New Jersey, in 1961. By 1965 he had led that community to adopt mandatory busing to racially integrate its schools—the only school district in the nation at that time to do so. He told me about that experience, saying that white opponents in the city "tarred and feathered me and put me a rail that carried me out of town. But I raised one hand high up out of the mess, stuck up my forefinger and said 'BUT I WAS RIGHT!' I grew up on a small island," he explained. "I knew what it was like to be thought of as a lesser person, a bumpkin or worse, and not have a good education, so I did something about it." I responded with a brief account of why I came to Vermont after being told to discontinue efforts to integrate beaches along the Connecticut shore. Scribner and I hit it off right away.

Scribner was a good administrator. His first step was to propose a plan to reorganize the jobs and functions of everyone employed by the department. The proposal served two functions. First, it made the entire staff uneasy that they would lose either influence or worse, their jobs, which helped make them eager to please him. The second function was to put people in positions where he felt they would be most effective and they would work hard to keep their job. I was a beneficiary.

Scribner moved me from my distant office to one adjacent to his that had been occupied by the deputy commissioner, who was relocated slightly farther away. Scribner was always available to talk about what I was doing or thinking, and liked to ask me things like, "Can I do this?" or, "Is there any law on the subject?" He liked to test his options and he always wanted to be on safe legal ground.

In his book, *Make Your Schools Work,* co-written with Leonard Stevens in 1975, Scribner set out the essence of the educational philosophy he brought to Vermont. Central to his thinking was the question, "For whose sake do public schools exist?" The conventional answer is they existed for youth who needed an education. Maybe so, Scribner would argue, but they also exist to provide work for educational professionals, to socialize and distribute an official culture, and to train citizens to serve in a democratic nation. The professional class, he argued, with its experts, specialties in learning systems, and accreditation rituals, was what really ran the schools and soaked up all the money. He once wrote, "The ultimate test of any reform idea is: what would it do to undermine the power relations of schools, to displace the professional class from its dominant and domineering position, to empower parents to govern, to orient schools to the needs of the young?" He believed that in education more emphasis must be placed on learning than on teaching. Each student is a different person with different ways of learning, who must be given a unique opportunity for success every day, no matter how slight. The school's function is to expand the differences between individuals, create a respect for those differences, and find successful learning experiences for all students.

The practical application of this point of view was that parents, through their school boards, should wrest control of the schools from the professional class and evaluate teachers and administrators by the simple standard of whether all children are learning. "Is every child accepted for what he or she is? Or do we label some children 'fast learners,' 'slow learners,' 'troubled,' 'hyperactive,' 'unorganized,' 'can't follow instructions,' 'disruptive,' or 'lazy'?"

He asked, "Do some children face chronic failure every day? Do we [wrongly, in his mind] emphasize rote learning—the teach 'em and test 'em approach?" These views were certainly compatible with my conclusion that the system had become dysfunctional for lack of clear rules concerning who had the power to do what.

Some specific events highlighted his philosophy. He asked me if there was any law that prohibited him from lowering the age of eligibility from twenty-one to sixteen years old to take the General Education Test (GED) by which high school dropouts could get a high school degree. I saw no statutory or other reason why he couldn't. But the educational establishment was furious. They argued, mostly in principle, that opening the test to high-school-age students would threaten multi-million dollar schools that either existed or were in the planning stages. Scribner's retort was that given the dropout rate for existing schools at the time, the kids taking the test weren't learning much anyway, so studying for and passing the test would provide at least some education. He was forced to compromise at age eighteen.

As I became known, I began getting phone calls from school superintendents seeking legal advice. Most questions from them, however, were not strictly law-related, in the sense of asking how a statute applied to a situation, they wanted to know how to use the law to navigate the maze of decision makers.

Part of my education in what laws to propose came from learning that skullduggery and shenanigans were possible where good-faith argument failed. In one infamous incident, residents in Grand Isle County—the county known as "the islands" on Lake Champlain, in far northwestern Vermont—voted to approve a union high school to serve all the island towns. The plan scuttled one popular feature of island life: existing law provided that if a town did not maintain a high school, it would have the tuition of a resident student to go off-island to a high school of his or her choice. This was popular with many who worked off the island and could transport their kids to and from school in towns where they worked, and others who would enroll their children in what they thought was the best nearby school. Other opponents simply did not like the idea of a new large school in the islands that might threaten some jobs or local influence. Vermont law required a revote on a proposal if demanded by a proper petition. A revote petition was filed. But there was a problem. The checklist in South Hero—that is, the list of eligible voters— was claimed to have been lost, so no revote was possible. The consequence was that the original vote was invalid, thereby defeating the union school. I was sent to investigate the situation, and if possible help the warring factions to compromise and approve the school. After mediating several long night-meetings with involved proponents and opponents, I was not getting closer to any solution.

I reported my futile efforts to Attorney General Oakes, who ordered an inquest to find the missing checklist. An inquest is a procedure similar to a grand jury in which witnesses could be subpoenaed to testify under oath. Frank Mahady, assistant attorney general (and later, the county of Windsor's state's attorney, and supreme court justice) from the criminal division was sent to conduct it. Many residents of South Hero were called to testify as to their knowledge of the whereabouts of the checklist. It is hard to keep a secret in a small town. Mahady began asking people under oath who knew what and when. There were passionate differences of opinion about the desirability of a single school for the island, among townspeople and within families, that caused various factions and individuals to report what they'd heard about what happened had to the checklist, understanding that there would be possible criminal charges against wrongdoers. Some witnesses became uncomfortable. Then, what a surprise! On the eve of her sworn testimony, the Town Clerk announced that by amazing good luck (and I suppose a fictitious new diligent search) she'd found the checklist that had inexplicably fallen behind the safe in her office. With the checklist found, the revote went forward and the union school idea was defeated. This incident led me to write a provision in the law I was proposing, requiring the checklist of each town to be filed with the clerk of the actual or proposed union school district.

Throughout 1967 and part of 1968, I often visited with Brownell and legislators on key House and Senate education committees, reciting broadly what problems I had discovered in administration. I offered to draft proposal for a bill that would repeal and rewrite all education statutes relating to governance of schools, and was encouraged to go ahead. I began by making lists of all governance issues I had encountered, then I assigned each of those issues to decision makers I thought should resolve it: state boards, commissioners, school superintendents, school principals, and school boards. Many governance problems were created by ambiguous laws that I proposed to rewrite or repeal. In the process, I contacted the people who might be affected, as well as legislators on the House and Senate Education committees, for advice and direction.

An obvious problem was that many lawsuits arose attacking school bond issues on the grounds that some procedure had not been properly followed, even after a revote had been petitioned and passed by voters. I did not participate in any of this litigation, preferring to settle cases by legislative action, and so suggested a simple solution. I drafted a proposal (that eventually became law) that provided that if a school bond issue was voted by a school district "no action at law or in equity attacking the legality of the formation of the district, or the validity of school district bonds, either directly or indirectly may be taken." When I finished my lists, I began writing statutory provisions to clarify duties and added provisions for the state board or the commissioner to resolve disputes. The resulting proposal enumerated the functions and powers of the board, the commissioner, superintendents, and voters. The proposal also dealt with many other issues, from state construction aid to the cost of student transportation.

In 1968 I submitted my proposal to members of the House Education Committee. As related below, I left the education department at the end of 1968. Beginning in 1969, the House Education Committee heard testimony and held hearings on the measure during the 1969 legislative session. In the 1970 session the committee brought out Committee Bill, H 476 incorporating much of my work, but much improved and added to by the committee. That bill passed as Act 298 of the 1969 adjourned session and became law on April 9, 1970. Act 298's statement of purpose was to "modernize certain parts of Title 16, [Education] relating to the state board, the commissioner, superintendents of schools, and school districts." It repealed approximately 123 sections of existing law whose provisions were moved, altered, or discontinued.

Below is one section of that law, illustrating its structure of assigning duties and responsibilities. One former commissioner of education told me she really enjoyed reading Title 16, because, unlike most laws, it was clear and easy to follow.

Sec. 39 16 V.S.A 316 is added to read:

Powers of electorate

At a school district meeting, the electorate:

(1) Shall conduct meetings in accordance with Robert's Rules of Order, unless other rules of order are specifically adopted at a meeting.

(2) Shall elect a moderator at the annual meeting who shall preside at the district meetings, regulate the business thereof,

decide questions of order, and make a public declaration of every vote. The moderator may administer oaths to district officers and newly elected school board members. In the moderator's absence, a moderator pro tempore shall be chosen to preside.

(3) May elect a school district clerk at the annual meeting who shall keep a true record of all proceedings at each district meeting, certify its records, make an attested copy of any records of the district for any person upon request, and tender of reasonable fees therefore, if so appointed serve as secretary of the school board, and perform such other duties as may be required by law.

(4) May authorize the school board to retain a public accountant, licensed in this State, to examine the accounts of the treasurer and the school board at the close of each fiscal year and at such other times whenever necessary, and report to the district whether the same are correctly cast and properly vouched.

(5) May vote annual salaries for school board members.

(6) May authorize the payment of actual and necessary expenses of school board members when traveling in the performance of duty.

(7) May authorize the school board to enter into leases of real property for more than three years, to purchase buildings or sites for school purposes, to locate and erect schoolhouses, and to sell, or otherwise dispose of, schoolhouses or sites for same.

(8) Shall authorize at each annual school district meeting an amount of money from all revenue sources to be expended by the board for the support of public schools; and, except for one-time purchase items that the board warns as a separate

article, the board shall determine how the authorized funds shall be expended.

(9) May authorize the school board to borrow money not in excess of anticipated revenue for the school year by issuing bonds or notes.

(10) Shall elect school board directors and other officers as are required for each class of school district.

(11) May grant general authority to the school board, at the request of the board, to incur debt at any time within the subsequent five years to finance the cost of school-building energy improvements not to exceed $350,000.00 per building in any three-year period and payable over a maximum term coextensive with the useful life of the financed improvements, but not to exceed ten years, provided that the avoided costs attributable to the financed improvements exceed the annual payment of principal and interest of the indebtedness. No indebtedness shall be incurred under this subdivision unless the entity appointed as an energy efficiency utility under 30 V.S.A. § 209(d)(2), an independent licensed engineer, or an independent licensed architect has certified to the district the cost of the improvements to be financed, the avoided costs attributable to the improvements, and the adequacy of debt service coverage from the avoided costs over the term of the proposed indebtedness.

(2) May take any action that is required for the sound administration of the school district. The Secretary, with the advice of the Attorney general, upon application of a school board, shall decide whether any action contemplated or taken by a school board under this subdivision is required for the sound administration of the district and is proper under this subdivision. The Secretary's decision shall be final.

By the middle of 1968, I concluded I'd done what I was hired to do for the education department. I had no professional educational training, or indeed interest in purely education disputes about how children learned or what they should learn. The subject seemed susceptible to fads, political opinion, and ad hoc reasoning. I was not enticed by the regulatory work of the department, and had no desire to make a career of being the department's lawyer. But I had enjoyed being center stage on a major reform effort, so I began to think about what I should do next.

CHAPTER 5

"To a young man who has in himself the magnificent
possibilities of life, it is not fitting that he should
be permanently commanded. He should be a commander."
President James A. Garfield

ELECTED AS STATE'S ATTORNEY

Among the legislative reforms of 1968 was the creation of the position for a full-time state's attorney in Washington County. Before that, the state's attorney was a part-time job taken by a lawyer in private practice who was paid a fee by the state to devote some time to prosecution. The publicity generated by the position undoubtedly provided relief from the sometimes humdrum picayune details of small-town law practice, while advertising the attorney's firm. But it was still part time. The legislature decided it needed a more robust system. The job of the state's attorney as a full-time employee with a reasonable salary was attractive. In 1968 there were no female state's attorneys. The incumbent prosecutor would be his own boss, and perhaps develop new skills to enhance his private legal career if he chose to pursue it. Friends and colleagues suggested I consider running for the office. I wanted to be a lawyer at the center of social issues. Ever since joining the Navy seven years earlier, I had vaguely dreamed of political involvement, and now saw a path toward that goal. As T. E. Lawrence noted:

"All men dream, but not equally. Those who dream by night in the dusty recesses of their minds, wake in the day to find that it was vanity: but the dreamers of the day are dangerous men, for they may act on their dreams with open eyes, to make them possible."

There would be no shortage of issues to face, as several law enforcement issues riled the public. The Supreme Court's Miranda decision, requiring that the accused have a lawyer if they wish and that suspects be warned that they need not incriminate themselves, had offended lots of Americans. In addition, many Americans were incensed by Vietnam War protestors who damaged property, looted stores, even blew up buildings. President Richard Nixon's call for law and order was popular, but so was Hubert Humphrey's call for peace and justice. In Vermont, some folks were loudly voicing concerns about draft dodgers and drug-using hippies moving into the state. Life as a prosecutor would be interesting and I welcomed the challenge. But first I would have to campaign and win an election. Another new experience lay ahead in my new home.

On the local scene, the incumbent Washington County state's attorney, Joseph Palmisano, a Republican, had chosen to seek higher office and was running for state attorney general. Palmisano had not yet distinguished himself. He was good at inflammatory rhetoric and actions catering to disaffected conservatives, blaming the influx of drugs and discontent on draft-dodging students and occasional protesters at the nearby Goddard College campus. He plea bargained away all his criminal cases but two—both involved similar "disrespectful" behaviors—with the intention of improving his image by pandering to his constituents. He charged one man who couldn't afford a lawyer with disorderly conduct for wearing an American flag sewn to the butt of his jeans, and used a jury trial to obtain a conviction. This generated laudatory letters to the editor of the Barre-Montpelier Time Argus and other favorable-to-his-cause publicity. The conviction was reversed on free-speech grounds by the state supreme court. His out-of-court behavior was also bluster. He rode on patrol with police and phoned a reporter with disparaging accounts about hippies and other young rebels in the county who needed to be curbed—resulting in his car being vandalized at least twice. He cited those episodes as signs of growing lawlessness in the state, rather than what they actually were: acts of retaliation, albeit illegal, for his own behavior.

As I considered running for state's attorney, I saw few obstacles. If I won, well, the next few years would be instructive. And if I didn't, I was sure I would find a job somewhere, either in state government or with a local law firm. Financial security was not a big issue. Barb was working, and family assistance in times of dire need was also possible. We were lucky in that regard. It was my decision whether to run; Barb raised no question. Colleagues in the attorney general's office, other private lawyers, and the legislators who helped create the full-time prosecutor position wanted a steadier hand in the local office who would provide professional management of law enforcement.

I didn't know much about the practice of criminal law but figured I could learn. I had one decisive advantage in my early career—working for Harvey Scribner, who mentored me to "Set goals and go all out!" as he frequently mentioned and acted upon. The day I decided to run seemed like the day I became an adult. It was 1968. I was thirty-three years old. Eventually I learned that I was wrong about becoming an adult, but I was certainly on the way.

But now a political question arose—was I a Democrat or a Republican? The Republican Party appeared to be rebounding after Hoff decided against running for reelection. Deane C. Davis, the former CEO of National Life Insurance Company, who promised both social and economic progress, was the Republican choice for governor. I had been a Democrat when I lived in Connecticut, however, in Vermont there were few signs of an organized Democratic Party at the local level; the Republicans I knew in the state were progressive, and many of the legislators who supported education reform were Republicans. So, I chose to run for state's attorney as a Republican.

I expected a primary and believed my opponent would be an accountant. No lawyer, besides me, sought the job. I checked my opponent's campaign filings, which no one else had bothered to do, and found that he had failed to obtain enough signatures on his nominating petition to be allowed on the ballot. I saw a victory with no effort simply by getting this opponent disqualified. I consulted a local lawyer for advice.

"Kim," said attorney John Patterson, "you are dead right about his failure. A suit to disqualify him would undoubtedly be successful, so you can win the primary and most likely the general election. But you are new in town, and few people know you, so if you knock him out with a slick lawyer's trick, it will probably be the last election you win." I got the message. I prepared for the primary. This would be a local election, but I knew national concerns would intrude.

The spring of '68 was rocked by the assassinations of both Dr. Martin Luther King, Jr. and Bobby Kennedy. Their deaths added to the consternation and alienation felt by a big segment of the younger generation troubled by the Vietnam War. The summer saw street demonstrations and mass arrests in Chicago during the infamous Democratic National Convention. "Hey, Hey, LBJ, how many kids have you killed today?" and "Hell no, we won't go [to Vietnam]!" were popular chants, not only in Chicago but also on college campuses across America. That fall saw Richard Nixon, a polarizing figure, become president with a promise of bringing "law and order" to the streets—code for cracking down on protesters and hippies. Though Vermont was far from Chicago and other cities suffering political and racial turmoil, the angst and anger spilled up this way, affecting local opinions and prejudices. Young urban refugees were flooding to Vermont, attracted by cheap land and beautiful scenery. Vermonters largely tolerated the newcomers, though many didn't appreciate their outspokenness, use of illegal drugs, and communal living arrangements. Bob Dylan sang, "the times, they are a-changin'"—as they were, but not without misgivings and opposition, including segments of law enforcement and others concerned about drugs, mostly pot, which appeared to be responsible for unwanted change.

I felt the focus on drugs was misplaced. My mom was an alcoholic. I knew firsthand the problems that come with abuse of that drug. I grew up before Mom's drinking was out of control, but my younger brothers had a terrible time. My dad did, too. There was yelling and tears, and for too long she chose the bottle over family, until fortunately one day she found her way to Alcoholics Anonymous, and after a long struggle became sober. As a consequence, my attitude toward the so-called "drug problem" included compassion for addiction, followed by treatment—whether it be booze or a mind-altering drug—with respect for the law which I would have to enforce should I become prosecutor. But I couldn't support putting people in jail for using pot if they did not otherwise endanger others. Despite all the talk back then about the sins of the counterculture, I doubted my opponent or a news reporter, or frankly anyone would bother to challenge my views about anything. I was not a big target. I would simply campaign on the need for professional law enforcement while avoiding any rhetoric that pandered to what I regarded as conservative angst.

My introduction to political campaigning occurred at the Fourth of July parade in Waterbury. I made an awkward start—I put on my lawyer clothes and set out alone, without supporters carrying banners or posters to entice people to vote for me. Some well-meaning advisor told me the political adage "a hand shook is a vote took." Simple enough, I thought, but I hadn't realized how hard it would be to thrust myself into the attention of unsuspecting strangers and asking for their vote. I was so shy, I walked the full length of both sides of the street before working up the courage to grab someone's hand. Finally I told myself, "Just do it!"

"Hello," I said to the first person I saw. He was standing with a child. "I'm running for state's attorney. I just wanted to say hello and let you know. My name is Kim Cheney."

"Oh," the stranger said, shaking my extended hand. "Glad to meet you; we need a good person there—hope it works out." To my amazement, many people I met that day were actually interested in who might fill that office, and were happy to meet me and engage in banter. I don't recall anyone asking me what my "platform" was. If anyone asked why I was running, or anything about crime, I said something about "better law enforcement by a competent lawyer" and moved on.

I shook about fifty hands that day, and many more before election day. As the campaign season progressed I honed a fifteen- to thirty-second opening comment promising competent law enforcement in the courtroom instead of posturing in the newspaper. I purchased only a few newspaper ads and radio spots. There was little opportunity to address big groups, though I did address one Rotary Club. I met with the twenty-three town clerks in the towns making up Washington County as I traveled to their town's country store or other local event, realizing they were important sources of gossip in their communities.

I won the primary easily, and was unopposed in the general election. As astonishing as the events of 1968 were to the country, to me the most noteworthy event was winning an election. Beginning in January 1969, I would be the top law-enforcement officer in Washington County, located in Montpelier, the state capital. For the next two months I said my goodbyes to friends in education, discussed my proposed education reform bill with key legislators, and tried to learn what I could about the state's attorney job.

A source of guidance was the American Bar Association's Criminal Justice Standards for the Prosecution Function. The standards are lengthy, covering many areas of duty. I focused my attention on the first standard:

"The primary duty of the prosecutor is to seek justice within the bounds

57

of the law, not merely to convict. The prosecutor serves the public interest and should act with integrity and balanced judgement to increase public safety both by pursuing appropriate criminal charges of appropriate severity, and by exercising discretion to not pursue criminal charges in appropriate circumstances. The prosecutor should seek to protect the innocent and convict the guilty, consider the interests of victims and witnesses, and respect the constitutional and legal rights of all persons, including suspects and defendants."

This was an aspirational standard rather than an ethical disciplinary guide. I was drawn to the idea that my job would be to seek justice and use discretion as I saw fit in the public interest. Vague as this was, and ambiguous as the idea of justice is, the standard fit my concept of what public service was about and to some degree mirrored the goals of the education reform bill. I expected to be a competent prosecutor following this standard, and was happy to be so engaged.

There was no official physical office for the Washington County State's Attorney because, until 1968, local prosecutors handled their prosecutorial duties from their own private offices. But the state was now obligated to provide an office. I rented two rooms in Montpelier in an unused area of a building that was uninhabited above the first floor. The landlord financed a partial renovation, creating a front "office" overlooking Main Street, and a rear room with a window overlooking the parking lot. I bought furniture from Sears, including two steel desks, two file cabinets, two high-back desk chairs and, for visitors, four steel chairs with arm rests. I perked up the spartan decor by hanging pictures of Vermont scenes on the walls, plus a print of a breaching whale obtained from an organization dedicated to protecting the species.

My companions at work were Hector, a large black Labrador Retriever, who also would accompany me on hikes, carrying a pack with his food on his back. He liked to come to work and sleep near my desk, hoping I would take him for a walk from time to time, which I did, tying him to a parking meter when I went to lunch. I hired Elizabeth Dodge as my secretary. She was experienced, competent, and a pleasure to have in the office, livening up every day with a laugh or acerbic comment. She was curious and knew much more about people in the community than I did.

After getting the office set up, I established a routine and soon received an unusual invitation. The state commissioner of corrections, who wanted to close the state's sole maximum-security prison at Windsor, invited all Vermont's state's attorneys to a tour of the prison. It had been built in 1808, during Thomas Jefferson's presidency, and had been in service since. It was a massive stone structure with steel bars set in rock, divided into cells perhaps six by eight feet. As the tour soon revealed, the facility, with its dim light, stale air, and clammy walls, was enough to repulse anyone. I was appalled that people were confined there, no matter how horrible their crimes, the environment struck me as inhumane.

To clinch his case for closure, the commissioner had one of the officers who had served in the prison many years display some of the contraband taken from prisoners over the years. The array included weapons used in fights between inmates; knives fashioned from stone and steel, ropes made from clothing, and—most terrifying—light bulbs with minute holes drilled in them with paper clips or pencils through which inmates could pour lighter fluid. The assailant would surreptitiously install them into a victim's cell; when the victim flicked the light switch, the bulb would explode, sending shards of glass and fire to "burn out" the victim. This was a common tactic of revenge and control by prison gangs, according to the officer.

One recently elected prosecutor, Robert Gensburg, after hearing all this, went home and resigned as Caledonia County state's attorney, saying, "I will not be a part of sending anyone to this place!" By this act, he earned my lifetime admiration. Many years later, I further admired his effort to investigate corruption in drug enforcement in Vermont. I decided to support the commissioner in his efforts to close Windsor Prison.

After the prison visit, and with my office ready for business, I began seeing police officers who would come to discuss cases and ask me to initiate a prosecution. One early visitor was Mark Brown, the county sheriff. Brown was maybe fifty years old, and, like me, was newly elected to office. Unlike sheriffs in many states who are the principal law enforcement officers in their jurisdictions, a Vermont sheriff's main duties were to arrange transport of prisoners from jails to court, maintain courthouse security, arrange for traffic control, and contract with small towns for law-enforcement services. The state police, with the assistance of local police departments, were the primary organizations that investigated crime, thereby allowing Vermont to avoid the maladministration and favoritism possible in a police agency headed by an elected official.

Brown was wearing his uniform; I was wearing a suit and tie. We were to discuss issuing a summons for a serious reckless-driving case. Brown had personally carried out a high-speed chase ending with the teenage driver crashing his car in downtown Montpelier. The law governing initiation of a prosecution at that time was simple and informal: the arresting officer would prepare a document loosely called an "information," pleading that the state's attorney send it to the court informing of the charge. The information included a brief report of what had occurred plus a description of the conduct of the accused in statutory form. If the state's attorney signed the information, the accused was arrested, or summoned if he or she was not already in custody. There was no other review or required court determination of probable cause for the arrest. Brown sat opposite me across my desk, pushing the information papers charging the teen to me to sign. I glanced at the various alleged offences. I'd heard something about the case on a morning radio program, but wanted to hear firsthand from the sheriff what the case was about.

Brown gave me the essence of the situation, relating that, about nine o'clock the previous night, he was in his cruiser at a gas station on Memorial Drive in Montpelier, looking up the hill on Northfield Street. He received a radio call that a car was speeding on Northfield Street and rapidly heading toward town. He saw the car coming down the hill and estimated it to be going sixty in a twenty-five mph zone. The tires screeched as the car made a right turn through a red light onto Memorial Drive, then accelerated along the drive following the Winooski River.

Brown flicked on the blue lights and siren and swung behind the speeding car. He guessed both vehicles reached speeds of up to ninety mph in short bursts, sometimes weaving around stopped traffic. After about five minutes, the driver of the car lost control and crashed into a roadside structure. The driver, seventeen, was slumped over in his seat, apparently unconscious, and the sheriff called an ambulance to take him to the hospital.

"He was messed up but should recover with time," Brown said. I asked Brown if he had been worried that another driver or pedestrian might have been injured during the ninety-mph chase. "Of course," he said, "but someone might have been hurt at the speed the kid was going when first sighted." He said he thought it was best to apprehend the kid, and said something like, "they can't be allowed to get away with reckless driving." I asked if there weren't other ways to deal with such a problem, to keep a bad situation from getting worse. After further discussion I picked up the papers on my desk and said, "Thanks, Mark. I appreciate you bringing this to my attention and risking your life as well as that of others."

"Kim, aren't you going to sign?" Brown asked in anxious surprise.

"I need time to think about this," I said. "I can't decide which of you to charge! There must be a way to deal with something like this without creating more danger to people." The sheriff angrily left the office. After two days and after discussing the issue of high-speed chases with other officers, I did charge the driver with careless and negligent operation and speeding. And not long afterwards, after consulting with Sheriff Brown, area police departments, and the state police, we worked out a policy for high-speed chases designed to minimize collateral damage to innocent people. It specified that police call for help and, if at all possible, set up roadblocks or use spikes to stop speeding cars. Nothing is foolproof, but I thought this was at least a step in the right direction.

That wasn't my last run-in with Sheriff Brown, and in fairness I probably share some of the blame for getting off to a bad start with him. I could have been more diplomatic. This job would be difficult to do without angering some people and pleasing others. It was an interesting first lesson for me.

CHAPTER 6

"From the mountain top, the wilderness spread
before you looks benign in its beauty."
Kimberly B. Cheney, 2019

ROUTINE COURT
BUSINESS

The courthouse in Barre, Montpelier's sister city, was a surprise: no
Greek columns, no historic architecture, no distinguished grand
statement—in short, no signs proclaiming the building's noble purpose.
The structure was an old, formerly unused, remodeled school building.
The layout was conventional, with the entrance through an unmarked
door leading to a staircase to the actual courtroom on the spacious second
floor. In the courtroom were rows of chairs for spectators facing the judge's
bench, a wooden railing dividing the room behind which were two desks
for lawyers, prosecution on the right and defense on the left, while further
to the left was the bailiff's table (with a doorway to the judge's chambers
behind it), the judge's raised dais, and a witness box to the right of the dais.
The jury box was against the wall to the right, with windows opposite, on
the left. There were no portraits of bearded, former distinguished jurists
and no decorations or furniture suggesting the majesty of justice or the
state. There was a Vermont state flag with its pine tree and cow, and of
course, the Stars and Stripes. The space appeared to be a statement to all

who sat in it to pay attention only to the legal matters at hand, giving no hint of the often decisive effect that room had on the people who entered it, whether they be police officers, prosecutors, probation officers, witnesses, defense attorneys, judges, defendants—guilty or innocent—and spectators. Vindication, validation, fear, hope, humiliation, despair, career enhancements or destructions, were all possible here. Judge John Connarn, a former Democratic attorney general and limping wounded World War II veteran of the Italian campaign, presided. He had the reputation of reasonably assessing the appropriate fate of defendants without tortured legal analysis. He dealt with all crimes except murder. Judges did not rotate to other districts back then, so Judge Connarn was a permanent fixture in this court for many years.

Monday was arraignment day. On that day, suspects arrested over the weekend or summoned to appear on that date assembled to wait their turn to be called before the court to enter a plea of not guilty, make bail if possible and be given a schedule for future appearance, or plead guilty and hear their punishment. The typical Monday lineup featured shoplifters, check forgers, drunks who got in fights, drunks who drove cars—sometimes injuring others, burglars, drug users, drug sellers, and parole violators. Few sex crimes were brought to court, not because they weren't being committed, but because it was rare for police to bring a domestic assault case against a man, especially when the case involved his girlfriend or wife. Violence against women was largely ignored by authorities, based on the then-faulty notion that if the woman continued to live with an abusive man, she condoned the mistreatment. Over time, dramatic changes have been made in laws and actions protecting women, but during my time as state's attorney, the silence fostered by culture and mirrored by police prevailed.

Arraignment day had a set procedure: Police officers would submit their prepared report of the offense to the court clerk, to me, and to the defendant. If I had not already done so, I would review the report and sign the prepared information if I found probable cause to believe that a crime had been committed and that the defendant had likely committed it. The accused would get a copy of information and the report. Time was available for a defendant, with or without the assistance of a lawyer, to speak with me to agree to or dispute the accuracy of the police report and negotiate what penalty I would recommend to the judge if there were a guilty plea. When ready, the defendant would be called before the judge and asked if he would plead guilty or not guilty. If the crime was minor and the person felt the charge and my suggested fine or other penalty were acceptable, he could plead guilty. The judge frequently followed my recommendation for low-level offenses to speed things along. If the plea was not guilty, the defendant would have bail set or condition of release imposed, such as abstinence from drink or other misbehavior, be given time to find a lawyer or perhaps have one assigned by the court, and then be told the schedule of next appearance. If a jail sentence was likely, the plea would invariably be "not guilty," bail would be set, and the case would be scheduled for further action.

Everyone was entitled to a jury trial, but both the prosecution and the defense had an incentive to save time or money by trying to negotiate an outcome. Plea bargaining was the result, which meant the defendant would give up his or her right to a trial in exchange for a guilty plea to a lesser charge or possibly reduced jail term or smaller fine. I initiated a policy to try some cases if I couldn't resolve them by negotiation, in order to strengthen my plea bargaining position. Vermont fifty years ago was small enough and intimate enough that everyone seemed to know everyone, and that included cops and scofflaws. This frequently added another dimension to meting out justice, with often ameliorative results.

A typical case would be like the charge of burglary brought against a person I will call "Randy Logan," twenty-five, who was spotted by police breaking into a pharmacy. (In this case, as in others I describe, I've used pseudonyms and fact sketches to describe cases and defendants who, after their brush with the law, may well have moved on to live exemplary lives.) Logan was represented by attorney Ed Free, who in his late fifties worked in the most prominent criminal-defense firm in the county. Logan was physically fit and had a relaxed manner that concealed underlying competitiveness, if not downright aggression. He was first in line that day. I always called first the offenders represented by private attorneys, as a courtesy to the lawyers and to lower the cost of legal fees to the client.

"Good Morning, Kim. Looks like a full house today," Free said, gesturing to the crowd in the courthouse. "The cops must have been busy this weekend." He mentioned that I probably had a lot of work ahead of me and that he didn't want to take much of my time. "I have to get out of here quickly today, anyway. I have a case pending in Superior Court [where civil cases are tried], but we should be able to plead Randy quickly. You know he's not a bad guy—he's a good worker, works in the granite sheds, just married, has a baby girl with serious asthma, comes from a large family, and has never had any trouble before.

"I know it looks bad," he continued, "but he wasn't after drugs. He needed money to pay his kid's doctor, and this was just a spur-of-the-moment deal. He was depressed and anxious and just decided to break in and get some cash. You can tell this break-in wasn't planned by how stupid he was and how quickly he got caught." He paused, checking my expression to see if he was making progress and then went on. "I think a misdemeanor attempted larceny is a better charge than felony burglary. Put him on probation and give him time to pay a fine and for repairs to the store," he suggested.

Now it was my turn. I pointed out that this break-in was at 2 a.m., and that Mr. Logan was caught thanks to a silent alarm. The officer's report didn't say anything about him being drunk or otherwise disturbed, or him saying anything about needing to pay the doctor. It was a nice story, but it was thin. I suggested Ed have Randy plead not guilty, and we'd release him without money bail. I added that the court would schedule a status conference in about a month, and we both should learn more by then. "We can have a serious talk and involve the judge if necessary at that time, but I'm not now buying your story," I said.

We did have that talk with the judge after I got more information from the police. Although the information wasn't rock-solid, it did indicate that Randy did have a drug problem and was suspected of being involved in other minor crimes. Attorney Free and I negotiated a plea agreement: Logan would plead guilty to the misdemeanor charge of attempted larceny, be given a sentence of one to three years, all suspended except thirty days jail time. I thought the lesser charge fair as long as he did some time to remind him of what would happen if there was a repeat offense, followed by a lengthy probation. The judge agreed with the recommendation.

Northfield's Police Chief, Burton Saunders, whose small-town department had six officers, was next. He and I sat down to talk. His uniform was clean and crisply pressed. He had been chief for a long time. I knew he seldom made arrests or issued summonses unless the offender was truly offensive, like the young Pete Williams who had assaulted and robbed a man with disabilities. "Pete has been trouble for a long time," Saunders reported. He added that he'd known him as a kid "but couldn't do anything with him." I agreed the matter required a serious sentence and asked Saunders what he meant by "couldn't do anything" with Pete.

"Well, usually when some kid acts up, I go see his parents and talk to them, or sit down with the kid to find out what's going wrong for him and see what can be done. But talking isn't always effective with a guy like Pete," said the chief.

I added, "And he's no kid."

"You are right," said Saunders. "But I do more than just talk to people. I find out what's going on. Is there too much drinking, a drug habit, no job, some girlfriend-boyfriend stuff, a wife-husband problem, you know—the kind of stuff that screws a person up. If it's booze, I get them to AA and keep an eye on them. If it's other stuff, I try to get some promises out of them and see that they keep them." Saunders was on a roll explaining his role. "Sometimes it works; sometimes it doesn't, but it's better than a jail sentence. Jail hardly ever improves someone."

"Jesus, you play social worker?" I said. He told me that was indeed part of his job. It took more work, but if you have the community behind you, you can get help from others, and family and friends can help with the follow-up.

I can't remember what happened to Pete Williams. After he obtained a lawyer and we had plea negotiations, the outcome probably was that he plead guilty to one felony count and was given a split sentence with one-year minimum and five-year maximum, meaning he'd have to convince the parole board to release him after the minimum time served, so he might do longer than the minimum. His crime was serious business, but a first proven offense. Saunders had done his best with Pete, it was now time for serious corrections. Mostly, I remember what a wonderful lesson I got from Saunders about small-town police work. I had to admire the chief's dedication and good sense.

State Trooper Edward Fish was next. He sat down and told me, "This guy, Raymond, I summoned for driving under the influence is a real turkey. He was weaving in and out of traffic, scaring everyone half to death. Had to chase him about five miles. I got him out of the car to do roadside tests. He was staggering and smoking. I asked him to put out the cigarette, and stuck out my hand for it. He put it out all right. He crushed it out in my palm! He was plenty drunk, so I don't want any dinky plea bargain for this dude."

"Don't worry," I said, though this would be my first DWI case and I didn't know what to expect. Early on, I had decided to try any case with a blood-alcohol breath-test result over the .10 limit. Not only were drunk drivers a menace to everyone on the road, but such a policy rewarded police for doing a good job, because they could see their efforts paid off. Raymond asked for a jury trial and was convicted. Judge Connarn gave him a split jail sentence followed by probation and a fine, some of which may have been enhanced by using Trooper Fish's hand as an ashtray.

Next in line was state Trooper Mel Morris. He, too, had made a highway stop, but not for DWI. "I stopped the guy for speeding, and he allowed a search of his car. I found a small stub in his ashtray which smelled like marijuana. He was okay though, no impairment that I noticed, just wanted to make a record." I asked Morris what he thought about a minor driving offense instead of a criminal drug crime. That made sense to both of us.

Then I had to deal with an after-school student fist fight. Ben Severge, eighteen, came in with his dad, Tommy Severge. The police report described the fisticuffs between Ben and another boy in which Ben got the upper hand. Sweaty and slightly bruised, Ben had calmed down by the time police arrived. The teen had been summoned to answer a charge of simple assault.

"Mr. Cheney," Tommy Severge said, "I'm really embarrassed. This is not like Ben. I spent an hour with him trying to see what's going on. I don't understand what has upset him; he doesn't want to talk—his mom can't get anything from him either. I wish I knew what to do."

"Mr. Severge," I said, "I'm glad to hear what you have to say. Maybe the school guidance counselor, or someone else at school, or you and his mom working on him some more, can help solve this. I'll put it on the docket for next week and you keep on trying to get Ben to open up and find out why he's so angry. I'll see what the other kid's family has to say and determine the extent of his injuries. We can talk again."

We did talk. With the help of the school counselor, Ben's parents got Ben to open up. He had a difficult relationship with his girlfriend, who had said mean things about him to himself and others. The injured boy had mocked him, but he admitted he'd been partly to blame. After talking with Ben and his family, and the victim's family, I saw no need for Ben to be given a criminal record, and dismissed the case. The boys were old for what amounted to an old-fashioned playground fight, but I let it go because there appeared to be genuine remorse on both sides and a criminal record might well lead to future anger and acting out.

By the end of a typical arraignment morning, about fifteen cases would be processed. Files of cases that were not resolved were given to Liz to store.

She would note any scheduled next court event or follow-up that I needed to address. It was largely a to-do list that we kept, mentioning whether further investigation was needed, whether new witnesses had to be interviewed, or whether I would need to respond to defense motions contesting the process or conduct of the police. One day, Liz looked overwhelmed. Files were piling up and she didn't know if she was expected to remember the facts of each or simply put them away alphabetically, to check as needed. I mentioned a filing system thought up by wags at the courthouse. There are only four kinds of criminal defenses, I said, so each of our folders should be put under one of the following headers:

(1) The SODI defense: "Some Other Dude Did it."
(2) The NOT FAIR defense: "You Didn't Catch Me, Right?"
(3) The NUTS defense: "I Was Crazy When I Did It."
(4) The U2 defense: "You'd Do It Too If You Were In My Position."

She didn't think this was helpful advice—even though it did list the usual defenses. She gave me a quiet raspberry and went back to work.

It didn't take me long to appreciate firsthand the challenges faced by police and other law-enforcement personnel. Their work can be dangerous, physically and mentally draining, and can take a toll on home life. The head of the state police once told me that one of his chief tasks was to be aware of and address the emotional needs of his officers, who were stressed by everything from tragic highway accidents to senseless murders and the feeling they were a thin blue line against social disintegration.

Despite my respect for the police, I knew my responsibility as prosecutor was always to assess the credibility of an officer when he or she gathers evidence to bring charges. Constitutional doctrine arising from a U.S. Supreme Court decision, *Brady v. Maryland*, a 1963 landmark case, requires that prosecution provide the defense with any evidence supporting an accused person's innocence. *Brady* did not apply to a prosecutor's suspicion that an officer might be making things up. A prosecutor's function, to be exercised if he or she has credible suspicion of an officer's duplicity—even without actual proof—may be to refuse to prosecute cases brought by that officer. This action will, of course, have serious repercussions for both the officer and the prosecutor, as I relate later in this memoir, and requires careful thought and at least some identifiable evidence. In my state's attorney tenure, I seldom encountered incidents of blatant police deceit. I found the officers with whom

I worked to be straightforward, trustworthy, and careful to state only facts—with one notable exception.

It was a fall day in 1971 when I selected a jury for a case in which the now-former Barre Town Police Chief Malcomb Mayo was the principal witness. In *voir dire* (meaning: a process to find the truth), as the process for jury selection is called, I routinely asked potential jurors if they believed police were generally honest or if they generally thought an officer might say anything to get a conviction. Defense attorneys ask potential jurors similar questions. At this *voir dire*, I went through the usual routine, something like this: "Mr. (or Ms.) Juror, because Chief Mayo is a police officer sworn to tell the truth, are you inclined to believe what he says simply because he is a police officer, or are you suspicious about officers?" Prospective jurors usually answered with something like this: "I would not believe him just because he's an officer; I would have to hear the evidence." That response was sufficient to show lack of bias, thus qualifying the person to be seated as a juror.

In this case, a lunch recess was called before all twelve jurors were selected. After the recess, but before we got started by calling out new names, an officer from the state Fish and Game Department and Nelson Lay, a state police detective, signaled that I should talk with them. I went over to them, and was handed a note that read something like the following: "Kim, we've suspected Mayo of poaching deer for a long time. We have witnesses. We sent police divers to the bottom of a local granite quarry this morning. They found a bunch of deer parts left over after the deer was dressed, wrapped in newspaper with Mike Mayo's name written on it in grease pencil, as the witness said we would. The local store owner says he put the name of all his customers in grease pencil on paper being held for them and that Mayo is a frequent customer."

The chief was a scheduled witness, but after receiving this information, I was not going to use him as my witness regardless of his actual guilt or innocence of poaching deer. There seemed to be enough smoke and possibly a fire, furnished to me by trusted officers, indicating he was not trustworthy. When it was my turn to resume questioning prospective jurors, I reported that I had been advised that Mayo was being investigated by authorities for poaching deer, but the outcome was uncertain. I asked if that new information might lead them to question evidence or testimony presented by Mayo. The answer by all was an emphatic "yes." After getting the answer I expected, I dismissed the case.

I could have dismissed the case without bringing the investigation to the attention of the jurors, but I thought it was an important opportunity to show the public and potential jurors that neither I nor the state police prosecute cases involving officers of questionable integrity. If there had been a conviction based on Mayo's testimony and this information followed, it would have had a devastating impact on future prosecutions. Later events proved my hunch correct.

In the 1974 elections, Mike Mayo was elected sheriff of Washington County, to take office in 1975. In 1976, in a rare Vermont impeachment proceeding, the House of Representatives found charges against Mayo. Impeachment is the sole method of removal from offices created by the state constitution, such as county sheriff. I don't have information as to why no criminal charges were brought against him, but three impeachable charges were found:

> Article I (1) Creating false reports about the date a deputy had been appointed, after the deputy made an improper arrest on a drug raid (2) Ordering the deputy to create a false report concerning the drug raid (3) Falsifying a statement he made to the Montpelier Police Department regarding an assault committed by him at the Thrush Tavern (4) Submitting a sample of marijuana to the State police laboratory, falsely claiming it had been seized on a raid.

> Article II Charged that, as sheriff, he ordered all his deputies not to cooperate with other law enforcement agencies.

> Article III Engaging in an assault and retaliating against other officers who intervened.

There was a trial in the State Senate on these charges. Mayo was represented by Barre lawyer Richard Davis; the House of Representatives, by one of its lawyer members. The case was not well-presented and was fraught with politics, resulting in Mayo being acquitted of all charges. Impeachment is a political proceeding, not necessarily a fact-finding proceeding, nonetheless, I doubt any state's attorney would thereafter use Mayo as a witness in a criminal trial. The proceedings can be found in the 1976 journal of the House, pages

389-390, and in the 1976 Journal of the Senate, pages 583-617.

Perhaps one of my biggest surprises occurred at an arraignment day several months later. A young man, whom I will call Ralph Ramage, appeared in court to answer charges that he had stolen groceries from a car parked in Montpelier's Grand Union parking lot while the shopper ran other errands. He lifted four bags of freshly-purchased groceries out of a car before bystanders accosted him and summoned police. He was arrested without incident, released with a summons, and appeared in court as ordered. He was about thirty years old and wore old jeans and a baggy sweatshirt. He looked ashamed and frightened, and I charged him with petty larceny.

When his case was called, he shuffled forward, agreed with the charges without argument, listened respectfully to Judge Connarn, who asked him if he understood the charge and wanted to plead guilty. "Yes, your honor," he said. Judge Connarn, learning Ramage was unemployed with two children, simply placed him on probation without imposing a fine. A reporter from the Barre-Montpelier *Times Argus* was in court and duly reported the story he evidently found to be the most interesting of the day: "Man Caught Stealing Groceries From Shoppers" was the headline, with a subhead adding, "Placed on Probation With No Fine." I thought the case and the news story unexceptional—until I received a call from Gov. Dean Davis's wife.

"Mr. Cheney," Mrs. Davis said evenly, "you don't know me, but I want to tell you that a group of my friends and I were very disturbed to read about the man stealing groceries from cars at the supermarket. He was let off with probation. We want to review what the court is doing and review the punishments being given. We think this was much too lenient, so perhaps there are other cases like this."

This was my first and only call of a political nature. I explained that of course this was a serious crime, and invited the governor's wife to come to court any time to talk to some key people, including, perhaps, Judge Connarn.

Soon, Mrs. Davis, accompanied by what I surmised were three other Republican women, appeared in court to review the Ramage matter. They were well dressed, polite, and appeared ready to correct a great wrong. I made sure the arresting officer and the probation officer would be present to answer questions. An informal discussion arose in the courtroom between the police officer, probation officer, the women, and me, all standing in a circle. Mrs. Davis was polite, but frustrated. She repeated that Ramage and others like him might be getting off too easy for their crimes, and we all, in our various capacities, should be harder on them.

"I've known Mr. Ramage and his family for quite a while," the officer said. "His wife left him with two children; he's had trouble keeping a job, but he's not a really bad sort. What he did made people pretty angry, but he was desperate. He told me he was sorry but that he didn't know what to do."

The probation officer spoke up. "I have been supervising Ralph Ramage now for about a month. At the time of the offense, Mr. Ramage was having a hard time; he'd lost his job at the quarry—I forget why—but he had no money, and no food for himself or his kids. His rent was due and he wasn't aware of how to apply for state assistance. He had no family to fall back on. He was totally ashamed. I think he's doing a lot better now."

The probation officer stressed that Ramage was sticking to the terms of his probation: he had found work, he was reporting for counseling, and he was staying out of trouble. I told Mrs. Davis I thought this came out about right. Jail wouldn't do any good, nor would a fine, as both would certainly have hurt the children. And the man was genuinely remorseful.

Underlying Mrs. Davis's concern, and the basis for all criminal punishment for that matter, was the concept of choice and free will—that people choose how to behave. I told Mrs. Davis that I agreed, if someone makes a bad choice there should be consequences that fit the crime, but there were times when it made sense to allow for exigent circumstances, like poverty, despair, or depression. She appeared convinced, thanked us all for meeting with her, and the group turned as if on cue and left the courthouse.

I never heard another word of criticism about being too lenient with offenders, and I was pleased with our visit, odd as it may have seemed. We made a point that "getting tough on crime" involved more than "locking 'em up." I've thought about that incident many times since. It exemplified what I liked about our small community in Vermont—people here could take the time to get the facts, have a discussion, respect each other, and moderate their opinions.

CHAPTER 7

"I love to deal with doctrines and events.
The contests of men about men I greatly dislike."

President James A. Garfield

JURY TRIALS

M y first felony jury trial was set to be heard. It was a serious and difficult case, and I knew I would need help. The facts were these: On a summer night in 1967, Abe German, fifty-eight, was working alone as an attendant at a gas station in the town of Berlin. According to him, he had gone outside to check on a noise when a man appeared from the dark and brutally attacked him with a tire iron, leaving him unconscious. German, who was incoherent for ten days after the attack, suffered permanent injuries and was never himself afterwards. The attacker stole $64 from the cash register. German identified Ernest Colby as his assailant. Colby was arrested, and the case investigated, before my term as state's attorney. Formal charges were brought by my predecessor, Joseph Palmisano. I had tried two or three DWI cases prior to this one landing at my feet, but no felonies. I asked the attorney general's office for help with the trial, feeling that a case of such importance to the community should be well presented. The chief of the attorney general's criminal division, Bill Keefe, a long-time prosecutor there, was assigned to assist.

Keefe was a short, heavy-set man who dressed in plain suits that looked well lived in. He favored unremarkable neck ties with white shirts, projecting an image of careful ordinariness which matched his personality—he had a police mentality and saw few shades of gray. He represented the good guys in a world full of bad guys who were all guilty, or they wouldn't have been charged. He was known for determination and thoroughness.

I met Keefe in my small office. We were seated on the opposite sides of my steel desk with coffee cups guarding the files spread before us that contained indexed police reports of each officer's investigation, recorded witness statements, an FBI forensic report on paint samples, and charts with diagrams of the assault scene.

After some banter about our shared profession, I summarized the basic facts of the case. "The defendant, Ernest Colby, age twenty-five, is well known to police. He pled guilty in 1962 to robbing his stepfather's gas station, and did time in Windsor prison. He's a rugged guy, reputed to be a Golden Gloves champion with a reputation for hanging out with questionable companions. His lawyer is Ed Free, who you and I know is competent. Free hasn't even suggested he might plea bargain, probably because he knows that with a prior conviction a second vicious crime will put Colby away for a long time."

Keefe's response was perfunctory. "I'm here to help," he said. "But it's your case, and you will be lead counsel. This case is a bag of contested facts that could go either way, but you ought to get this guy." This response wasn't encouraging—Keefe wasn't engaged; the trial didn't mean that much to him. It was just another case, one that he hadn't lived with or helped investigate. In a way, I was in the same position, for I had not been involved in the investigation or worked with police to bring charges. However, it was my first big trial and I wanted to avoid rookie mistakes in the conviction of a man I thought a major danger to the community.

I got right to the point with Keefe, telling him German said he could identify Colby as his attacker. But there was a problem. The assault occurred in semi-darkness behind the gas station, and in the shadow of a fuel tank. German, bleeding, was discovered by customers seeking gas, who called 911. German told police that he had gone outside because he heard someone banging on the tank. He said he knew Colby and could identify him because lights from the station's restroom partially illuminated the area by the tank. But the police report stated that when he made the identification he was still suffering some confusion from the smash to his head. I told Keefe, "I'm worried that German may not appear to the jury as completely credible in his identification."

"Yeah, I see that," Keefe responded. He then brought up another difficulty identified in the police reports. There was a witness, a waitress named Linda, who claimed that several weeks after the attack she overheard German talking to his son while she was serving them. She heard him say he wasn't sure who attacked him. She knew Colby, but there was little in the report describing their relationship, whether they were mere acquaintances, casual friends, or lovers. Keefe pointed out that the cross-examination of Linda would be crucial. "Have you had much experience with cross-examination?" he asked.

I replied that I had not. I'd read some books, tried some misdemeanor cases where the facts were not complicated, but had not learned any techniques for examination of a witness like Linda, who could upset our case. My plan was to rely on German's doctor, who would say German wasn't capable of clear speech at the time Linda said she heard him admit he couldn't identify Colby, but that he had recovered sufficiently to do so now, and there was no indication his memory was compromised.

Keefe said he, himself, would not do the cross-exam, and there wasn't time for him to teach me much, so that meant I would just do the best I could by cross-examining Linda about her relationship with Colby until I found things that might compromise her impartiality. I was upset. I had no information regarding this possibility. Could I just pursue this without strong evidence?

There were other problems. Colby claimed to have an alibi. There were two friends who would testify that Colby was with them at a hunting camp. They would say Colby showed up at 1:45 a.m.—about the time the crime occurred—and joined them for a few drinks and conversation. Those witnesses would also need to be cross-examined carefully. The police estimated it would have taken at least fifteen minutes to drive from the gas station to the hunting camp, which would have meant Colby would not have been at the gas station after 1:30 a.m., which was the estimated time of the attack. And that would mean someone other than Colby had attacked German.

Favorable evidence was provided by an FBI report. A piece of tape used to hold rusted parts together on a car was found near the site of the attack. The object used for the assault, a tire iron, was also found by the tank. The FBI stated the tape was of the same type found on Colby's car. How it got there, though, was not clear. Could it have fallen off at the pump when Colby gassed up, and then was it stepped on by German who later walked it over to the fuel tank? When police searched Colby's car, they found no tire iron. And the iron found on the ground and used in the attack was suitable for use in the jack in Colby's car.

A few weeks later, the four-day trial began in the Barre courtroom before Judge Connarn. Spectators began arriving, including German family members, a *Times Argus* reporter, and a couple of police officers who had not been involved and would not be witnesses. Although the courtroom might have appeared sparsely filled to a visitor with no knowledge of what was occurring, to me its spaces were filled. The pressure was on. I believed Colby was guilty and I wanted him convicted. Colby had attacked a man who was just trying to stitch out a living, and left him possibly to die. All for $64. I also had my own egotistical need for success.

Mine were not the only emotions that filled the courtroom. The twelve jurors were undoubtedly anxious about what they would be called upon to do, and were possibly resentful, or flattered, by the lottery that had lifted them from their daily routine and placed them in this drama. Perhaps they feared they would make the wrong decision. Perhaps they feared being duped by smart lawyers. German's emotional accusation of Colby only heightened the tension. It was a fair guess that a conviction might bring him some satisfaction, but it wouldn't restore his health.

Judge Connarn, who had witnessed many similar scenes, undoubtedly was concerned about his own reputation and wanted to be careful not to make rulings that would result in successful appeals. Perhaps he also wondered whether the new state's attorney had the right stuff. Keefe, meanwhile, was a quiet enigma, an apparent automaton doing his assigned job. Colby's fear was palpable—although the jury process was intended to find the truth, he was the only person there who actually knew, with 100 percent certainty, what it was.

I won no critical admissions from Colby's witnesses through my cross-examinations. I thought I was doing well enough, but I just couldn't tell. Keefe—bless his soul—said later that I had done just fine. With more maturity, I now know the extent to which an effective cross-examination requires thorough investigations. Linda's relationship with Colby should have been fully explored in the investigation, by questioning people acquainted with them. This had not been done. Were they lovers? Were they economically dependent on each other? None of this had been ascertained. Nor had his relationship with his hunting camp buddies been thoroughly investigated.

By contrast, attorney Free found success by hammering on German's testimony, pointing out the challenges inherent in recognizing Colby while being beaten in the semi-darkness. He cited Linda's testimony that she overheard German express doubt about what he had seen; and Free mentioned the various possibilities that would account for the piece of tape being at the scene of the attack. He described Colby as brave for taking the stand with the knowledge he would have to admit to his prior burglary conviction that resulted in jail time. Free said Colby's willingness to take the stand was evidence that Colby had learned his lesson and he wouldn't do anything that might send him back to the Windsor hellhole.

My closing argument was light on drama and heavy on facts. I made a plea for justice, but it was pretty much emotion-free. Free, on the other hand, was full of scorn about what he claimed was the unconvincing, circumstantial evidence presented by the state. He praised the wisdom of requiring proof beyond a reasonable doubt, while stressing that a person is presumed innocent until proven guilty.

The jury deliberated for about five hours. Tensions on all sides rose as the hours dragged on. The conventional wisdom is, "the longer the jury is out, the better for the defendant." I watched the minutes go by. I had not slept much the night before. I'd gotten up early and jogged a couple of miles just to wake up, hugged my two little girls, gave Barbara a quick hug goodbye, and was out the door spinning my final argument in my head. I was now growing even more exhausted waiting for the jury to announce its verdict.

At approximately 6 p.m., the jury reached a verdict. The foreman stood and said, "Your Honor, we the jury find the defendant not guilty." The emotional balloon popped, and I slumped in disbelief. Keefe briefly put an arm around my shoulder. There was stunned silence in the courtroom.
"Mr. Colby, you are free to go," Judge Connarn announced, and the bailiff cleared the courtroom.

I met Keefe the next day in my office. The *Times Argus* accurately reported that the jury evidently had difficulty believing either that German could identify Colby or that the tape or tire iron evidence meant Colby was at the scene of the attack. "Damn," Keefe said to me. "I know that son of a bitch is guilty. I don't know what went wrong—you did great! Cross could have been a little better, but it was good. There was evidence for both positions. What do you really think about Colby? Did he really smash that guy?"

I told him I didn't know. When we started this case I was convinced he brutally attacked German for a lousy $64. There was no other suspect. The guys who called the cops were the only ones known to be at the scene around the time of the assault. There could have been a phantom attacker, but it was unlikely. What I did know is that the jury said he wasn't guilty, and the jury had the final say. German died about four months after the trial without ever fully recovering from the attack

After I had closed the file and talked with German's friends and family and the involved officers, I mulled over and over the meaning of truth. Was truth something a person could know absolutely, and if so, how? A trial lawyer's clichéd response to this question is the old saying, "I always know the facts of a case, but only God knows the truth." Unfortunately, God never seems to speak out definitively about the "facts" that are so important in a criminal case. Jurors, of course, although they say what "truth" is in individual cases, don't know the truth either. I know that because of an encounter I had with a juror after I won a conviction in a drunken driving case. The validity of the results of the breath test in that case were hotly contested. The defense insisted that the officer giving the test had not followed protocol required for an accurate result, while the officer insisted he had. After a lengthy deliberation, the jury unanimously found the defendant guilty. As the jurors were leaving the courtroom, one of them asked to speak with me in private. I took him to a quiet place. When he was sure we couldn't be overheard, he asked, "Tell me, Mr. Cheney, was he really guilty?" I of course said he was, because I believed that was true. Here was a juror who had voted to convict but wanted to know what "the truth" was, thinking I knew something he didn't.

From the beginning of human history, various horrible ordeals have been established by powerful people whose status was threatened, to discover "truth" and punish liars. Truth-finding methods included burning heretics at the stake, trial by fire—walking barefoot over burning coals to see if the suspect's feet burned, near-drowning by dragging suspects through water, piling rocks on a suspect's chest until the truth was forced out or he or she was crushed, and various other hideous means of torture. Often, "the truth"—for example, trials in Salem, Massachusetts, purporting to answer the question "Are you a Witch?"—was really a ceremony to vindicate beliefs of people in power, not a search for a factual answer. Perhaps my query from the juror about drunken driving was really a suspicion that the practice was alive and well.

Certainly, humanity has come a long way from Salem. Cultural paeans to freedom and precise definition of crimes has led to the idea that a trial is simply an inquiry as to whether a certain action had actually taken place. The judicial system, with juries of people randomly selected from the populace who are disqualified if they are discovered to have any bias, and trials governed by complex rules of evidence, is the best humans can do in a search for factual truth. True, the system has its imperfections: Outcomes may be determined more by theater and emotions than a meticulous weighing of fact. Procedures can be manipulated to contaminate results. Some lawyers are more clever than others. People with one world view will have an emotional reaction and find meaning in a cluster of events boiled down to something called "facts," while people with another emotional reaction, or world view, will see a different fact. There is a conceit that people can tell if someone is lying by looking at body language ,which they assert by saying, "I'm a good judge of people"— on the other hand, they may be simply validating their preexisting bias. The jury system is posited on the premise that twelve people faced with a factual controversy can distill, out of their views of humanity, a result that spills out the truth. Still, I believe it's the best system human beings have devised to maintain a civil society.

I had another encounter with Colby a year or so later. He had been involved in a fight at a local bar with some college students from Norwich University. Barroom brawls are notoriously messy to unravel. The police investigation showed that Colby initially retreated in the face of provocation by the students—Colby had been attacked first, and he fought back. No lasting physical harm was done to anyone, but the students got the worst of the bruises. As usual, there was the predictable mélange of contradicting facts concerning who said what and who did what, indeed, what caused the entire incident. I decided to charge four of the students with disorderly conduct. The trial was presided over by Judge Connarn, a graduate and loyal supporter of Norwich University. The state's case depended on the jury believing Colby's version of events.

The rules of evidence, with some exceptions, forbid submitting evidence of the character of a witness to establish that he or she is the type of person who would act in a way that is at issue in a trial. A similar rule excludes evidence of the character of a witness with regards for telling the truth. The rule is modified to permit testimony limited to a person's reputation in the community for truthfulness, but specific acts of misconduct are not allowed. Accordingly, the defense called four local police chiefs who testified that Colby's reputation for telling the truth was bad. They weren't permitted to give examples illustrating this, unless asked the basis for their opinion by me. I didn't ask. There was no evidence presented about the outcome of the German trial. The jury convicted the students.

Later, Judge Connarn asked why I'd been so hard on the students. I said I thought they were wrong based on the facts I knew, and regardless of what many thought of Colby, he was legally innocent of a prior assault, which I was bound to respect.

"Fair enough," the judge remarked.

My next non-homicide felony case triggered considerable public interest, which is why, in part, I chose to bring it. I charged Sheriff Mark Brown with assault on a prisoner in his care at the county lockup. The state police investigation concluded that Brown used excessive force on a prisoner to force him into a cell. The witnesses were principally other inmates. The allegation was that he struck the prisoner, twisted his arm, and knocked him down while placing him into the cell. Sheriff Brown asserted he used only such force as was needed to subdue an unruly prisoner and prevent more unrest in the jail. Given the incendiary emotions generated both for and against the police during contemporary events, like the 1968 Chicago Democratic Convention, and certain unruly protests here in Vermont, I thought bringing a police officer to account would instill confidence in the legitimacy of the social order. Filing the charge was a mixed public-relations bag, and generated balanced press coverage: criticism was leveled both at the sheriff for his alleged behavior, and at me for being a publicity hound.

A change of venue was granted and the trial was held in Middlebury. Trooper James Whittaker, assigned as an investigator to my office, shared a hotel room with me during the two-day trial. After the first day, it wasn't much of a contest. My "jail bird" witnesses were not persuasive; the complainant did not excite sympathy, and Sheriff Brown seemed credible. On the second day I struggled out of bed, thinking only about how I was going to survive the trial, and planned my usual morning jog to clear my mind. As I opened the hotel room door to leave, Whittaker lifted a sleepy head and said, "Kim, I hope you come back!" I wasn't so sure I would. I was tempted to run back to Montpelier.

On this second day of the trial, I chose to question Sheriff Brown, asking him to demonstrate exactly how he'd handled the prisoner. That was a mistake. We stood in the middle of the courtroom with the sheriff grasping and pushing lightly on me. The sheriff's shove was pretty benign. He was acquitted.

I later realized how naïve I had been to expect a law enforcement officer to be found guilty on account of one marginal incident. On the other hand, the fact that a case had been brought demonstrated that police conduct would be scrutinized, which appeared to support public confidence in law enforcement. I had made an enemy of Sheriff Brown, though, for a spell at least, we managed to navigate around this episode.

As I thought more about the Brown case, I concluded I probably wouldn't do it again if the circumstance arose. I'd let my belief that the world should be a perfect place take over. Maybe I wanted to be a bit of a hero. But I did learn something—I should have fully considered any harm I might do to Mark Brown's reputation (or anyone else's) as an elected official, by bringing a charge that was unlikely to succeed. In Mark's case, I think he was vindicated by the acquittal even though an unproven charge is obviously not helpful. I learned that losing a couple trials is the best way to become a good prosecutor and trial lawyer. It sharpened my judgment, made me dig deeper into facts and cultural contexts of cases, and fostered a deeper humility—all good things.

CHAPTER 8

Speak only truth; do not yield to anger; when asked to do so,
give of the little thou hast. With these three steps thou shalt
approach the gods.

Buddha

THE PROSECUTOR IN A TIME OF CULTURE SHOCK

For three days, in August of 1968, television news showed scenes of cops outside the Chicago Democratic Convention tear gassing young people who were protesting the Vietnam War. The cops were using batons to smash protesters' heads, carrying the wounded on stretchers to waiting police vans, herding other rioters with jeeps equipped with front-mounted barbed wire meshes into confined areas from which there was no escape from either the police or the tear gas. It was a portrait of a war against radical youth protesting Lyndon Johnson's lies about the war over seas.

Elsewhere in America, young men were coming home from Vietnam in caskets. Many of those who came home alive suffered PTSD or physical disabilities. Instead of being welcomed as heroes, they were often denigrated by others of their generation who thought they were idiots to have gone to war at all. These images remained seared in the nation's memory long after Richard Nixon beat Hubert Humphrey in the November presidential election.

Earlier that year scores of U.S. cities erupted in flames during riots following the assassination of Dr. Martin Luther King, Jr.

Students at high schools and colleges in Washington County, and elsewhere in Vermont, were also protesting that year, at various times disrupting street traffic, holding sit-ins, and blocking entrances to public buildings. I heard complaints from police officers about changes in attitude toward them which made their job more difficult. They faced accusations of police brutality on one hand, while on the other, of failing to do their duty to crack down when laws had clearly been broken. Conservatives mounted a counterattack of opinion. People were confused. "What is going on?" people would ask me on the street.

One businessman, who'd supported me in the election, dropped into the office to talk. He said teachers in town were worried that students had lost all respect for authority. On the other hand, many students were convinced that just speaking out against the war could be grounds for arrest. He wondered if there were ways to ease the tension.

After mulling over his visit and listening to other gossip and rumors, I concluded that it might help if high school kids could see me as I saw myself. I hoped that if students could see that I and others in law enforcement were basically decent people trying to keep a modicum of order in a chaotic world, their hostility to authority might ease. With the cooperation, or at least acquiescence, of the six police agencies in the county, and principals of local high schools, I started an educational program that set understanding as a goal. I asked each high school on a rotating basis to allow one student, preferably one identified as a leader, to miss classes for a week to come to my office and observe firsthand the cases that came in, how they were handled, and get some idea of what our policies were. The schools cooperated.

I screened out ongoing investigations or sensitive cases, but otherwise students were able to follow the office's process. They could read police affidavits, sit in on discussions with me and officers about what charges should be made, and attend court hearings to see and hear what the state's attorney, defense attorneys, probation officers, and victims actually said and did. If they were lucky, they might observe a jury trial. My idea was that the students would return to their schools with a new perspective and real information, and could share with their peers accounts of real people doing hard work as they attempted to enforce shared values. After five or so interns had come and gone, the chance to join the program became a prestigious opportunity. I got reports from schools that the program was helpful in calming conflicts, and many of my "graduates" went on to eventually become lawyers.

The most successful result occurred when one intern approached me with a special concern. Peter, a student from Montpelier High School, warned me that the "jocks" at his school were threatening to beat up any kids who protested the war or dressed like hippies, so some kids were afraid to express themselves. I called the school principal, told him of Peter's concerns, and suggested sending state troopers to walk the halls to let students know they were there to protect anyone who wanted to speak out about anything. I thought it would be useful for students to see the police protecting dissent, not just "harassing" protesters, as many felt they were doing. The state police barracks commander agreed to send troopers for a couple of days. The purpose of their presence was stated to be supporting students' First Amendment rights; to encourage talk instead of disruptive protests. I also suggested the school sponsor a day or time when students could voice their concerns, be it protest or support for a cause, with a local police presence. The principal quickly agreed this was a good idea and arranged for a "Protest Speech Day" to be held in the auditorium. The auditorium was filled with students, faculty, and some interested people from the community. Several students came onstage, using the microphone to publish their ideas and argue their positions. The principal later told me the process helped reduce tensions among students, while improving dialogue on issues. One flattering indication of the success of this outreach effort occurred at the end of the school year, when Union 32 High School in East Montpelier invited me to give the graduation address to the senior class.

Soon after I was sworn in as state's attorney, a group of perhaps fifty people protesting the Vietnam War showed up on the statehouse lawn while the legislature was in session, and I went to the event as an observer. The protesters carried posters fixed to sticks and two-by-fours, or long banners held by two or more people, protesting the war. They were restless and agitated. After a few speeches and chants of "Hell no, we won't go!" from the statehouse steps, they decided to go inside.

To my surprise, the head of the state police detachment came over to ask my advice—he wasn't sure what to do. I responded that the statehouse was known as the "people's house," that it functions as a place where diverse opinions are welcome as long as they were peaceful. Accordingly, I discouraged any attempt to prevent people from entering the building simply because they were protesters. I suggested the officer explain to the apparent leaders of the protest that they were welcome to enter the statehouse to observe whatever debate was going on, but all banners, signs, weapons, or anything else that could disrupt the proceedings must be left outside, any disruption would be met by arrests and prosecution, and no one would be permitted in the balcony. These instructions were given and followed. The protesters entered peacefully and remained so while watching a debate.

The incident educated me with the surprise realization that I was expected to formulate policy responses to civil disruption. This was not something I'd given any thought to, thinking some chain of command ending with the governor would be in charge. I'd assumed my responsibilities were limited to the courthouse. Overcoming my naivete, I met with the county state police barracks commander, Lieutenant Richard Curtiss, to discuss how to plan for demonstrations. Curtiss outlined plans to accommodate hundreds of arrested protesters in a local armory, or armories if necessary, to be held until they could be brought to court. "I'm not anxious to arrest a lot of people," he said, "but that's the plan if we need it."

I agreed, the policy should not include mass arrests simply as a show of force. Most of these people, I argued, just wanted to make a point about the war. They wanted press coverage, and a few might have even wanted to provoke a confrontation to get front-page photos of being roughed up by the cops. We agreed that the police should use restraint if at all possible, telling protesters they were free to voice their concerns peacefully, but they could not be disruptive. True to form, most events were peaceful, but others were disruptive and led to several arrests followed by court appearances.   As part of the planning process I met with Judge Connarn to outline a response. The corrections department was not well-staffed to accommodate mass arrests. Neither were the courts, nor would law enforcement, be improved if anger and retaliation became the norm. I proposed that if a protester had been arrested and held in custody for a short time and if he or she pleaded guilty to disorderly conduct, the judge should impose a sentence of time served, in which case the protester would be free to leave. Judge Connarn agreed with this policy. I called it my catch-and-release policy, giving the protesters the notoriety they craved and law enforcement a practical and effective way of responding. When a protester appeared in court and I explained our policy, most protesters went along with it.

But one protester didn't—Ralph Arby insisted he'd done nothing wrong and wanted a jury trial. He'd been arrested for sitting in front of the door to the post office wearing a football helmet and shoulder pads to protect him from the expected police attack. Two officers asked him to stand, which he refused to do, so they lifted him up, handcuffed him, took an arm on either side, and guided him to a waiting bus to be taken into custody at the county jail. When he appeared the next morning in court, I explained our policy and asked if he would plead guilty. Arby said he had done nothing wrong and wanted a jury trial. I told him he was entitled to a trial, but he'd better win because if he didn't accept the policy, the court would probably impose a jail sentence.

Arby had his trial. He lost. The jurors found his beliefs were no excuse for his behavior. When he was sentenced, the judge imposed a short jail term. He appealed to the Vermont Supreme Court. My comments, he argued, and the jail sentence were an unconstitutional threat that was part of a conspiracy to deprive him of his right to justice. The supreme court upheld the jail time, saying it's the judge who sentences people, not the state's attorney, and that the outcome was appropriate.

While that appeal was pending, I had what I thought was a brilliant idea. It turned out to be dumb. I thought that protest issues had settled down after police had avoided violence, and punishments had been modest. While driving home through Plainfield one night after an out-of-town meeting, I decided to make an impromptu stop at the student center at Goddard College, the liberal arts school. My deputy, Robert Gagnon, was with me. "Let's stop and show a human face to the students," I suggested. "It seemed to help with the high school kids; maybe it will with the college kids, too." Bob believed the idea risky, but agreed to go along with the stop.

Bob was right. We parked my unmarked car, took off our rain coats and threw them into the back seat. We then entered the student center, dressed like lawyers, which signaled to students that something was up. I saw a handful of students getting a late meal, introduced myself to one or two who approached and explained who I was and that my visit was purely social. I pointed out that I came with no cops and only wanted to talk with them about their concerns. One student, well-groomed and outgoing, stepped forward, and declared, "Don't appreciate you coming here. Got nothing to say to you."

"Oh, come on, not so fast," I said. "I'm coming as a friend, I hope you will see it that way." Others formed a circle around us in a threatening manner, as though the speaker needed protection. I got the good idea to get out of there fast. We headed out the door into the parking lot, and as I approached my car, I saw all four tires breathing their last breath as the vehicle settled to the ground. Our raincoats were gone. Before I could do anything, I saw several students and the president of the college, Jerry Witherspoon, walking quickly toward us. I knew Jerry. We'd worked together on education issues before I became the state's attorney. Jerry said what I already knew: "We've got a bit of a problem here."

My initial plan was to call for police assistance on my car radio, but Jerry's presence was reassuring. Several students grouped behind Jerry. "What ya gonna do now?" they chanted. "What ya gonna do? What ya gonna do now?"

Jerry and I shook hands while he emphasized, as I had already concluded, that it would be good for us to leave quickly. The chanting, "What ya gonna do now?" continued. I told Jerry in a voice loud enough for the students to hear, "I'm not going to do anything, but someone here is going to give us both a ride home. I have an 8 a.m. meeting tomorrow and will need my car. I'll expect it to be in my driveway with four new tires by then."

Jerry told the students to leave, then invited us to follow him to the college security office, where we were given a ride home. The next morning, my car was in my driveway. Surprisingly, there were also two new raincoats in the car. I wore my new coat for years afterwards, not exactly as a badge of honor but as a reminder of recovery from a poor decision.

Nationally, things turned more serious. This time, it was the Black Panthers causing trouble, not me. In mid-1968 there'd been several shootouts between the Panthers and police in California. Ronald Reagan, then governor of California, responded by proposing that state legislature pass a law outlawing possession of guns in public places, except those weapons held by police. With the support of the NRA, the proposal became law. Violence would be avoided, in theory, because arrests could be made for being armed in public without otherwise disturbing the peace or assembling to do real harm. The Panthers, in turn, approximately a year later, proclaimed a certain night nationwide to be "Off A Pig Night," during which Blacks everywhere would be tasked with shooting a police officer. This outrageous, well-publicized planned act did not excite the general public in Vermont because few people of color lived here. The police, however, were well aware of the Panthers' proclamation, and feared Black assassins would come to Vermont for murder that night.

The phone at my office rang during the day of "Off A Pig Night." Liz was busy, so I answered the call by identifying myself. Instantly, an agitated voice came on the line. "Kim, it's me, Bobby, from the college. Remember me?" asked a familiar voice. I did remember Bobby. He was a Black man on the Goddard College faculty. We'd met at a forum discussing civil rights in local education.

"Yeah, Bobby, of course I remember you. What can I do for you?"

"Hey Kim, glad I caught you, we're really scared out here."

"Scared? What do you mean?"

"I, other faculty, and students of color are scared stiff about the so-called 'Off A Pig Night'. We think local redneck racists will try to shoot us down so we can't kill cops, or they'll try to kill us if we go out, or maybe come looking for us. You know damn well there are lots of them in this town, and there aren't any police out here. I've had lots of phone calls—people are really scared. It's bad enough being Black in Vermont, but tonight could really be hell. We're scared, you gotta do something!"

"Bobby, I get it. I don't blame you for being scared. I hate to say this, but stay inside and I'll see what I can do. I'll call you back with any news." I didn't think it was a serious threat, though I was aware of plenty of racial prejudice in the area, so I understood the fear. This would be an emotionally charged night. I immediately called the head of the state police, Colonel Edward Corcoran, who held the title of Commissioner of Public Safety. "Hello Mr. Cheney, what can I do for you today?" he said pleasantly.

"Uhh, Commissioner," I responded, " I need some information on your plans for tonight. I'm concerned about 'Off A Pig Night'."

"Oh, don't worry—I got that covered," Corcoran said. "Local police stations will be closed down, with no lights on inside. Local officers will stay off the streets, they won't be visible targets. The state police barracks will also be closed. We'll have snipers on the rooftops of nearby buildings. We'll stop any trouble real fast. We're ready for any crazies that may show up."

"Well commissioner, that's great, but I got a call from some Black folks at Goddard who are scared of local whites with guns. I don't think there's a big danger, but on the other hand, I don't think their fear is unreasonable. We need to give them some reassurance that police protection is available."

"Okay, I hadn't thought of that. I'll take care of it," he said. "I'll have a couple of patrols in marked cars in the college area. They will be in radio contact in case of trouble. Tell your people to call the main state police number at the first sign of any trouble—we'll respond right away."

I returned Bobby's call and told him there would be a state police presence nearby. He was relieved. Then came a call from a man I didn't know. He said he'd heard of the possibility of violence because of "Off a Pig Night," and asked if he could help. He said he had friends with guns who could be available if needed. I thanked him for the call. I asked for his phone number and address, and said I doubt he'd be needed as the police had things under control, but suggested that he and his friends assemble at his house, make sure there was no drinking, and wait for my call in case we needed them. He agreed to do so. It turned out to be a peaceful night, after all. There were no Black Panthers, no vigilante actions, no desperate calls for help from anyone. I never heard if there was a good party.

The calm following "Off A Pig Night" was soon interrupted in the springtime by yet another outrage—skinny-dipping. Yes, yet another major crime had occurred. I arrived in court for the usual Monday morning arraignment, when people arrested over the weekend were brought before the judge. About eight young men, in various stages of undress—barefoot and decidedly unkempt—were seated in the first spectator row waiting to have their cases called. Two state troopers were keeping an eye on them.

"What the hell is this?" I asked one of the troopers.

"We arrested them late yesterday just before dark," one trooper volunteered. "They were skinny-dipping in the Mad River. We got a call from local folks, that their favorite swimming hole where they liked to bring their kids, or wives, was full of these young men scampering about in the nude, making the place unsuitable for families. They were angry about it, said 'fucking hippies' were fouling up their favorite swimming hole. It seemed a clear case of disturbing the peace."

At that point, Judge Connarn appeared from the judge's chambers and took his seat on the bench. He was proud of his Army service and of the Army's discipline, and was not tolerant of dissent or disturbing public events. He motioned me to the bench for a conference. When I appeared, he leaned over, barely concealing his anger, and asked, "What the hell is this? What are those guys doing coming to court half-naked? Why do they think they can show their bodies in public and disrespect the court as well?" He was getting angrier as he spoke.

I explained that the boys didn't have much choice, since the police arrested them the day before for skinny-dipping in a place the locals thought of as a family swimming hole, even though it was on private property. Judge Connarn was not amused. He wanted them out of his court as soon as possible. I called the first name on the list and spoke briefly to the young man. "I suggest you plead not guilty," I advised. "The judge is pretty upset; you will probably be released on bail, and you can come back another time with a lawyer, or without one, and we can figure out what to do."

And that is what happened with almost all the boys. After they pleaded not guilty, I dismissed their cases a few days later. However, when one lad from Waitsfield was called, contrary to my advice, he pleaded guilty. Judge Connarn saw his opportunity and angrily told the young man his actions seriously disturbed the public's right to enjoyment and to be free from people like him upsetting their summer pleasure. He ordered the young man jailed for twenty days. "Bailiff," he said, "take the defendant into custody." He banged the gavel and left the bench, leaving no opportunity for me or anyone else to object.

I was dumbstruck. Typically, before accepting a guilty plea, the judge must advise the defendant of possible punishment and, by personal questioning, make sure the defendant understands the charge and that there is evidence to sustain it; what a guilty plea means; make sure the plea is voluntary; and make sure the defendant has full knowledge of the consequences. This ritual was entirely omitted. Now this kid was going to jail. He was earning a criminal record for an offense that merited at best a scolding. The judge appeared adamant.

I knew a Waitsfield lawyer who had represented criminal defendants in court and phoned him as soon as I returned to my office, suggesting he file a habeas motion immediately to have the defendant released. I explained I had no authority to dismiss a case once it was adjudicated. The lawyer asked me for the basic facts of the situation, took down the contact information, thanked me, said he would get on it, and hung up.

"It is kind of weird for a prosecutor to be telling a defense attorney how to overturn a conviction," Liz muttered as I put down the phone.

The lawyer filed a motion in Superior Court that day asking that the conviction be overturned for failure of the court to obtain a valid guilty plea. That court, with a different judge, has jurisdiction of habeas corpus-like cases. The Superior Court judge vacated the conviction and ordered the case returned to Judge Connarn's court for further consideration. Bail was set by the Superior Court. I dismissed the case before the defendant was scheduled to appear.

When Patrick Leahy, the Chittenden County State's Attorney, saw the press account of this nutty episode (which did not include the Superior Court proceeding), he called a local *Times Argus* reporter and told a folksy story about how, as a kid growing up in Vermont, he went skinny-dipping all the time. It was a Vermont tradition, he said, adding, "What was that crazy Cheney doing over in Washington County busting skinny-dippers?" When the reporter called me for a reaction, I didn't try to explain that the young men had been dragged into court without my knowledge, and of course I was in favor of skinny-dipping—but I was tempted.

The story, absent the reversal of Judge Connarn's order, went statewide as fast as a nude plunge into a refreshing lake on a hot day. I respected Leahy, who has been a U.S. senator since 1974, but I didn't appreciate his comment. I would tell Leahy the whole story later, but at the time I couldn't afford to have Judge Connarn know how I'd thwarted him. All in all, though, I had to admire Leahy's ability to grab the headlines and leave me holding the bag. He was a skilled politician and I figured I had a lot to learn from him.

CHAPTER 9

*The wrong course vigorously pursued
is grately to be prefered to indecision.*

Maimonides (Spanish philosopher), 1135-1204

DRUG CRIMES POLICY

The gods were angry and so were their hapless subjects. Mars was on the loose, creating warfare in the far-away rice paddies and jungles of Vietnam, but he was spurring riots here at home, as well—turning youth against their elders, most maniacally in the streets of Chicago at the 1968 Democratic National Convention. Dionysus triumphed in the biggest way a year later, at the Woodstock Music Festival in Bethel, N.Y., where he liberated thousands of youthful libidos at Max Yasgur's dairy farm. Both gods were evident, albeit less so, in Washington County's five high schools and at one local college, Goddard in Plainfield, known since 1935 as being educationally and politically progressive. The explosive cultural changes brought by war, its casualties, and liberated libidos spawned a backlash of counter-forces insisting that accepting being drafted and going to Vietnam was patriotic and drug use was an escape from reality by disillusioned youth.

To some observers the growth of drug use was part of a plan hatched by narcotics cartels against America, spreading drugs like a bacillus to undermine America's Vietnam War effort and the nation's domestic order. The country was worried. Gallup polls revealed that nearly half of all Americans believed that drug use was a serious problem in their respective communities.

Newspaper headlines supported this perception, including one in the *Times Argus* on May 8, 1969: "Marijuana Use in Montpelier Reaches Freshmen." A subhead reported alarmingly that "Heroin Use Rises." The story underneath, the first installment of a series of reports by one prominent reporter into "the drug problem," was based on interviews with local students, clergy, and law-enforcement officials. The surprising revelation that even freshmen in high school were using marijuana suggested a problem was becoming a "crisis"—a favorite word in journalism.

I understood there were many ideas on ways to control the widespread and growing phenomenon of drug abuse ranging from use of overwhelming force, more and better treatment, to ending the war and stopping the draft, to name a few. The cacophony of opinion was not leading to any consensus about social policy.

I needed to educate myself about different drugs, addiction, and treatment to form a local law enforcement policy that I could live with and that would be accepted by the community. To start, I went to a several-day seminar in Connecticut sponsored by the Yale University Drug Dependence Institute. The program started with the pharmacology of common mood-altering drugs, followed by descriptions of treatment for heroin addicts. The institute recommended that the first step in any program was to see addicts as humans plagued by poverty who became inadvertently addicted, rather than as criminals. It urged communities to expand mental-health services, establish group rehabilitation programs, and encourage cultural changes that would foster a sense of self-worth. Presenters insisted this was not a problem that could be improved by mass incarceration. One addict on the recovery cycle spoke movingly about how much he was helped by feeling that people around him cared about, even loved, him. He said it gave him the courage to keep on with treatment.

The institute also encouraged methadone treatment and the use of other therapeutic drugs as practical temporary tools in combating heroin addiction. I was encouraged that the lead *Times Argus* article favorably mentioned methadone maintenance as a strategy despite all the moralistic notions, widespread at the time, that trying to combat drugs with more drugs would only create more problems. The article may not have convinced anyone, but it did broaden the discussion.

The institute's approach to the "drug problem" resonated with me emotionally. My mother's alcoholism had a profound effect on me and my siblings, and her descent into drink was nothing she had planned for herself. All addicts have their own bugbears, but I believed her drinking was largely a response to a fact that she could not accept the consequences of being born female. Mother never clearly said so, but based on what I knew of her and her life, it seemed obvious. She was the archetypal female depicted in Betty Friedan's *The Feminine Mystique*, the book that launched modern-day feminism.

She was far more creative, and had a quicker mind, than her husband. Father was not especially talented, yet he did have a satisfying professional life. Although trained as a lawyer, he abandoned the profession to sell life insurance with the religious fervor he brought from church. The combination was not appealing to me, nor, I assumed, to my mother. She felt frustrated in her role as a housewife, and alienated. Her abuse of alcohol, her generation's drug of choice, was understandable to me. Nevertheless, the prevailing notion throughout the country, and certainly here in Vermont, was that alcohol (and drug) dependence was the result of moral failings, that abusers were weak and shameful. This prevailing attitude may have been supported by the fact that probably half of Washington County's families had at least one alcoholic member whose sober relatives found easier to blame than to embark on the difficult and frustrating road to sobriety with.

While in the '50s it may have been beer, martinis, and Manhattans that helped people cope, now in the late '60s and early '70s it was marijuana, hashish, LSD, amphetamines, and heroin drawing concern. I determined that my best approach to "the drug problem" was, first off, to ratchet down suggestions that police "crack down" on drug abuse with wide-scale arrests. Like Prohibition in the 1920s and 1930s, I thought this policy would fail, and might lead to more corruption and crime. Although drug use, and the buying and distributing of it, often created collateral crimes like burglary, theft, and assaults, I considered the rise in drug use to be principally a social problem rather than behavior that could be controlled by calling it a crime problem, even though the drugs of abuse were illegal. With a federal grant of $7,000 available for county law enforcement, I considered bringing in experts from outside the world of law enforcement to hold public forums to suggest social changes that would lessen the misuse of drugs. But the amount of money available was unlikely to have any major impact, and might just add to the cacophony of "cures."

I opted instead to use the grant to study the extent of burglary and look for ways to stop it. Local police agencies accepted that idea. Catching a burglar would please an innocent homeowner and maybe even recover stolen property, with the additional benefit of putting a bad guy in jail who might give a lead on a serious pusher. It also seemed possible that traditional police work might be an avenue for success. The study did show a rise in burglary, but no clear plan for an effective response. Not surprising results, but I hoped it at least encouraged an effort to support police in doing things they were trained to do.

I certainly wasn't the only one working on the drug issue. There was public demand for a viable drug policy. The Chamber of Commerce organized a roundtable discussion on drug abuse involving educators, clergy, mental health agencies, and law enforcement. What emerged from the discussion was a consensus that everyone, including users, parents, cops, clergy, educators, and community leaders, has a role and should begin talking with one another to understand the social forces behind the growing use of drugs. In addition, marijuana was identified as the principal drug of choice for youth.

As an involved community official, I also was invited by Rev. David Brown, the rector of Christ Church Episcopal in Montpelier, to meet informally with several students at the church to assess their attitudes and gain information. I learned that students considered pot smoking a rather harmless, non-aggressive response to a confusing and violent world, which, indeed, it seemed to be in 1970. I came to believe that high school students were bewildered by the current unrest in social attitudes. The despised "hippie" class, if there was such a thing, were sorting out their values in an effort to find a place for themselves. Marijuana, they argued, allowed the kind of contemplative life that was absent in a confusing world in which they saw no part for themselves to play. The question I kept asking myself was "Is marijuana use by kids really any different than alcohol use by adults?" My answer was that society must provide meaningful goals for youth to live by, rather than the violence and conflict inherent in the daily news. This is the message youth are giving us, and they should be supported. I voiced this opinion to the kids at the meeting.

Soon after that meeting, an event known locally as the "Easter Crisis" occurred on Easter weekend, involving three students arrested for possession of marijuana. I declined to bring charges after talking briefly with the teenagers, who seemed apologetic enough and willing to talk about the overall scene—which, as an older person, I felt I was beginning to grasp. The press billed the event as a "crisis" because it was kids who were arrested, indicating a prevalent drug culture. The local media criticized me for advocating talking with and supporting kids rather than prosecuting them. I was labeled "soft on drugs," not a label helpful for a prosecutor's career.

In response, Rev. Brown organized another meeting between me and about twenty students for yet another discussion of drugs and the community. At the session, I encouraged everyone to speak freely, assuring them that no one would be prosecuted for anything said. Still, I reminded the students that marijuana was illegal, and I was obliged to enforce the law in other circumstances. One student commented, "It seems pretty nice to sit down and talk with the state's attorney and not worry that you might be arrested." Some students said the only thing to do around the high school was booze and sex, and they wanted something healthier to do. We discussed the peer pressure they faced to flirt with the law. They also brought up and supported the idea of a coffeehouse featuring music, conversation, and organizations to advocate for healthy community activities.

Rev. Brown told the *Times Argus* afterwards that the meeting "transcended the most optimistic hopes and showed the possibility of cooperation between students and community groups." He said he saw "a real bridging of the chasm between prosecutor and student worlds." I attended many other such meetings, for as local prosecutor I was expected to take a lead in bringing order out of this turmoil elsewhere in Washington County. Other people and organizations came to adopt this approach, and public meetings were held to discuss the "drug problem" and what could be done about it. One of the most effective meetings that grew out of the "Easter Crisis" was held at the Montpelier High School and attended by 350 parents and various experts on drug use. The parents' principle concern, expressed at the meeting, was clearly the safety of their children. Many asked the school physician what to look for to detect drug use, so they could intervene; others wanted stronger law enforcement; still others urged more church attendance. Someone suggested tasking teachers with watching kids for odd behavior and reporting them to their parents. Another person blamed television drug ads saying, "If you turn on the TV you get a bombardment of ads for one drug or another . . . a drink, a beer, a sleep aid, an anxiety drug, you name it. The tube urges drug use. It must be stopped." Others urged development of teen centers with activities other than sports.

When called upon to speak, I once again said I would grant virtual immunity to student drug users who sought help, but dealers and "pushers" would be severely dealt with. (I knew this promise was mostly bravado, because so few such offenders were ever arrested.) The meeting ended after two hours with distribution of schedules for upcoming community meetings featuring law-enforcement officers, psychiatrists, clergy, me, and Chittenden County State's Attorney Patrick Leahy. These meetings did ratchet down hysteria as people began to understand that combating drug abuse was a task for the whole community, not merely a job for police who could not be effective on their own.

I continued to think about the issue. The state had been increasing the amount of resources devoted to curtailment of drug trafficking, but it was evident that it had not diminished supply. All it did was raise prices. Indeed, those efforts seemed to be having an opposite effect. Instead of curtailing the drug supply, the policy was perfectly suited to increasing it. Law enforcement efforts essentially acted as a retail price support system for illegal trade. The small risk of being jailed justified high prices. Even when the rare pusher high on the distribution system was arrested, he was quickly replaced. High prices also encouraged people to get in on the trade. When officers made routine narcotic arrests, offenders were prosecuted as a matter of course, but with little effect. The war against drugs had other problems. Sometimes officers would stop a person for a traffic offense, or even a serious crime, like a break-in, and then negotiate to "forget it" if the suspect would provide a lead for a drug bust. This kind of freewheeling negotiating weakened law enforcement, undermined police credibility, and occasionally allowed people who deserved a long jail term to go scot-free. Like Prohibition, all that law enforcement was accomplishing was insuring there was money to be made in selling drugs. Like alcohol prohibition, drug prohibition caused crime to flourish and the wrong people to get wealthy.

Although I prosecuted flagrant law violations, I understood that my personal skepticism about the drug war could not stop law enforcement efforts. Police "undercover work" sometimes worked and sometimes didn't. It was, of course, always a betrayal business. The officers would hang out in bars, music venues, or wherever else young people might congregate and pretend to make friends while searching for leads on drug crimes. In one case, an officer overheard a conversation at a bar where one man was complaining about the lack of rain and that his grass was hardly growing. "Really?" his companion said. "Mine is about five feet high." The resulting police search discovered a crop of marijuana on his property, leading to his arrest and conviction. Undercover work could be dangerous not only to officers, but to people suspected of snitching. On one occasion, around 1970, State Trooper Melvin Morris determined that a major drug deal was going down in a local bar on Barre Street in Montpelier. Police were stationed in unmarked cars while others in plain clothes stood outside the bar, keeping up a surveillance with binoculars. The plan was for Morris to determine there were drugs and dealers in the bar at the time, and then go outside and take off his hat as the signal for the raid to begin. Unfortunately for the police, but fortunately for the suspects and possibly himself, Morris got into an argument with a suspected druggie who thought Morris was a narc. The suspect suggested they go outside and settle things. Once outside a scuffle broke out; the suspect swung at Morris, who lost his hat, and a crowd of cops descended on the scene, racing into the bar yelling orders and shining lights. They'd intended to search people identified by Morris as sellers, but Morris called off the raid because he hadn't had time to identify sellers and potential buyers. His cover, and that of other undercover officers, was blown. Morris was reassigned, for his own protection, to a uniformed position in another area, and the undercover operation required a complete remake.

I was not happy the operation had been blown. The police were following legislative and public demand to demonstrate social outrage at the burgeoning explosion of illicit drug use, which brought with it fears of many parents for the well-being of their children. A dramatic public action in that context would've helped political actors support a consensus of respect for governing. Perhaps the arrests of several users and pushers would stimulate thinking about the need for broader programs for rehabilitation of users as well as stimulate ways for youth to find personal meaning in the chaotic social climate.

Another law enforcement approach was to obtain search warrants for possible locations and plan raids for contraband and "druggies." About a month after the blown raid described above, State Police Lt. Richard Curtiss called. "Kim," he said, "we're going to have a drug raid at Goddard College tonight. Want to come along? We have some good information about users on campus that may lead us to their suppliers. I have a search warrant for specific dorm rooms."

The plan was to assemble in a nearby parking lot, screened from view from the college and the road. When I arrived, there were three or four unmarked police cars, plus a van for transporting prisoners. The rooms on campus to be searched were distant from one another, so a team of three officers was assigned to each room, one to knock to engage the person who opened the door, another to stand guard with weapons ready, and a third to enter immediately. Curtiss told me he had other units close by in radio contact with each searching unit, in case they were needed. The searches were scheduled for 10:30 p.m.

At 10:30, Curtiss gave the word and searchers moved in. Suddenly the quiet campus was in an uproar; lights flicked on in dorms, sirens blared, and blue lights flashed. I remained in my car, listening to the police radio. The raid was a failure. In one student's room, the searchers found a small amount of marijuana, but there was a question of to whom it belonged. All the other rooms were clean. After a short time, Lt. Curtiss called off the raid, and everyone returned to the parking lot. It was evident that no serious crimes had been discovered. He looked at me in disgust and muttered something about hippies getting away with drug use, and possible tip offs, but it was clear it was time to go home empty handed.

There was one other state police raid at Goddard, months later. I had not been involved and knew nothing of it. A search warrant had been obtained from a judge based on an informant's tip. This time a few students were found with only small amounts of marijuana and were issued summonses to appear in court the next Monday. An officer brought me a copy of the search warrant approved by a judge I'd never heard of, with a batch of police affidavits of probable cause. As I was reviewing these, a lawyer whose name I cannot now recall, phoned. He said something like this: "Kim, I represent one of the Goddard students summoned to court. I've got news for you. The person who signed the search warrant was not a legitimate judge. He was someone who had been specially assigned to act as judge but had not taken or filed the necessary oath of office at the time he acted, so he had no authority. I just pointed this out to the local news reporters, radio, and television stations, and this news is being aired as we speak." I didn't know how to respond. "Your warrant is no good," he continued. "It was clearly an illegal search. You'll have to void the summons."

"Thanks for the information," I finally said, with a degree of sarcasm. "I'll check this out." The lawyer's description of the flawed search warrant was technically correct. I could have undertaken some process to validate the search, if it were critically important, maybe a review by an appropriate judge would be enough. But there was sure to be a lot of litigation over the warrant's legitimacy. I knew it would cause a stir, but I decided to void the summons.

The convictions for possessing minor amounts of marijuana would've had little effect on drug trafficking, but could possibly have serious collateral effects on the students' lives. More important to me was that efforts to prosecute the case would suggest that the "drug problem" was being caused by rebellious college kids, as the former State's Attorney Palmisano had suggested. The deciding factor was that, if I voided the search, doing so would send an important message to police to follow meticulously every legal step in making a search. It would also encourage officers to keep me informed beforehand of planned searches.

The *Times Argus* did, in fact, report on the case, but without criticizing the police. One person quoted in the news account suggested that I had created an arrest-free zone for drug use at the college, that I was soft on crime in general, and that I favored rich college kids over poorer local kids who would have been charged. I didn't respond because, other than braggadocio, there was little I could do practically. Planning more raids at the college didn't seem like a winning strategy, nor did reminders that I'd promised high school kids that if they came forward for help they would not be prosecuted. I didn't push back. I figured the issue would quiet down if I kept quiet, and it did.

Even more bizarre was a case involving a judge's son that occurred a few months later. A state police narcotics officer reported to me that they were quite sure the judge's son, who was living with his dad, was a major drug dealer. I discussed their investigation with them and realized there was probable cause for a search warrant for the judge's house. I thought if we were serious about the drug issue, we could make a statement that no one is above the law. I suggested the officers get a warrant.

I promptly received an urgent call from State Police Sergeant Nelson Lay, with whom I had worked in several investigations including the recent discovery of two buried bodies that had not yet been identified. The narcotics people had asked his opinion about a warrant and Lay, the senior detective, was shocked by the idea of searching the judge's home. He had a cool head and I respected him.

"Kim," Lay said in a steely, even voice, "are you crazy? We aren't going to search the judge's house. You can get a warrant if you want, but we won't serve it. It will be a disaster no matter how it turns out. If you okay it and we find drugs, you personally, and the state police lose by alienating the judiciary. If we don't find drugs, we're both even worse off. You'll look like a reckless state's attorney seeking press coverage, and we'll look like poor investigators. Either way, law enforcement will be trashed. If the kid is really involved, we're likely to find a better way to find evidence. We'll keep on him; he's bound to screw up sometime, particularly if he's a user."

I agreed, realizing it had been foolish to consider such a plan. I learned an important lesson: don't get so excited about a principle like "no one is above the law" that you ignore real-world constraints. The search might have harmed the judge himself, by implication, when there was no reason to believe he was aware of his son's claimed activities. As it turned out, the judge's son, then in his thirties, was arrested years later by federal officers in a sting that occurred in a public place. Investigation showed he was aware of the police plan and had arranged for a sting of his own, slipping the substantial buy-money to some unidentified person just as the police closed in on him. The money was never found. He suffered from asthma as a small child and was treated with amphetamines obtained by his parents, which allowed him to breathe. He became addicted and remained so until his arrest, which he appeared to have arranged as his only way out of a life he couldn't control. Insane in that he truly could not conform his behavior to the law, he was sentenced to a long prison term which seemed to me obscenely unjustified.

One of the challenges of being in politics is that, in the long run, you have to be true to yourself and your own ideals, not just to the hottest winds or issues craving attention at any moment. I knew drug prohibition would be no more effective than alcohol prohibition had been. It seemed to me though, that my problem was not how to solve the social evil of increased drug use, but how to convince people that I cared and was doing what I could to make it better. I think the community meetings were helpful in this regard. They were augmented by drug busts that were a necessity for police and prosecutorial survival. Such events did little to curtail supply, except for a short time, but were nevertheless extremely valuable as critical to maintaining law enforcement credibility, and incidentally, garnering votes for a state's attorney's re-election.

CHAPTER 10

"Other sins only speak; murder shrieks out."
John Webster, 1632

MURDER

The pain and despair arising out of the Vietnam War was expressed locally, on April 16, 1969, as a shriek of horror. Murder. A Vietnam veteran, home on leave, hiding in the woods 200 yards from his eighteen-year-old girlfriend's home, fired one shot, killing her instantly with a bullet through the heart. Gerald Blondin, an army sniper home on a three-day pass, killed Robin Farnham as she stepped out of a car in the driveway to her home, in the presence of her mother, sister, and brother. Blondin, twenty-one, was arrested by state police forty minutes later as he emerged unarmed from the woods on a back road where he had parked his car, about a mile from where he fired the shot. After being given the Miranda warning, he admitted he was the shooter and directed police to a place where they found the high-powered rifle with a high-resolution scope.

The shooting occurred about four months after I was sworn in as state's attorney. I had no prior experience, either personally or as a lawyer, with violent crime. The Farnham murder, or what came to be called "the Blondin case," would be uppermost in my mind and on the front pages of the *Times Argus* for months. The first news I had of the shooting came on commercial radio news. Almost instantaneously, I received a state police call on my car radio requesting that I come to the State Police K Barracks in Montpelier.

K Barracks was a shabby, almost windowless one-story building on a busy corner across from Montpelier High School. The entrance door, made of bullet-proof glass, was controlled by a dispatcher who allowed visitors entry, or not, depending on their business. There was an office for the lieutenant in charge, Richard Curtiss, small offices for other officers to write reports, and a small, secure holding area for up to two prisoners.

I was greeted by Sgt. Nelson Lay, the lead detective, whom I knew slightly. I respected Lay as one of the more experienced officers who saw cases as problems to solve rather than moral dramas of good and evil. Instead of being emotional and immediately judgmental in a case, he would explain simply what he actually knew, didn't know, and what might be done to know more.

To my surprise, the police appeared immune to the horror of a young woman being destroyed in full view of her mother and other family members—they had work to do. I tried to match that effect as I walked in. My first responsibility was to find out what happened and then fashion some kind of public response to this horrific crime. My performance would be judged in the court of justice but also in the court of public opinion, an opportunity for any elected official to profit by "earned media" as distinguished from advertising promotion. Sgt. Lay was accompanied by several uniformed officers standing in a ragged circle with military bearing, no hands in pockets, each with a straight face. Lay acknowledged my presence and began introducing everyone. Present were Lt. Richard Curtiss, the barracks commander; trooper Gene Lessard, who arrested Blondin; Cpl. Newall Freer, an assisting detective; Dr. John Dunleavey, the medical examiner and state pathologist; and a *Times Argus* reporter. I'd met them all before, but Lay introduced me to everyone, probably to make sure the reporter got their names correct. There were no handshakes, only acknowledging head nods.

Lay spoke first, outlining matter-of-factly what he knew. "The shooter was Gerald Blondin. We have him in the holding cell. Lessard caught him approaching his car coming through the woods on a dirt road, parked about a mile from Farnham's. I gave him Miranda as soon as I arrived. Blondin appeared in control of himself, told me he understood the Miranda warning, was willing to talk, and then he admitted he was the shooter and said he had hidden the rifle in the woods. Lessard followed Blondin's directions and recovered it, several yards into the woods."

Lay directed his remarks to me, but for the others to hear. He told me he'd learned this much from Farnham survivors and Blondin's brother: He'd fought in Vietnam, was home on leave, and apparently was given medals—a Purple Heart among them—for bravery and service which included being a sniper. In all probability, he helped save the lives of many of his comrades. The ambulance squad checked out the Farnham girl, but she was dead when they arrived. Her body was taken to Burlington for autopsy. Seems a clear first-degree murder. Blondin must have known the Farnham girl's schedule and hid up in the woods about 150 to 200 yards behind her house with a scoped rifle. He shot her with one shot. Lay went on to say police arranged for a judge to come to K Barracks to arraign Blondin, set bail, or whatever. Police would then transport him to the Burlington jail. He added that Blondin's father's guns had been taken from him temporarily, as a safety precaution. The father had called earlier that day, complaining that Blondin was in a rage after the girl told him she didn't want to see him anymore. They'd looked for Blondin then, but weren't able to find him.

After Lay finished, he assured me that any further investigation would go forward. I asked if we knew why Robin broke up with Blondin "Not that it matters now, but it will be part of the story." Lay said they had nothing specific. The group then discussed the fact that public opinion was turning against Vietnam veterans, in part because of the My Lai Massacre, the recent killing of several hundred innocent civilians by U.S. soldiers in Vietnam. I agreed that some people are thinking stuff like "Those Vets are all heartless bastards" and speculated that maybe Robin had said something along those lines as she broke off the relationship. If so, it could generate sympathy for Blondin.

I said I would take responsibility for dealing with the press thereafter and did not want police who might have been witnesses to give detailed accounts to reporters. "All of you may be witnesses, and I don't want some defense lawyer finding statements given to the press that may be a problem as we learn more." Lay acknowledged that as standard protocol.

As we waited for the judge, I found a private moment to ask Lay if Blondin showed any signs of insanity. "Nothing obvious," he said. "Unless you want to consider why a soldier who was given medals for killing enemy soldiers would ever use his skills to kill his girlfriend in front of her family. He wasn't raving or talking incoherently, if that's what you mean."

I commented that some things about Vietnam may make some men go insane, mentioning again the demeaning treatment many returning veterans were receiving. They came home after serving their tours and were often treated like vicious fools instead of honored veterans, many of whom were drafted and never wanted to go to Vietnam in the first place. I anticipated that Blondin's mental state would certainly become an issue, so he would undergo some psychiatric exams. Everyone was aware that the legal definition of insanity relates to what the person's state of mind was, not how crazy the crime was. Finally, I suggested that police help make arrangements for counseling for the grieving Farnham family.

A judge was admitted into K Barracks and Blondin was brought before him, surrounded by officers. An information sheet previously prepared by the police and signed by me charging Blondin with first-degree murder of Robin Farnham was read to him. A *pro forma* "not guilty" plea was entered for him by the judge. Blondin's brother said that Richard Davis, a capable Barre defense lawyer, would be retained. Bail was set at $50,000, and Blondin was transported thirty-five miles away, to the Burlington correctional facility. With nothing more to do that evening I went home, ruminating on recent events. This job had turned out to be more interesting, and perhaps more challenging, than I'd anticipated.

Both the *Times Argus* and *Burlington Free Press* reported that I was in charge of the murder investigation. The news stories repeated facts learned at Blondin's arraignment and offered new details reporters had gathered about Robin from her family. It also gave more extensive biographical information about Blondin. It seemed odd that so much more attention was being focused on the killer than on the victim, but maybe information about Blondin was easier to get.

In 1969, unlike now, the law did not give the victim or her family any formal part in the process by requiring that the state's attorney inform them of proceedings. The law treated a crime as an act against the state, not the victim. This attitude was enshrined in the conclusion of every information charging a crime, which ended with the words "Against the Peace and Dignity of the State" to signify that the State of Vermont was the victim of the crime and the prosecutor's duty was to avenge the state, not the victim's family. Accordingly, the Farnhams' horror and anguish were an assumed part of any crime rather than something to be proved. Perhaps in recognition of this attitude, it was rare for the victim's family to comment on or demand a severe punishment like the death penalty. Newspaper and broadcast accounts were not inclined to carry reports of a family's personal anguish at the loss of a loved person. Hence, there was no talk of the death penalty, which had been abolished in Vermont in 1965. Later, in 1972, the U.S. Supreme Court effectively invalidated most state death penalty laws on due process grounds.

Obviously, though, the legal ritual of prosecution of Blondin was of enormous consequence, not only to the Farnhams but to society in general. I was aware, or course, that prosecution was the means by which family members could see that society intended to provide revenge for their egregious life-long harm. A successful prosecution was also vital to give the public a sense that they lived in a just society. I was offended by news stories and thoughtless commentary to the effect that the conviction and the imposition of extreme punishment of Blondin would "let the healing begin" for the family, as though revenge could actually assuage their grief. I felt it fatuous to suggest the Farnhams could ever be whole again.

From the prosecutor's perspective, prosecution of murder cases is often legally complex, even if the facts are simple. Police conduct will be microscopically reviewed for constitutional mistakes. Appeals to the Vermont Supreme Court testing that conduct often follow. All appeals, of course, required extensive comparison of U.S. Supreme Court cases and rulings. One advantage I did have is that, in general, juries favor the state. Few, if any, jurors would condone murder or be so secretly hostile to the police as to vote not guilty when reasonable evidence of guilt was presented. Still, I could assume nothing and had to prepare carefully for the trial in case something unexpected occurred. What I did expect from the get-go was that the defense would emphasize the common sentiment that soldiers fighting in Vietnam were also victims of that senseless war. That sentiment was legally irrelevant but emotionally highly pertinent, which might actually promote sympathy for Blondin. A skilled lawyer like Richard Davis could be expected to do just that.

The motivations of any murderer are always facts a jury would want to know. What mental process or feelings caused Blondin to act as he did? I didn't know what horrors Blondin might have experienced in childhood or in Vietnam. I anticipated the psychiatrists would gain this information and fill it in, but whatever else was true, his was an old story: an angry male attack on a female. Perhaps a simple story. I would need to prove not that he did it, but that the homicide happened viciously, with premeditated intent. The bare bones of the killing seemed to make this obvious. One does not plan to hide in the woods with a high-powered rifle, await the arrival of the victim, and shoot her through the heart without advance malevolent intent.

Davis, on the other hand, would want jurors who saw the world as an unjust place where people did bad things because life is an uncontrollable mix of crazy forces that, to some extent, affect all of us and cause crazy things to flit through our consciousness, undercutting our responsibility for what we do.

The defense responded as expected. Richard Davis filed a notice of intent to plead insanity and a motion to suppress the statements Blondin made to police at the time of his arrest. State law required the attorney general to participate in a murder case. Deputy Attorney General Fred I. Parker was assigned to assist me in trial preparation. He was a superb lawyer and person, who went on to become a federal judge, and I was delighted to work with him. The suppression motion claimed Blondin had not been given proper Miranda warnings and sought return of certain papers he'd left in his cell. The trial judge took evidence on the circumstances and denied the motion. Davis appealed, but on October 6, 1970, the Vermont Supreme Court declined to intervene, saying the issue could only be resolved after a trial. I don't recall the ruling on the papers, but it was not important to the case. Davis applied for a change of venue, which was granted. The defense so far had been unable to establish a viable claim of insanity, at least not one that seemed convincing to me or Fred Parker.   Trial began in November 1970, in Middlebury, before Judge William Hill. The charge was first-degree murder with a mandatory life sentence if convicted, but would allow a jury to find second-degree murder, allowing a judge to sentence Blondin for life or a lesser term. The jury was to be sequestered, meaning the jurors would be in the custody of the bailiff, who would provide hotel quarters and meals during the trial so no outside information could get to them. I took two days to select a jury. On the third day, police witnesses testified about the arrest, the Miranda warning, what Blondin had said, and a description of the murder weapon and how it was found. The afternoon began with the testimony of Cynthia Trepto, Robin's sister. She said that Robin and Blondin had been dating for about six months when Robin had tried to break up with him, asking for her class ring back. She did not provide any statement of why Robin wanted to break up or what she'd said to Blondin—both of which would have been subject to exclusion by the hearsay rule. Next came testimony by the state medical examiner describing Robin's wounds: a bullet passed through the two lower chambers of her heart and ripped through a major blood vessel, killing her instantly.

I decided to press on with my prize evidence—a photograph of Robin taken at the autopsy. The black-and-white photo showed her nude torso, visible from collarbone to waist, with the bullet hole between her breasts, precisely above the location of her heart (the damage done by the exiting bullet was not shown). The photo dramatically told the story of senseless destruction of youth and beauty. I thought it would negate any possible sympathy for Blondin the defense might produce. During the medical examiner's testimony, I offered the photo as evidence. Attorney Parker and I felt autopsy evidence showing the cause of death was customarily admitted, but Davis objected to admission of the photo.

Judge Hill called for a bench conference. Davis and I came forward, while the jury remained seated perhaps ten feet away. Davis's whispered argument was that the photo was unduly prejudicial to the defense, evoking emotion rather than facts. I quietly countered that it showed the effect of Blondin's evil intent and was competent to show the cause of death. Judge Hill leaned toward us and spoke in a low voice so the jurors a few yards away could not hear. He asked both of us to expand our positions, meanwhile, he held the photo of Robin in his hand nearest the jury box as whispered impassioned arguments from Davis and I continued. Everyone in the courtroom had to know the argument was about the photo. Finally, after fifteen minutes of discussion, the judge ruled the photo could be admitted, then adjourned for the day. Davis told the judge he would have extensive evidence of Blondin's insanity to produce at the proper time, and I gave a brief summary of our rebuttal.

It was early afternoon, which gave Davis and me a chance to discuss the case. He proposed that the charge be amended to second-degree murder and Blondin would plead guilty. The only real question was whether Blondin would be found guilty of first- or second-degree murder. Parker and I believed Davis could put forward a lot of evidence of insanity going through Blondin's life and the effect of the Vietnam War on him. It could take a long time, with the jurors in custody, and the chance that, like any trial, something could go wrong. Since the judge still had the authority to sentence Blondin to life in prison for second-degree murder, we saw no point in continuing the trial. I also wanted to avoid further trauma to the Farnham family by having members testify any further. We agreed to amend the charge to second-degree murder and Davis agreed Blondin would plead guilty. The judge had left, so we would have to inform him about the agreement the next morning.

I came to court early on Thursday, before the jury and others assembled. I then received one of the shocks of my career as a young lawyer. As soon as

I entered the courtroom the bailiff told me Judge Hill wanted to see me in chambers without Davis or Parker, an invitation I knew was highly unusual. I stepped into the judge's chamber wondering what would justify such a departure from the rules prohibiting a judge from having *ex parte* conversation with a lawyer, and took a seat. We were alone, there was no court reporter and no witnesses. Judge Hill sat behind his desk. Without any preliminary chatter Judge Hill fixed me with a glare. "Mr. Cheney," Hill said sternly from behind his desk, raising his voice and staring at me, "you are an idiot, and may have caused a defense victory!"

I was shaken by this statement and asked what he meant. "You didn't keep your eyes open as to what was going on in the courtroom. Instead of looking at what I was doing with that picture, you just kept repeating your arguments about the photo without looking around. If you'd been smart, you would have seen that all during the bench argument I was holding the photo up so the jury could see it, and I'm confident they did. You didn't need it to prove your case. Now I've ruled it in evidence as you insisted, but it's a close call. You may very well have given the defense a good appeal that could get any conviction overturned. Damn it, be more alert! Use some judgment for once!" He concluded with almost a snarl, "Now, get out of here."

I left in a daze. This was crazy, I thought. But as soon as Davis appeared, he told the bailiff Blondin was prepared to plead guilty to second-degree murder. Judge Hill, advised of this possibility, recessed the trial to hear counsel immediately in chambers about the offer and what other evidence might be expected. I could amend the charge without his consent, but he would have to approve any guilty plea based on evidence, and he wanted to know what that would be. In chambers, without a court reporter, Davis elaborated on his insanity claim, emphasizing the public's disapproval of the Vietnam War and even the soldiers who fought it, which had a devastating effect on Blondin's pre-existing childhood vulnerabilities. Too many returning veterans, like Blondin, came home as lonely figures with no comrades, parades, or cheers. Too often they were jeered as accomplices in war crimes like what happened at My Lai. Many became depressed, angry, and confused after serving in battle, triggering latent destabilizing tendencies. Blondin's case was even more distorted, as he'd been given medals by a government for doing on the battlefield what he did to Robin. Davis suggested the reason Robin Farnham broke up with Blondin was that she shared an attitude of many in the public who despised Vietnam vets, and said his evidence would take up to a week to present. Parker and I emphasized the police evidence showing purposeful and premeditated activity seeking revenge and Blondin's articulate, in-control confession to the crime. We also had expert psychiatric evidence to present. Judge Hill thought a not guilty but insane verdict was unlikely and concluded the conference, telling the jury the case had been resolved, and in open court began hearings in which Blondin agreed to plead guilty to second-degree murder. A presentence investigation was ordered, meaning sentencing would be months later.

In view of the plea agreement, I didn't worry about whether Judge Hill's prediction of a reversal of a jury verdict on appeal was possible and went to the sentencing hearing expecting a possible sentence of life in prison or a split sentence, like a minimum term of twenty-five or thirty years to life. To my astonishment, in a highly unusual twist, Judge Hill did not set any minimum time to serve, and instead sentenced Blondin to a maximum term of thirty years. The result was that Blondin would be immediately eligible for parole.

The Blondin case occupied my thoughts for years to come. The bizarre behavior of Judge Hill concerning the nude photo of Robin Farnham at the autopsy and the lenient sentence Blondin actually received puzzled me. This was not a case, like you'd find in fiction, of whodunit, but rather about the vicissitudes of life, legal proceedings, and the unexpected. At the trial, Judge Hill's behavior about the photo taught me something valuable: it is often the case in court that you just don't know what will happen. On one level the judge was right—never overtry a case. On another level the lesson was, don't be too confident that the judge will see things your way, especially if you are absolutely certain you are right. He or she may have attitudes that are triggered by yourself or the evidence. Perhaps the whole episode of Hill and the photo was not only about how I needed to brush up on trial skills, but because he had a heart and felt compassion for Blondin as the rejected war hero, he wanted to control the result. In the courtroom, judges can be as much a wild card as a surprise witness.

What eventually happened to Blondin was equally surprising. In 1975, the year I left law enforcement, Blondin was paroled after serving only five years in prison. The stated reason given by the Department of Corrections was he had to be released on furlough in order to participate in a violent-offenders correction program, and to help ease pressure on the overcrowded Vermont prison system. This didn't make sense to me then or now. I don't know if there was another more plausible reason, but I know that Attorney Davis stayed in contact with him and would have done anything he could to help him. Blondin did fine for about twenty years—even working as a prison guard for several years—but in 1995 he was arrested again and charged with assaulting his wife, and being a felon in possession of stolen firearms. He was convicted of those offenses and served some additional time, but was released before being in the system either on parole or in prison for thirty years. Ultimately, he was allowed to live in Florida, where he died at age sixty-six.

I cannot explain the leniency shown Blondin. I can only speculate that others who interacted with him saw reasons for both sympathy and admiration, and decided to help him. The lenient outcome is, to me, the real mystery in this murder case. One explanation may lie in the theory of the "just world hypothesis," launched on the psychological world by Melvin Lerner in 1965. In brief, the theory is that people have a powerful belief that the world is just and people get what they deserve. To account for this belief, people may rationalize injustices by blaming the victim for the catastrophe that occurred. For example, when a person reads a newspaper account of a horrible traffic accident, what most people look for in the story is to see if the deceased was at fault—that he must have been drinking or arguing, or doing something stupid, or else he would have avoided the accident. In such cases, the accident was a just event.

In the Blondin case, many people would search for ways to prove Robin said or did something horrible to him with regards to being a Vietnam veteran, thereby triggering her own murder. Such an explanation may provide a comforting resolution of a horrible event. As prosecutor, I would want "just-worlders" on the jury, under the assumption that the accused deserves what he or she is going to get, or they wouldn't have been charged with the crime. A defense lawyer, on the other hand, wants jurors who see the world as an unjust place where bad things happen to good people because it's a crazy world. The theory explains Attorney Davis's suggestion that Robin did something to outrage Blondin, and so got what she deserved. In every trial the outcome is uncertain. In the more disturbing but rarer cases, where the murder involves complete strangers (seldom the plot of murder novels), there is a threat to everyone, to the very tranquility of the world we inhabit. Then, the search for a just world turns to governmental or other collective action to restore justice either by providing protection or discovering and preventing the criminal tendencies of similar people. In the more prevalent type of case, such as Blondin, where the murderer and victim know each other, the possibility of some form of "just world" theory being part of the defense is likely.

Before the Blondin case was over, Central Vermont was stunned by another major crime—the murder of three people in the town of Cabot. While reading accounts of police investigations and legal maneuverings surrounding Blondin, *Times Argus* readers were stunned by a headline announcing three bodies found in a small cabin just off Route 2. Everett Morse Sr., 45; Joyce Martin, 22; and Anthony Martin, 18 months, had been dead for five days before their bodies were discovered. The adults had been shot between the eyes. The baby and a chained dog had been left to die.

Everett Morse's history was nasty. It included assaults on his ex-wife, robbery, and burglary, charges for which he'd been imprisoned. He had finished his term in prison about a year before his murder, but had vowed to kill those responsible for sending him there.

I was called by police radio to Morse's rented cabin, where I met Sgt. Lay and other officers involved in the investigation. The landlord, who'd seen no activity at the home for several days, had gone to take a look, only to find the three bodies and a whimpering dog. The dead had been removed before I arrived. Even in the cold December day, the place smelled of death, neglect, and decay. It was a nauseating blood-stained sight, but I knew that if a trial were necessary, personal knowledge of the scene would help me make a compelling and effective narrative.

Lay told me that Washington County Sheriff Mark Brown, with whom I'd had that major disagreement over high-speed chases, had immediately gone to interview potential witnesses in Orange County, where the Morse family had lived. But Brown had no authority in that county—he was checking with witnesses before the state police could reach them. Brown had not asked Lay how to proceed. Lay asked me to call the sheriff with instructions to leave everything to the state police, because he wanted to contact witnesses in a planned order. Brown backed off, but he was not happy. He told me he could crack this case almost immediately if I let him go to work. I still said no.

Within two days, Lay approached me with a request for murder charges and arrest warrants for Everett Morse, Jr., James Morse, and Julie Morse, all children of the deceased. They had been interviewed by Sgt. Lay, but after getting the Miranda warning, had said nothing. They asked for lawyers.

Probable cause was based on what other witnesses had said about the siblings' plans for a trip to Cabot and their comments about their hatred of their father. Someone told police the murder weapon had been thrown off the Granite Street bridge in Montpelier, where it was soon recovered. All three siblings were arrested and lodged in the Washington County jail, behind the Montpelier courthouse, administered by the sheriff pending arraignment the next morning. Not-guilty pleas were entered by all, and the trial was set five months hence.

With no incriminating statements made by the Morses, I determined the best way to proceed was to offer Julie Morse immunity from prosecution in return for her full and complete description of the murder and willingness to testify against her brothers. I was sure the brothers had planned and carried out the murders and Julie had little to do with it. The trio had been brought to Montpelier from their places of confinement elsewhere for a pretrial proceeding. While the boys were in court, I visited Julie in her cell. She didn't have a lawyer at that time and had not been given Miranda by Sgt. Lay. I told her I only wanted to talk about my willingness to offer immunity from prosecution if she was willing to help, and until she agreed to do so, I would not ask her about the actual facts of the crime. I was dressed in suit and tie, and had a neatly-trimmed mustache that I thought looked pretty sharp—I expected my sincerity and impeccable appearance would win her confidence. She wore prison clothing, looked scared and morose.

I began by asking if she had been treated well. She nodded affirmatively, but didn't speak. I went on, saying I was there to ask for her help in seeing that some wrong things that had been done might be corrected, and asked for her cooperation. If she helped, I could make sure charges against her were dropped. If she wanted a lawyer, I would get her one. Julie seemed confused. She looked blank. Friends and school reports showed she was intelligent. I didn't know why I got no response, so I tried again. With the most ingratiating and friendly voice I could manage, I repeated that I just wanted to help her. I didn't want to see her life ruined. Julie still wouldn't answer. She just looked intently at me. I waited patiently. At last she leaned forward to speak.

"Mister Cheney," she said, "can I tell you something?" She paused.

"Of course," I said. "That's why I'm here." She went blank again, looked furtively around the cell, then leaned towards me, looking at my face but not my eyes, and said quietly, "Mr. Cheney, I really like your mustache!" That was it! She wouldn't say more! But two days later she got a lawyer who called me saying Julie would cooperate if I gave her immunity. A later interview laid out the entire crime, incriminating her brothers without any comments about my appearance. As the trial approached, as required, I gave the defense and the court a list of my expected witnesses, indicating Julie with an offer of immunity. Other witnesses who'd overheard the Morse boys talking about the crime were on the list. When Sgt. Lay saw the list, he contacted me and asked why I wasn't calling Mark Brown. I told him I didn't think he had anything to add. I'd told him to leave the investigation to the state police and believed he'd done so. Lay said I ought to call him, that he might know something.

So I did call the sheriff. I hadn't heard anything from him since asking him to leave the investigation. He asked to meet with me, and I went to his office in the jail. When we met, before any conversation, he handed me a few typewritten pages. I took them out of curiosity and quickly read them over. What I had in my hand appeared to be an account of a conversation Sheriff Brown had with James Morse on an occasion when he was held in the Washington County jail months ago. It recited that Brown gave James the full Miranda warning, James agreed to talk, and then described the crime in all its lurid details. I had never seen this admission, or known of its existence. The confession appeared to meet all the Miranda requirements sufficient to allow the confession to be admitted into evidence. I was both shocked and angry and asked the sheriff why he never mentioned he'd obtained a confession or provided me with a copy of it. Brown replied that I told him to stay out of the case and that I'd never asked him. He also said he'd given the confession to the state police, even though I told him to stay out of the case. But it was not mentioned in any state police reports. I pointed out, as calmly as I could, that his concealment of the report from me had caused me to give Julie immunity when I didn't need to. "Mark, whose side are you on?" I asked.

"I might ask you the same thing," he replied, indicating the conversation was over. He had finally found an opportunity to pay me back for the way I treated him in the high-speed car chase, and the charges I'd brought against him for excessive force against a prisoner. My conduct in those cases may have been worthy of criticism, but, I thought, not at the expense of justice being done in a pending murder case. At least he told Lay of the confession on the eve of trial so I would learn of it, but I had to come to him with hat in hand, so to speak, and recognize he was a good and competent cop. It was a lesson for me in how multifaceted and competitive law-enforcement could be.

Because of James's confession and Julie's expected testimony, there was overwhelming evidence against James and Everett Jr., who agreed to plead guilty to second-degree murder. Everett Jr. was sentenced to prison for the remainder of his life, James was given a sentence of life with a minimum of twenty years to serve.

I've driven past the scene of the crime many times since then. Soon after the trial, the owner had the building demolished. In the spring, the ground was cleared and fresh grass planted, adding to the bucolic pastoral farm scene beside the road. But it never looked that way to me. As I describe in the next chapter, there were more murders to come. It is not easy to believe in a just world.

CHAPTER 11

*"I'm going to have a whole mess of vicious
dogs people want to give back."*

Jill Martin, Central Vermont Humane Society, 1969

MORE MURDERS

In the fall of 1969, word that a murderer was preying on innocent victims in Washington County had people scared. I caused some of that concern. The *Times Argus* accurately reported that I'd announced that a "sexual psychopath" was responsible for a double murder of a retired Florida couple on September 19. I told the reporter what a state police investigation in the deaths of James and Iola Hipp had found: Both had been bludgeoned to death with what appeared to be a ball-peen hammer in their camper trailer. The camper had been parked in a pull-off area on U.S. Route 2, just east of Montpelier, but had evidently been towed to a remote place by the killer, where their bodies were found several days later. Iola Hipp had not been raped, police said, but her body had been slashed postmortem with a knife, in a peculiar pattern. The manner of death and mutilation were reported as being similar to those suffered by Alice Baker, a victim of an unsolved murder in February of 1958. There were no suspects.

More was to come. On September 29, the body of a decapitated young woman was found by hunters in a field. On October 4, another missing woman's body was found in a shallow grave not far from her home. On November 19, a Goddard College student was raped, shot in the head, and left for dead, but survived when passersby heard her calls for help and rushed her to the hospital. All these killings occurred just months after the Farnham/Blondin murder, and were closely followed by the Morse murders on December 15, adding to the perception that something was horribly wrong in Washington County. The Hipp homicides were the third double-murder statewide within a year—the Morse case was a triple. The *Burlington Free Press* reported people were reacting, saying that "there are no more moonlight walks" and "brutish watchdogs are now sleeping indoors." Another article said Vermonters were "wishing investigators would capture the killer, yet hope he has already left the area." And I was quoted as saying, "The police are trying, but it's almost like trying to snatch a wisp of cloud from the sky."

The manager of the local humane society, Jill Martin, described the mood of the county succinctly. She was receiving phone calls from people willing to adopt vicious dogs, or asking how they could train their dogs to be aggressive toward strangers. "I'll have a problem when the killer is caught, or things calm down," Martin said, "because I'm going to have a whole mess of vicious dogs people want to give back." A store selling guns and ammunition reported an upsurge in sales, while hardware stores announced they were running out of locks.

I'd been the state's attorney for less than a year when these events shattered everyone's sense of peace and security. Since I was the spokesman for the police investigating these crimes, people looked to me for assurance that the killer, or killers, would be caught—this was an utterly novel function for me. Never before had I been a focus of dramatic events creating turmoil in a community. Of course, the police—not I—had to do the day-to-day investigative work to solve these crimes, but I had to be in regular contact with investigating officers, like Sgt. Lay and his assistant, Cpl. Ted Hislop. We met frequently to discuss what had been done or could be done, asking myriad questions to make sure all avenues of inquiry were explored. My duty was also to assure the public as completely and honestly as I could that competent people were working hard for their safety. Personally, I was excited by the challenges. Vermont certainly provided what I had come for: a chance to be a lawyer doing meaningful work.

The details made public about some of these crimes added to people's concerns. In a report I passed on to the *Times Argus*, Lay and Hislop summed up their findings regarding the Hipp murders this way: "This is the most horrific crime scene we've ever seen. The inside of the trailer was covered with blood. It was a vicious attack; and with a week gone by it's going to be really hard to find the killer. If we are lucky, he'll say something stupid to someone that will furnish a lead, but if he doesn't, it's going to be a real tough one." That's when one *Times Argus* headline read: SEX PSYCOHPATH BELIEVED IN AREA.

The police worked hard, interviewing 250 people and performing traffic stops near the murder scene, asking if anyone had seen anything suspicious. They hadn't. But one curious fact did emerge—a young Northfield man, Kenneth Jennett, twenty-three, had gone missing from his parents' home without explanation about two days after the Hipps were murdered, but three days before their bodies were discovered. There was no information from parents, friends, co-workers, or anyone else concerning why he left or where he'd gone.

The Hipp murders were never solved. Years later, state police retained Brian Linder, a meticulous historian, to examine all missing persons reports in the state originating from around the time of the Hipp murders. Linder focused on Jennett as a suspect, asking anyone living in Northfield who knew him for information. He told me as I worked on this memoir that most people refused to talk openly about Jennett, giving various deflecting responses. Linder did learn that two days after the Hipp murders, Jennett gave each of his parents $5,000, and then disappeared forever without saying goodbye. Vermont State Police speculated he slipped across the border to Canada, which they investigated, only to learn from the Royal Canadian Mounted Police that they had been unable to locate any trace of him.

In 2018, when no longer holding public office, I made an inquiry to the state police Cold Case Officer about possible DNA evidence, and was told that DNA research would be undertaken, but my request to see the file was denied. When asked about this, Linder told me the state police had actually lost the file and there were no DNA tissue samples preserved, so, short of a corroborated confession, there would be no possibility of solving the case. The only comforting fact is, in the four decades since the murders, no similar crimes have occurred. Perhaps the people got their wish and the killer left the area. At the time, though, two highly publicized cases contributed to the fear of a maniacal sexual predator roaming the county.

The decapitated body of a sixteen-year-old woman found in September was identified as Lorette Baker of Barre, missing since April. She was found by hunters in a shallow grave in a field. Investigators learned she was a frequent companion of a man who had committed suicide on September 1, 1969, a month before Barker's body was found. He was the only possible suspect, so police ended the murder investigation, and to some extent calmed popular hysteria concerning a roaming psychopath.

Another body, discovered on October 3, was that of another sixteen-year-old, Roberta Blakeney, of Barre, whose parents had reported her missing in July. Her body was also found in a shallow grave in a field, just 200 feet from the front door of her parents' home. Ms. Blakeney's parents said they thought she'd run off with a young man, whom they didn't know. Her body was identified by a tag on her clothing, but was so badly decomposed, forensic examination could not determine the manner or cause of death, thereby crippling any further investigation. The circumstances supported conjecture that the killing was the work of a person known to Roberta, rather than a random killing. That hypothesis assisted in calming lingering fears of a roaming psycho. I called a grand jury to interrogate the parents and other acquaintances of Lorette's, but no evidence was found suggesting the name or identity of a possible killer, or the cause or manner of her death. Ineluctably, the grand jury issued no indictments. I was quoted as saying police may never know what happened.

I had little courtroom work to do on these unsolved cases, but did follow police reports and discussed any new investigation findings, if any, with local press. I emphasized that there was no evidence of any connection between the deaths of the young women found buried in shallow graves and the Hipp murder. Given the mood of the times, however, I doubt my comments had the calming effect I was seeking.

The November 17 rape and near-murder of the Goddard College student, which had superficial similarities to the Hipp Murders due to graphic descriptions of violence, further exacerbated community fears. As part of her studies, the student had been off the Plainfield campus at the time, demonstrating dance techniques to third graders in Barre Town. She'd decided to hitchhike back to the college after completing her lessons. She was picked up, raped, and shot in the head. Her assailant fled, leaving her for dead. Amazingly, despite the bullet wound to the head, she was able to cry for help, bringing some children and their father to her aid. They saved her life, getting prompt police and emergency medical help. She was hit by a .22-caliber bullet that entered the left side of her head, traveled through it, and lodged on the right side. Miraculously, no vital structures or parts of her brain were destroyed, and she was able to describe her assailant, as well as his car. Fortunately, this information allowed the crime to be quickly solved, identifying her attacker as Dale Findsen, twenty-three, of Barre.

On November 18, approximately twenty-four hours after discovery of the crime, Findsen was arrested by Corporal Ted Hislop, as he left his workplace at a granite company. Hislop immediately took Findsen to his father's house in Barre, where he lived, to look for the murder weapon. Hislop feared trouble when he saw that the garage floor had recently been refinished and filled with concrete, creating the possibility that the weapon had been buried. However, with the father's permission, Hislop, went inside to inspect clothing that might provide evidence Dale's guilt. He found Dale's jacket hanging in a closet, with a .22-caliber pistol in its pocket. Hislop showed the weapon to Dale. His father asked incredulously, "Did you do this?" Dale responded promptly, without evasion or emotion, that he had in fact done just that! He was taken to the State Police K Barracks in Montpelier where, at 7:00 p.m., he was arraigned on charges of rape and attempted murder, then lodged in jail for lack of bail, set at $40,000. Dale's employer said he was a "good worker." He was married and the father of two, with no known criminal history or disturbing behavior.

Barre Attorney John Bernasconi was assigned to represent Findsen. On November 20, Findsen was brought to court where he entered a plea of not guilty by reason of insanity. I arranged for a psychiatric evaluation by Dr. William Woodruff, a well-known forensic psychiatrist frequently used by prosecutors for such purposes. In 1969, DNA evidence was not available. I decided to have a lineup. This is a process of placing people of similar stature and appearance in a line for the victim to survey. Defense lawyers, if available, can be present to ensure there are no obvious or subtle clues to tip off the suspect to the victim. Given the student's ability to identify her assailant for police, I was confident she could identify Findsen as her attacker, to corroborate his confession.

On December 5, Dr. Woodruff called me and attorney Bernasconi to say that, although he had not yet finished his report, his opinion was that Findsen was legally insane. Bernasconi immediately filed a motion with the Vermont Supreme Court, asking that prosecution be enjoined from holding a lineup on the grounds that Findsen would be found insane, necessitating the appointment of a guardian ad litem before any further court-ordered procedures could take place. The supreme court agreed, issuing an order on December 16 prohibiting a lineup until a guardian ad litem was assigned.

The student wanted to go home to New York City to recuperate, which I permitted.

In late 1969, Woodruff furnished a nine-page report concluding that Findsen was insane at the time of the crime, that is, that he was unable to control his impulse to commit a horrible act. Woodruff reported that Findsen had matter-of-factly admitted all the facts of the crime. A lineup was then unnecessary. His opinion was that Findsen, while hallucinating, heard voices telling him to rape and kill, and that a voice told him to pick up his victim when he saw her hitchhiking. His history showed several serious head injuries from childhood to the present, but without demonstrable organic brain damage. He'd had a probable sexual relationship with his brother as a child, Woodruff reported, and as a result, was wary if not fearful of certain males, which led him to buy several guns and often carry with him a .22-caliber pistol.

Dr. Woodruff diagnosed Findsen as having borderline personality disorder and schizophrenia, paranoid type, which in the legal sense would amount to insanity. Court proceedings followed in which Woodruff testified to his opinion, of course, without contradiction. On April 3, 1970, Findsen was indefinitely committed by Judge Connarn to the Department of Mental Health, to be held in the high-security ward for patients who were a danger to themselves or others, unless determined at a later time that he was not such a danger. On September 7, 1972, Findsen met with the Board of Mental Health, and in November was permitted to fly immediately to Thailand to live with his brother. I was not consulted, nor given any authority to contest that decision. There has been no further news concerning him.

Every social system creates a rationale and system for punishing people who do things that threaten to undermine the political state. To be legitimate, the system must assume that people have free will and so can choose whether to misbehave, that is, to act or not act in a way the state demands. The insanity defense is a necessary corollary to that assumption. Its existence recognizes that some mental states negate free will and therefore punishment is not merited—but confinement in order to protect society is. In principle, the concept is simple: a four year old who picks up a gun and shoots his mother is not a criminal, nor is an adult who suffers from some irrational mental state (which he did not cause by his own behavior, such as taking drugs or alcohol) and who, because of mental disease or defect, is unable to control his behavior and intentionally drives his car into an oncoming car, killing others.

With the assistance of hundreds of highly-qualified experts, the American

Psychiatric Association publishes a catalog of diseased mental states, known as the *Diagnostic and Statistical Manual of Mental Disorders.* The DSM, as it is called, is generally accepted among psychiatrists and the legal community as the gold standard for diagnostic criteria. For example, it lists a condition like schizophrenia and provides a comprehensive description of behaviors warranting that conclusion. The DSM is useful for diagnostic and treatment purposes, and in a criminal case where an insanity defense is presented, it can be overcome by showing a lack of an accurate diagnosis. A battle of experts is common, but if there is disagreement, the fate of the accused will be determined by a jury that must determine beyond a reasonable doubt which of the expert psychiatrists' testimony to accept. In Findsen's case, I could've retained another psychiatrist to dispute Dr. Woodruff, who would then be a defense witness. These legal processes add up to the practical reality that the real test of insanity is that insanity is whatever behavior twelve jurors can agree merits treatment rather than punishment. Evidence from psychiatrists will give them guidance, but contextual human and political factors, including the nature of the crime, are also involved. In Findsen's case, I accepted Dr. Woodruff's opinion because he was trusted by many other prosecutors and his reasons seemed convincing.

The concept of insanity is based on the premise that humans have free will and are able to choose to behave or misbehave. Whether or not that premise is an objective reality is not subject to challenge, because the entire social order rests on it being accepted as true. Years later, when I was no longer prosecuting and was defending, I did try to dispute the idea of free will. Although my client at that time had no identifiable disease or defect, he had a horrible life history, which I thought determined how he had committed a crime. I asked the state's psychiatrist, who had testified that my client was not insane this question: "Doctor, do you believe in the concept of free will—specifically any reasonable ability to control behavior under certain circumstances?"

"To answer your question," the psychiatrist responded, "I do believe in the concept of free will, although to bring it about may require extensive counseling and a change in friends and in attitudes over time."

I didn't disagree, but how could my client be found sane without having had those services? At the time of the crime, the doctor admitted, the accused could not control his behavior. The judge wasn't convinced of my logic, but gave no reason for ignoring it. I could rationalize the outcome as it rested on the assumption that resulted in the conviction of drunks and addicts. They had chosen to drink or use drugs, and my client chose not to engage in therapy. The difference was, my client's mental condition prevented him from foreseeing the consequences of not having therapy. Different than the drunken criminal? My conclusion: social necessity prevails over logic; any failures discovered in the logic of the law may be made up at sentencing—or parole, in a humane system where it costs a lot of money to keep a person in jail.

After the Findsen case, there was a hiatus in grisly crimes in Washington County, until July 30, 1970. That was the date Martin Kennelly Jr., fifty, of Barre tried to kill his former wife from whom he'd been divorced for fifteen years. She was then living with Victor Cano in their shared home at West Hill in Barre, known as the Morrison farm. A little before 1:00 a.m., a neighbor of Kennelly's phoned Cano, warning him that Kennelly had been practicing with a pistol and was on his way to Cano's house. Cano immediately called the Barre police. Officer Joseph Colombo, age twenty-two, responded, didn't see Kennelly, knocked on Cano's door, announced himself, and was admitted into the house. The home entrance was not secured. Kennelly, who must have seen Columbo arrive and enter the house, snuck into the house soon after Columbo entered. Other officers arrived. As soon as Kennelly became aware of the presence of other officers in the area, he slipped back outside, took Columbo's police cruiser and drove it a small distance away, hoping to draw the newly-arrived officers from the scene. He was successful. They searched for Kennelly in buildings near the Cano residence.

Kennelly then went back inside the house, calling out, "Come on you cops!" Kennelly heard Colombo on the house phone calling for help. He fired through the wall at him, wounding him severely. Colombo returned fire, possibly hitting Kennelly who then ran outside, where he sought cover behind a five-inch-diameter flagpole. By then, State Police Capt. Newell Freer and another Barre officer, Al Wolters, had arrived armed with shotguns. Freer found cover behind a tree. Wolters was sheltered by a porch. Kennelly fired several shots at both of them. Freer and Wolters returned fire, Freer using his service pistol and a shotgun. Shots, possibly by Wolters, hit Kennelly, who fell to the ground. An ambulance took Colombo and Kennelly to the hospital. Kennelly had been hit several times and died soon after arriving at the hospital. Five bullets were later found in the tree sheltering Freer. Six holes were found in the flagpole sheltering Kennelly, in a five-inch circle. Colombo survived, but took a long time to recover. Cano and Kennelly's former wife escaped physical injury, though were undoubtedly traumatized by the gun fight.

I went to the scene as soon as I was notified by phone and car radio. After getting a briefing from Freer, I asked how big the tree was he was standing behind. He looked at me with a slight smile then brought his two hands together palm to palm about four inches apart, signaling not only his best recollection but also his feelings at the time, that the tree offered no real protection. This was an extremely dangerous gunfight for both the officers and the Cano family. In my comment to the press about the gunfight, I voiced my admiration for the officers, saying they should all be commended for bravery and superior judgment through the entire incident that prevented the probable triple homicide of the Canos and officer Columbo. Ever since that morning, I've had images of cops facing gunfire from crazed shooters with protection only as wide as Freer demonstrated. In truth, there is no perfect protection from a hail of bullets. Freer was describing the possible experience of all police officers.

Central Vermont was free of violent crimes for about four months, until August 10, 1970, when the *Times Argus* headlined yet another murder. Police had been called by a resident of a trailer park who reported a shooting at an adjacent mobile home. Robert and Sylvia MacDonald lived there with three or four children, one of which was home at the time of the shooting. Upon arrival, police entered the trailer and quickly arrested a distraught Robert MacDonald, a well-respected state employee. A .22-caliber pistol was found on the bed in the main bedroom. Sylvia and a knife were found in another room. An ambulance took Sylvia to the hospital, where she was pronounced dead on arrival. Robert was taken to court for arraignment. Officers present determined that Sylvia had been shot in the back.

I charged MacDonald with first-degree murder on the basis that Sylvia died of a gunshot wound to the back, indicating she was getting away from Robert when she was shot, contrary to Robert's story. He'd said his wife became enraged at him over an inconsequential event and was about to attack him with a knife when he shot her in self-defense. He was represented by Barre Lawyer Richard Davis.

I requested Robert MacDonald be released on bail, saying I could not form an opinion as to what took place without ballistic analysis and an autopsy. Davis didn't object. The autopsy report stated the wound in Sylvia's chest was an entrance wound, not the exit wound the police had identified on the night of the shooting—the basis for the murder charge. Since MacDonald had been publicly charged and probable cause found by a judge, I felt both MacDonald and I each needed public vindication. I called a grand jury to review all the evidence, including police witnesses who detailed their investigation and recited MacDonald's version of events as he'd stated on the night of his arrest. The medical examiner who performed the autopsy also testified. As I anticipated, the grand jury refused to indict Robert. Accordingly, I dismissed the murder charges.

I had little professional courtroom involvement in either the unsolved crimes or the police gunfight with Kennelly. In 1969-1970, little notice or comment was made about the fact that all these crimes involved women's gruesome deaths. The Blondin case was the start; Iola Hipp appeared to be the target for a sexual psychopath who incidentally involved her husband; two women were apparently strangled by their male lovers; the Goddard student's rape was classic violence against a woman; whatever rage led Sylvia MacDonald to apparently attack and provoke her husband was never explored; Kennelly was a thwarted lover's revenge; the Morse murders appeared to be motivated by rage at their father's mistreatment of their mother.

I recall no social, political, or journalistic attempt to raise awareness of the obvious and dramatic display of women's exposure to violence and the consequences these cases illustrated. A cultural cloak of female invisibility was thrown over violence against women. Decades later, that cloak has been ripped away by the vigorous work of skillful people. Murder is rightfully considered the most serious of all crimes. At the time, I saw these cases as merely problems to be solved by arrests, if possible, not as larger social issues. But I believe a state's attorney has some responsibility to change social attitudes. I made some efforts to do so regarding drugs, in part because of personal experience with my mother's addiction to alcohol, but I'd had no personal experience with violence toward women. Probably for that reason, it never occurred to me, even with two daughters, to sound an alarm and seek change.

These murders did propel me into media focus as I became the spokesman for police investigations into these disturbing cases. Headlines and stories about the killings and discoveries of buried women's bodies were constantly in the local newspaper. Readers had a chance to read about State's Attorney Cheney almost every day. Press accounts of an elected official being involved in his or her work are the coin on which reputations are built, and provide the foundation for higher office. Newspaper readers would get the erroneous impression that my principal occupation was investigating or prosecuting murder cases, when in fact other business involving drugs, social disturbances, petty crime, and jury trials (many of which also merited press coverage) as described earlier were ongoing. These cases increased my sophistication about criminal law policy as well as police operations. They also generated statewide publicity that undoubtedly helped in my subsequent successful campaign to be elected as the state's attorney general in 1972. I was pleased with the excitement and satisfaction of doing important work in the public eye—a reason I had come to Vermont.

CHAPTER 12

*"Far and away the best prize that life has to offer
is the chance to work hard at work worth doing."*

Theodore Roosevelt, c. 1910

1972 CAMPAIGN FOR ATTORNEY GENERAL

Murder, mayhem, theft, drug and alcohol abuse, as well as increasing numbers of drunk driving cases, are not a nourishing diet. When taken excessively they are apt to cause some malaise. By 1971, the legislature created a deputy position for the Washington County State's Attorney's Office, to assist with the growing workload. The position had been created because better prosecutorial law enforcement brought about by a full-time state's attorney encouraged police to make more and better cases. The result was that disturbing behavior, previously ignored by police—to the disgust of peaceful citizens—was now less tolerated, and more miscreants were being brought to court. I hired thirty-year-old Robert Gagnon, a recent graduate of the University of Washington Law School, as my deputy. Bob came with a career goal to become a prosecutor. He had excellent judgment and professional expertise that had grown out of his study of criminal law issues.

Gagnon's arrival encouraged me to think about my own professional ambitions and about who would be the next state attorney general. The incumbent, James M. Jeffords, announced he would run for governor, instead of for re-election. 1972 promised to be an active political year, with contests for Vermont's lone congressional seat, governor, and attorney general. I saw an opportunity and decided to talk this over with my friend, Johnathan Brownell, who'd resigned as deputy attorney general to enter private law practice in 1968 because his mentor, Attorney General James Oakes, was leaving his post in 1969.

"You're new at this political business. Don't you think you're rushing it?" he asked during a meeting in his Montpelier office. "You've only been in the state six years."

"Well, JB, I don't really know what my chances are, but personally I think it's time for me to make a try," I said. "I've done my thing as state's attorney. More to the point, if I don't run, someone else will get the job, in which case it will be years before there's a vacancy." I told him I didn't want to be state's attorney for life. "I either need to get into private practice and build my skills and income, or do something I really want when I have the chance."

Brownell pointed out that Robert West, a Republican lawyer and state senator from Rutland, would be a tough opponent in a primary. He was also the former Republican state's attorney in Rutland, Vermont's second largest city. West had served four years on the Judiciary Committee in the state senate. We didn't talk politics for long, as Brownell asked about the impact of a statewide campaign on my home life.

"Thanks for your concern," I replied. I didn't really want to get into details, so I said, "The short answer is, Barb won't miss me but the kids will. I'll find time for them. Barb's got a good job. We'll be okay financially, as my state's attorney pay will continue during the campaign. Of course, I'll have to do state's attorney work, but I can get away for campaigning."

The fact was, Barb and I were never soul mates. We'd stayed together to bring up the children, live a cooperative economic life, and share family, but were unable to confront the circumstances and

Barb and me with the girls and Hector

disappointments of our marriage. There were no sexual relations between us after the children were born. We lived cooperatively but without real affection, only a common interest in making the best of the situation we found ourselves in, and to some degree acting out a marriage because we didn't know what else to do. I was interested in my work and excited about the work I'd done in the Education Department and the legislature, loved being a father to our girls, and simply avoided thinking about my relationship with Barb. Barb appeared to enjoy her counseling work at the local mental health agency, and being a mother. I had little idea what other things she did to sustain herself. We didn't talk much, except about managing our busy lives.

Brownell and I continued talking. "Kim," he said, "if this makes sense for you, I'll see if I can help you raise money. You'll need a bit." We didn't talk amounts. I thanked him for his support, saying I would contact him as I got my campaign organized. I naively thought I could raise what I needed, but had no idea what it would cost to run a viable statewide campaign. I assumed my good local reputation would help, that I would shake a lot of hands, and work for newspaper, radio, and TV stories. And so it began—my first ever statewide campaign. Another new job to learn.

In the national political background to the November general election were two dramatic events: the Watergate burglary of June 17 tied to President Nixon, and Secretary of State Henry Kissinger's efforts to end the Vietnam War. Watergate was emerging as a serious political event, and of course the war was of enormous public concern; but any local effect was not yet apparent. Issues raised by these events were not forecasted to be factors in the contest for Vermont attorney general.

In May 1972, I announced I was running in the September 12, 1972, Republican primary for attorney general. Former Caledonia State's Attorney, Sten Lium, had already announced, and State Senator and attorney Robert West, then a member of the Senate Judiciary Committee, announced the following week. Former Superior Court Judge Nat Divoll was yet to announce, but he, too, would soon be in the race. A long shot, Peter Diamondstone, a progressive to the left of Bernie Sanders, would also enter the Republican Primary. There was only one candidate in the Democratic primary. The winner of the Republican primary was almost certain to become attorney general in November, because the Democratic candidate was not attracting much attention. In a five-way primary contest where a plurality determines the winner, a candidate needs fewer votes to win than in a head-to-head race.

The Republican Party at that time was really two parties—one conservative and one moderate-to-progressive. The progressive wing had some signal achievements: rural electrification, a ban on billboards along the roads, and a statewide law controlling major development to name a few. A tradition had grown of having these fundamental political persuasions fought out without the hindrance of Democrats. The "hippies, freaks, and radicals" who'd migrated to Vermont in the sixties had not yet become the recognized reliable voting force that would eventually change the state. After Phil Hoff's election as the first Democratic governor, in 1963, and retirement in 1969, the old order began to crumble, confuse party labels, and pile up rubble in unusual places. The Republican gubernatorial primary between Jeffords and Luther Hackett, a Burlington businessman and favorite of outgoing Governor Deane Davis, was a traditional party fracture between conservatives and progressives. Vermont attorney general elections tended to be issue-oriented, without choosing sides in the split Republican party. Still, the gubernatorial campaign had one enormous future consequence for me.

Attorney general Jeffords sued New York State and the International Paper Company, claiming money damages because International Paper had dumped tons of polluting paper waste from its mill into the southern end Lake Champlain, on the New York side, and New York State had done nothing to prevent it. Jeffords filed the suit in the U.S. Supreme Court, as the U.S. Constitution prescribes for suits between states. Republican Governor Davis supported the effort, knowing it would require extensive funding. New York State, the suit claimed, had acquiesced in this practice, and profited from the income earned by International Paper, without paying for collateral damage done to Vermont. Litigation costs were expected to be enormous. The next attorney general and governor would have to decide how to raise the necessary money. Jeffords campaigned on the importance of the suit, seeking to protect Lake Champlain. Hackett was to win the primary with about 53 percent of the vote, but went on to lose the governorship to Democrat Thomas Salmon.

My statewide campaign was primitive. Neither e-mail nor social media existed, but newspapers were everywhere and their political stories were often picked up on radio or TV. Campaign stories were earned by giving radio interviews, an occasional candidate's forum (usually populated by friends of the candidate rather than the general public), or being involved in a criminal case that reporters found interesting. Paid messaging was by radio, TV, or direct mailing. I had no collection of political friends ready to help with a campaign. Fortunately, a local attorney, Fred Bertrand, who worked at National Life Insurance Company, volunteered to be my campaign manager.

His work provided extensive statewide connections. He volunteered in an effort to dilute the overwhelming grief that engulfed him and his wife caused by the recent death of their child. He needed to be engaged, he said, to help others, to be absorbed in work apart from his usual routine, to think only about how to help a friend. Fred's sometimes demonic energy—making yet another phone call, even when exhausted; or planning a day's events, lining up people to see; or suggesting responses to an opponent's nonsense—energized me as well. Fred had many local contacts, because his father was a much loved pediatrician who cared for many families. His energy and friendship were critical. Another friend, who wasn't tied to a daily work-life, was available to be my driver on trips around the state for events. He was a great help, allowing me to rest a bit between trips, and warming me up for up-coming events with interesting conversation.

Since the campaign would be a contest between relatively unknown candidates, I believed endorsements would be effective, and sought them out. At one Republican Committee meeting, outgoing governor, Deane C. Davis, refused to acknowledge the other candidates, but gave even-handed praise to both West and me, saying we were good candidates—in context, practically an endorsement. The most persuasive effort came about in the letter shown below, signed by four former attorneys general, the chair of the House Judiciary Committee, and Jonathan Brownell.

I made this letter into a poster and brochure, proud of it because it showed support from people who knew both me and what the job entailed. As I traveled the state, I posted a copy anywhere public announcements could be left, and passing out the brochure wherever I could. I arranged a schedule of visits to every small weekly newspaper I could find, and sought interviews on local radio shows whenever I could arrange a time, hopefully coordinating with a speech at the local service club. I used bulk mail and purchased as many radio ads as I could afford, but I didn't have money for more than a few television spots. I spent about $10,000 on the campaign (in 2020-dollars, that would be equivalent to $62,000), about 75 percent of which was raised from supporters.

Barb was a real help in my campaign. She went on campaign trips from time to time, occasionally posing for photographs with me, looking pretty and filled with youthful charm. Her appearances gave important context to me as a candidate, as an ordinary married father of two. She found time to keep her job while keeping the house going with happy kids. One long article about her sympathetically detailed her career as a folk singer, therapist, and mother of two, dividing her time between work, family, and her husband's campaign. The headline read: "She Likes Campaigning, But Her Legs Get Tired," explaining that she often had to stand alone, outside of the conversation, while I talked with people. I expect many wives would feel the same way. An article about Robert West's wife was headlined: " She Stacks the Dishes and Goes"— a sad, cringeworthy relic of women's roles. Barb was kind and attentive to people who helped with my campaign, and also monitored messages and helped with communications. Her help was certainly a factor in my eventual success.

In addition to touting my endorsements, I did address law enforcement issues. "Drugs" were, and are always, a political issue requiring a candidate to find a safe haven amidst conflicting opinions on what could be done. Like everyone else, I called for more effort to find and jail large-quantity sellers, characterized as "pushers," linked to the narcotics infrastructure, noting that law enforcement alone would not solve the "drug problem." I supported lowering the blood alcohol count (BAC) in sobriety tests to determine a presumption of driving under the influence. My pet plan was to propose a complete revision of the criminal code. Constitutional law requires the legislature to define exactly what conduct is prohibited to constitute a crime, for which the state may impose punishment, like a fine or a jail sentence. As a result, the statutes were filled with "designer crimes," to fit the latest new outrageous act committed. My favorite of these was "Painting and Disguising Horses," followed closely by a specific crime for blowing up a steamboat. More troublesome from a prosecutorial point of view was a plethora of theft crimes tied to specific kinds of property and another long list of specific ways to inflict bodily harm or sexually abuse a person. I urged elimination of some specifics in favor of more generic definitions of crimes, such as theft and assaults, to be matched to a penalty scheme carefully related to the harm done. Doing so would curtail disparate penalties for similar crimes. Criminal code revisions common in several states would provide a model for Vermont.

The major issue of the campaign turned out to be a gift from Senator West. In the 1971 session, he sponsored and got through the Senate his own criminal code revision bill. His version changed many drug related crimes formerly classified as felonies into misdemeanors. In addition, the law removed the crime of armed robbery from the books. When the law passed and was scrutinized by the press and public, these changes were subject to harsh criticism. On May 2, 1972, a St. Albans newspaper, *The Vermont Sunday News*, an unabashed conservative voice, wrote an editorial saying, in capital letters:

BUT AFTER THE SCREW-UP OF THE STATE'S CRIMINAL CODE, TOTALLY REMOVING SOME LAWS AND DROPPING MANY FROM THE FELONY CATEGORY TO MISDEMEANOR, ONE WOULD THINK THAT SENATOR WEST WOULD KNOW BETTER THAN TO ESPOUSE HIS BRILLIANCE AS A CANDIDATE FOR ATTORNEY GENERAL.

The editorial went on to urge West to drop out of the race "after pulling one of the biggest legislative bloopers in state history . . . Senator West is one politician whose 'vast experience' the State can well do without in the office of the state's top prosecutor." The editorial also made a snide reference to me. "He doesn't strike us as any great shakes of a prosecutor, judging from some of the goings-on in his county that he has chosen to turn his back to." To what outrages I had turned my back was not mentioned, but given the paper's rabid insistence on severe criminal prosecutions to solve the "drug problem," evident a year later as I will relate, one would suspect that my more moderate approach explained the slur.

I had the good fortune to get the support of Senator T. Garry Buckley, the Republican Judiciary Committee Chairman, and Democrat Patrick Leahy, the Chittenden County State's Attorney. Both were newsworthy individuals; Buckley because he was at the center of many legislative fights, and Leahy because he was very good at getting his name in the paper—he managed to be at every news-making scene covered by his hometown paper, the *Burlington Free Press*, where he was often photographed and available to make some quotable remarks. He was so good at this, his state's attorney colleagues jealously referred to the *Burlington Free Press* as *The Leahy Press* (also a play on words since his family did own a company called The Leahy Press). Both Buckley and Leahy inadvertently helped my position by issuing press attacks against Senator West throughout the primary campaign. Buckley, because he was seeking reelection and feared being blamed for the legislative outcome, told the press that West was solely responsible for the law "and he screwed it up." Leahy, seeking reelection, (and with no affection for West) chimed in, lambasting West for writing and sponsoring the bill, claiming it severely weakened drug prosecutions. West never recovered from these attacks, which were repeated and revived in other papers around the state. I was alert to repeat these views whenever appropriate. As the campaign progressed, former judge Natt Divoll emerged as my principal opponent. He had extensive support from conservative Republicans and people his age who'd grown up with him and admired his tenure as judge.

I enjoyed the intensity of life during a campaign. The adage that a "hand shook was a vote took" mandated seeing a lot of people and hoping to find some common ground with them. There was no "baby kissing school," that is—how to run a campaign, except as shown in real life on television; but the idea of affable behavior before any audience, even of one, was alive. One rule was to never argue with a constituent; if he or she said something that grated on you, simply acknowledge the position and move on to something else. The topic of Vermont's changing weather was always a good escape from a noxious opinion. On the other hand, a campaign about issues required a candidate to know something about them, to study legislative nuances—for example about land use planning, consumer protection, drug enforcement, education, criminal law issues, and an endless array of other problems—and be ready with a concise, sensible response to questions asked in good faith. I found all that study and learning to be a real pleasure.

Barb and I scheduled a primary election night party at our home. Maybe twenty-five people came. As we got the vote totals over the radio, I was doing well and it became a joyous occasion with much laughter, congratulations—especially to Fred Bertrand, and resolutions to keep up the campaign. Barb made it all possible by planning and being gracious to everyone. There certainly were good aspects to our marriage. I won the primary with 36 percent of the votes, over Divoll's 29 percent and West's 23 percent out of a total of about 60,000 votes cast. I did well in Washington County, getting more votes than either candidate for governor in that county, and about 2,400 votes more than Divoll. Strength in Washington County was the key to my success.

There'd been no Democratic primary for attorney general, however the party convention did nominate a St. Albans lawyer, Richard Gadbois, to be an attorney general candidate soon thereafter. He proved not to be a serious threat, with no statewide credentials and being late to the campaign. The Republican primary campaign had raised my visibility and electability. I continued campaigning as before, except I emphasized my environmental credentials, announcing support for the suit against New York and International Paper.

I spent election night at "election central," set up behind the Capitol Plaza in Montpelier, with a few friends and supporters. The meeting space had room enough for all the reporters, projection screens, electronic equipment, candidates, supporters, and the public to watch as votes were tallied for the statewide candidates and recorded on a big screen showing the towns reporting. Alcohol was available in the hotel across the parking lot, a factor that seemed to make the process more interesting to a lot of people, judging by the vigor of the cheers, backslapping, and yes, groans and curses of disappointment that filled the room. I enjoyed the happy noise and congratulations as my vote totals came in. I was elected attorney general with about 58 percent (101,401) of the 175,305 votes cast. Gadbois had 38 percent (67, 884), and Peter Diamondstone 3 percent (5,898).

Following my victory in November, I worked on a smooth transition from the state's attorney job, which would be taken over by Mr. Gagnon, while preparing for a new experience. Thomas Salmon was elected governor, having run a brilliant, essentially single-issue campaign designed to curtail the rampant development destroying Vermont's bucolic heritage, and was the surprise winner of the gubernatorial election. I looked forward to working with him.

CHAPTER 13

"Through our great good fortune, in our youth our hearts were touched with fire."

Oliver Wendell Holmes, Jr.

OPENING CONCERNS

I was inaugurated as attorney general on January 3, 1973. I will tell you how it felt: exhilarating. Barb and the children came to the ceremony. Inauguration took place in the House of Representatives, in the company of the entire 180-member legislature, plus other constitutional officers with their friends and families. I recall sitting with Barb, participating in a ceremonial proceeding that was the essence of democracy, feeling I deserved to be there and looked forward to being there in the future, as I carried out my new job. There were handshakes, congratulations, happy snatches of conversations with friends, and gracious remarks to opponents. Any successful candidate in his or her right mind would concede that chance and timing play a part in electoral success, but the perception that the outcome was the result of personal merit and disciplined work was, at that time and place, uppermost in my feelings. It is fair to say I was very proud of myself. The roll call of newly elected and officially declared winners of constitutional officers added drama to the event. The ceremony was followed by being sworn in by the governor in his ceremonial office in the statehouse. That evening was the inaugural ball held at Norwich University, and Barbara bought a beautiful new dress for the occasion. To all appearances, we were a happy, handsome couple at the beginning of a promising new career, mixing with other newly elected and happy people.

To have that experience required that I spend the prior year studying the "issues of the day"—matters that voters and politicians before me had raised to high levels of concern. "Studying" in this sense meant not only avidly absorbing press accounts of events and people involved, but also reading as many background papers as I could, to understand the nuances of proposed solutions to problems. It also meant talking to people throughout the state to learn how they might react to the framing of any political issue being debated. My task was to determine what positions to take on any issue that conformed with integrity to my own values, as well as how to frame responses to possible opponents.

My first task was to understand how to manage the political and legal aspects of the lawsuit initiated by my predecessor, James Jeffords. He'd brought suit against International Paper Company (whose budget was probably greater than that of Vermont), the State of New York, and the U.S. Environmental Protection agency for causing or allowing the pollution of Lake Champlain. This suit promised to be costly, risky, and thus controversial. I also had to begin work on writing a complete revision of the state's criminal code to fulfill a campaign promise. The rewrite would have to be approved by the legislature. I would also need support on this and other matters from Democratic Governor Thomas Salmon, who had his own agenda: new legislation to protect Vermonters from unrestrained development, and various policy initiatives to address Vermont's drug problem. One other matter concerning the state as a whole was the recent opening of the Vermont Yankee Nuclear Power Station in Vernon, in the state's southeast corner. The danger of nuclear accidents and how to dispose of nuclear waste were fast becoming public environmental concerns.

My introduction to the Lake Champlain lawsuit occurred when Attorney General Jim Jeffords, who'd just been defeated in the GOP primary to succeed Republican Deane C. Davis as governor, invited me for an orientation period prior to inauguration. It was my first visit to the attorney general's office on the second floor of the Pavilion Office Building. The Pavilion was a newly reconstructed, impressive five-story red brick building adjacent the statehouse. Jim gave me a quick tour of the office spaces and introduced me to the assistant attorneys general. There was no time for conversation, merely a handshake and a 'glad to meet you.' I remember one young man, I never did learn what his responsibilities were nor did I work with him, who seemed alert and intelligent. He was recently hired by Jeffords. It was Jeffrey Amestoy, who became attorney general and chief justice of the Vermont Supreme Court. As we entered the elevator and the doors closed behind us, Jeffords turned and said, barely concealing a rueful smile, "Kim, you'll notice it's a long way from here to the fifth floor." Indeed it was. Many attorneys general have tried, but only one succeeded in my memory—Robert Stafford, now a U.S. senator, in 1959.

After a short, pleasant visit with outgoing Governor Davis, we set off on the other planned event for that day: a trip to the International Paper Company (IPC) mill in Ticonderoga, N.Y., for a site visit. Jeffords and his able deputy, Fred I. Parker, were to meet at the plant to have IPC experts explain its waste disposal systems to attorneys representing all the parties in the lawsuit. Lawyers for IPC and the Vermont and New York attorney generals' offices were present, as well as each state's environmental agency, and representatives for the IPC operators. Jeffords's complaint was considered an "original action" between two states, which the U.S. Constitution required be filed directly in the U.S. Supreme Court without interference by a lower court. The Supreme Court justices would not personally hear evidence in the case, but appointed a recently retired justice of the Massachusetts Supreme Court, Justice R. Ammi Cutter, to preside over the proceedings, conduct an evidentiary trial if necessary, and recommend a decision to the Supreme Court which could accept, reject, or even modify any decision. Since, as a prosecutor, I adhered to the maxim "Always Go to the Scene of the Crime," I was happy to make the trip.

The suit alleged IPC was dumping toxic polluting material consisting of sludge and chemicals into Lake Champlain on the New York side of the lake, which affected Vermont waters and carried pollution in the form of high phosphorus deposits downstream to Canada. Over the years, the dump site had produced a large accumulation of sludge. The concern was that the sludge beds must be removed to prevent continuous leakage of pollutants into the lake, and the suit alleged that New York's environmental agency had taken no corrective action, as required by New York's own regulations. It also charged that the U.S. Environmental Protection Agency had failed to enforce federal regulations controlling pollution of interstate waterways, and that the extensive beds of sludge were a continuous source of phosphorus leaching, which in turn accelerated eutrophication of the lake. In addition, Vermont was being subjected to the noxious odors of paper production, thanks to the prevailing west wind. The suit was based on common law notions of nuisance, that is, the principle that you can't use your property in such a way as to injure your neighbor. The suit demanded remediation and an unspecified amount of money for damages. In 1972, state and federal regulatory actions were rare and not robust enough to remedy the problems. Neither provided for an award of monetary damages to compensate Vermont for the diminishment in Lake Champlain's water quality, which was expected to require costly remediation measures. Jeffords insisted the state was entitled to an award, which was the driving force of the suit.

Lake Champlain is Vermont's jewel of nature, with dramatic views of the Adirondack Mountains across the broad expanse of water. The lake is a source of recreation for thousands of Vermonters, and is also used for commerce. The value of nearby real estate was tied to the quality of the water, and the lake, along with the state's mountains, forests, and farmlands were nostalgically promoted to encourage tourism and businesses in Vermont, which the Davis administration touted as "The Beckoning Country." Accordingly, preservation of Lake Champlain as a clear, inviting body of fresh water was and is considered vital for Vermont's well-being. The purpose of the trip to the mill was to drill that point home, as well as to orient all of us to the mill's waste-discharge systems.

All the meeting's participants except me had previously met. Each official greeted one another with professional courtesy and chatted amiably about weather, travel, and other inconsequential matters as they waited for the tour led by the mill's environmental managers to start. I was struck by the attire of some, such as Taggart Whipple, a partner in the law firm of Davis Polk and Wardwell of New York City, who wore a snappy three-piece suit, in sharp contrast to the more casual outfits chosen by me, the other government lawyers, and the mill's scientists.

Like Madame Sosostris, the famous clairvoyant in T. S. Elliott's 1922 poem, *The Waste Land*, I had a bad cold. Sosostris's bad cold prevented her from predicting a way out of the British despair and disillusionment following World War I. My cold did not prevent me from foreseeing the consequences of degradation of Lake Champlain, but it did provide an excuse for me not to be especially convivial or to engage in close-quarter discussions with the other lawyers. Although I was introduced as Vermont's next attorney general, medical excuses were made and accepted, to allow me to remain anonymously quiet in the background. My obvious illness allowed me to comfortably embrace the aphorism, "It is better to keep your mouth shut and appear stupid than to open it and remove all doubt."

Although I was new to the lawsuit and certainly no scientist when it came to lake degradation, I did enthusiastically support the suit. Such a fight had the virtue of being well within Vermont's legendary tradition of fighting with "Yorkers." In the 1770s, Ethan Allen saw New York State residents—contemptuously referred to as "Yorkers"—as usurpers of land titles to Vermont land occupied by his Green Mountain Boys. Ticonderoga also had historical significance, as on May 10, 1775, Allen and his Green Mountain Boys famously surprised and overcame the British garrison at Fort Ticonderoga. They later used oxen to drag the purloined canons of His Britannic Majesty over the snow to the hills around Boston, where they could bombard the warships supporting the British siege of Boston, thus ending the siege. The Vermont Statehouse Hall of Inscriptions boasts of Vermont's historically stubborn repulse of any attempt to undermine its sovereignty, either by "Yorkers" or British military forces. Theodore Roosevelt's remarks, inscribed on the statehouse wall referencing the Green Mountain Boys, were particularly appropriate for the suit against New York:

"They hewed this State out of the wilderness, they held it against a foreign foe, they laid deep and stable the foundation of our state life, because they sought not the life of ease, but the life of effort for a worthy end."

As are Ethan Allen's remarks, also inscribed there:

> "I am as resolutely determined to Defend the Independence
> of Vermont as Congress are that of the United States and
> Rather than fail will Retire with hardy Green Mountain
> Boys into the Desolate Caverns of the mountains and wage
> war with human Nature at Large."

Such inscriptions, known to any Vermonter who's visited the statehouse, provided rhetorical inspiration for spending large amounts of money on lawyers to battle New York, only this time to protect the lake. Such sentiments would be revived to inspire the Vermont legislature to appropriate money for it. Perhaps some similar jingoistic references would be appropriate, as it was certain that political controversy would arise because of the cost of the suit as well as the invisibility or uncertainty of any results.

At that meeting I learned the basis of the issues. Papermaking creates unpleasant smells and noxious waste, and this for-profit enterprise was only too happy to dump industrial waste into the environment in order to increase profits. After returning from this meeting and conferring with Jeffords and Parker, I agreed that four assistant attorneys general, whom I'd never met, would be assigned to the case which was to be tried in New York City. I would hire a deputy who would be in charge, and offered the job to Martin K. Miller, a former assistant attorney general. I was delighted when he accepted and designated him as deputy attorney general to add stature to our commitment to the suit.

It was clear the case would require radically altering the priorities of the office, reassignment of personnel, expenditures to develop persuasive evidence, more expenditures to prepare convincing graphs and documents, and still more expenditures to pay for living expenses for attorneys and witnesses in New York. The cost to process the suit, excluding salaries of the five assistant attorneys general, and to obtain support from several state agencies, would be more than the attorney general's entire annual budget. I'd need to spend time at the statehouse defending costs and explaining what we hoped would be the positive results of the suit, in order to get money to go ahead. The arrangement also meant I would not have a deputy to assist in any local crises that were sure to arise.

When I moved from the small rented state's attorney's office in Montpelier to the Pavilion Office Building, which had just been renovated, I brought Hector the dog without asking permission. The Pavilion was created from a razed 1874 hotel and rebuilt in 1972 with modern materials and construction techniques. In a compromise with preservationists, the new building was built behind a faithful re-creation of the hotel's former Victorian Eclectic facade, with extensive porches (piazzas) on the south and west sides. The five-story building, which houses some of the important executive offices of state government, is artfully situated on the statehouse lawn. Symbolically, to get from the statehouse to the Pavilion, one has to pass by the supreme court building. The journey of all laws follows this route. The Pavilion housed the attorney general's offices on the second floor, treasurer's on the third, secretary of administration's on the fourth, and governor's on the fifth.

As soon as I entered my office I began hearing from constituents about the IPC suit. Many expressed the view that the suit would amount to a sinkhole. People were also skeptical about the harm caused by the sludge beds, and felt the whole enterprise was just lawyers taking a lot of taxpayers' money while squabbling about cause and effect. Having no idea how the case would end up, I had no idea whether I'd be seen as a hero or a villain in the end. Still, I charged ahead. I hoped the lawsuit at least would require this small part of the paper industry to become a responsible corporate citizen. My feeling was like that expressed by a handwriting expert I once had testify to help convict someone forging checks. I'd asked the expert why she chose that as her specialty, and she'd replied, "It's good to see the miscreant get his comeuppance."

I stayed in touch with the case through Marty Miller, with whom I met at least once a week, usually by phone, to discuss legal developments. I was not familiar enough with the particulars of trial tactics or evidence to give much direction, but I needed to understand enough to deal with publicity in Vermont. Frequently, press accounts from the New York City hearings would appear in local papers, requiring a comment from me. I would talk with Marty to understand the issue from his perspective and then, working with legislators and speaking to the press, try to frame it in a manner that would assure continued funding for the suit. In the meantime, IPC lobbyists appeared before Vermont legislative committees in their own campaign to undermine political support for the lawsuit.

On September 24, 1974, the IPC case ended with a settlement. After seventy-five days of trial in New York City, and with political support from Governor Salmon, the chairmen of the House and Senate Appropriations committees, the speaker of the House, and technical support from the Vermont Environmental Conservation and Transportation agencies, an agreement was signed by all parties. I issued a statement that began with the phrase, "Public officials, as well as sports fans, would like to proclaim that their team won a great victory. I prefer to avoid such rhetoric in discussing this case." I then explained that Vermont did achieve virtually all it set out to, but that the environmental health of Lake Champlain was endangered by myriad sources of phosphate pollution, and not just from IPC. This circumstance complicated a compelling computation of damages. Accordingly, the health of the lake would require eternal vigilance. I named pollutants that flow from farms, roads, cities, and homes into rivers and then into Champlain, including agricultural runoff, municipal sewer and waste discharges, detergents, and commercial and industrial dumping. "Human beings," I said, "appear to have a great capacity to foul the air they breathe and the water they rely on for health and prosperity." I chose not to criticize the U.S. Environmental Protection Agency and the State of New York on lax enforcement of their own rules. Vermont would have to work with them in the future to insure the settlement was carried out.

In substance, evidence presented in the suit demonstrated that IPC's own records showed it was discharging massive amounts of pollutants into the lake. There also was agreement that remediation was needed, although what, if any, damages would be paid by the company or New York State remained in dispute. What to do about the sludge beds was also a disputed issue. After inspection and much testimony, experts agreed the wisest course was to leave them alone. Trying to dredge them would only liberate more pollutants that, with the natural flow of water, would travel downstream into the broad reaches of the lake. Given the substantial number of bad actors polluting Champlain, it was hard to establish the degree to which IPC should be held accountable, or to measure the damage in money. The issue of money damages became the hardest one to prove or resolve. Vermont sought a settlement that would leave jurisdiction with the U.S. Supreme Court to resolve this question as new data became available, however the court rejected that idea, leaving Justice Cutter to put pressure on the parties to push for settlement.

The settlement that was finally reached required IPC to spend somewhere around two to five million dollars (about ten to twenty-five million in 2020 dollars) to meet its obligations to control pollution, and for the State of New York to construct a sewage treatment plant for the village of Ticonderoga, at an estimate of four million (about twenty million in 2020). These expenditures would certainly help reduce further degradation of water quality. Nevertheless, the attorney for IPC, Taggart Whipple, was not above a little chicanery. Taking a glass of water from the lake, he drank it down in front of Justice Cutter, to vouch for the purity of the water since remediation. A Vermont attorney, Sheldon Prentice, told me this long after I'd left the attorney general's office, and that Taggart Whipple immediately left the hearing room and had his stomach pumped! IPC also agreed to make substantial investments in air quality, to mitigate the vexatious odors drifting eastward into Vermont. Finally, IPC agreed to pay Vermont the costs it incurred to prosecute the suit, approximately $500,000 (about $2.5 million in 2020 dollars).

I considered all this a breakthrough, but press accounts of the settlement were not generous. Few papers saw this as a victory for Vermont. For example, the *Times Argus* editorialized that the failure to have IPC pay reparations for all pollution it had put into the lake was a disaster, and the failure meant similar problems in the Great Lakes and elsewhere would now likely go unpunished. Vermont, the editorial said, should have insisted that industries that pollute be held directly responsible for cleaning up their messes and should pay damages, just as an ordinary citizen would be required to. On the eve of a campaign for reelection, I saw such comments as a sour note. However, I thought it would be strange indeed if anyone thought a single lawsuit would reverse human nature, the power of wealth to get what it wants, or the necessity of politicians to compromise. The exhortation that "No one can do everything, but everyone can do something" seemed a reasonable explanation for why the suit was successful.

At the very time Vermont was suing IPC for the mess it created in Lake Champlain, another corporation, that in the eyes of many offered an even graver environmental threat—the Vermont Yankee Nuclear Power Station— began operating in the town of Vernon, near the Massachusetts border.

The huge (by Vermont standards) plant was of a boiling-water design, capable of producing 500 megawatts, which was enough to both meet about 34 percent of Vermont's electrical needs and export the excess capacity to the New England grid. Early in 1973, Governor Salmon invited me and other newly elected state leaders to a tour of the plant led by its operations personnel. The tour included a brief description of how the plant functioned, and we learned how nuclear reactions in the core heated water and how the temperature of the reactor core was controlled by the fuel rods inserted into it. We non-nuclear scientists and non-electrical engineers learned that raising the fuel rods out of the core reduced power, lowering them increased it, and removal of the rods shut down the nuclear reaction. The plant was maintained at negative atmospheric pressure, to prevent airborne radioactive contamination. This boiling water, contaminated by radiation, was circulated in an isolated system which exchanged the heat generated into an adjacent system holding uncontaminated water, converting it to steam to turn a turbine, thereby generating electricity. The steam was then cooled and condensed for reuse within the containment of the facility, to prevent release of radiation. The principle was the same as that for any other method producing steam to turn turbines, the basics of which I'd encountered in the Navy—except for the fact that the fuel source for this was a nuclear reaction, not from burning wood, coal, or fuel oil.

Nuclear plants require complicated and reliable systems to assure safety;

not only to protect the workers at the plant, but for all of Vernon and the entire area of potential contamination in the event of a core meltdown. To function properly, the facility needed the cooling waters of the Connecticut River, a reality that had its own environmental consequences, since the water would be heated, thereby disrupting the ecosystem. We were given a description of the training and functions of employees, with a simple discussion of how the plant safety features were monitored. We were taken on a walk around the then-empty cooling pool where spent fuel rods would be stored until the plant was decommissioned in an estimated forty years. Safe disposal of these radioactive waste rods having a life of hundreds of years was, and still is, of concern.

This show-and-tell was interesting, but beyond the usual press chatter and interest-group commentary there wasn't much discussion, and my understanding of the regulatory process for the plan remained rudimentary. The federal Nuclear Regulatory Commission (NRC) was responsible for safety issues; the State Public Service Board and the Public Service Department were able to participate in NRC proceedings, but the attorney general had no statutory regulatory responsibility. Nonetheless, the attorney general, as a top state enforcement figure, by default would be required to respond to the political controversy certain to arise from time to time. This trip to the "scene of the crime" would be helpful, as would diligent rudimentary study of anticipated issues. I figured that, with a little more work, I might even understand competing points of view, if offered at an NRC hearing.

As news accounts of the Vermont Yankee visit appeared, I began to hear from casual acquaintances about their hopes and fears about nuclear power. I listened sympathetically, but avoided endorsing any point of view. I knew little about the issues, so felt it unwise to provoke an argument with constituents. Some people wondered if we were all going to survive what they were certain would be the Vermont Yankee mushroom cloud. I deflected these concerns, saying something like, "Yeah, probably. Anyhow, even if something does go wrong, I doubt there will be a mushroom cloud. But if it's any comfort to you, I think if something does go horribly wrong, it will likely be an invisible airborne dose of radiation, without a big bang, and you might be far enough away, or the wind might be in the right direction, and you won't get poisoned." I doubted this would comfort anyone—it certainly would not offer comfort to anyone living downwind, but I would say it anyway, figuring anyone would take it as doomsday or gallows humor. My only real contribution to the issue of safety was to urge the legislature to create and fund a position for a competent nuclear engineer to advise policy makers on NRC issues, which it eventually did.

Vermont Yankee did produce one political benefit for me. Of the many issues that arose was local concern that the NRC was too industry-oriented and not responsive enough to the public's safety needs. In early 1974, I decided to go to Washington, D.C., to meet with our Republican Senator George Aiken to discuss these issues, in hopes he would influence the NRC to be more safety conscious. When we met, I'd immediately started in on my concerns when he interrupted with concerns and explanations of his own. I recall being irritated that he wasn't paying enough attention to my concerns, and then it dawned on me that he was well informed on the matter, and I would do better to keep my mouth closed and listen.

Taking my own advice, I spent a fascinating half hour discussing nuclear issues with the senator. Later, I met with Republican congressman, Richard Mallary, who, with Governor Davis's retirement, had become the highest ranking Vermont Republican. As we walked down 16th Street one afternoon, Mallary and I glimpsed the White House. The Watergate scandal was raging at the time, and I'd been growing more and more anxious about how to respond publicly, as a Republican, to Nixon's conduct in office. Could I publicly voice my contempt for the dishonesty of President Nixon? Or would doing so risk the support of Vermont Republicans who'd helped me get elected? As we two Republicans walked along, I did not have the courage to ask the leader of our party if I would be politically smart to come out in favor of impeaching Nixon. As if reading my mind, Mallary paused and pointed to the White House, saying something like, "Well, you know, Kim, before long that house will be empty! It's just a matter of time."

Neither of us went deeper into the conversation about apparent treason, or engaged in talk of how to conspire to bring down Nixon, but I got the signal that I was not alone among Republicans fearful of their political fate because of Nixon's crimes. It was a small relief. I decided events would take their own course without a response from me.

CHAPTER 14

"I loathe people who keep dogs. They are cowards who haven't got the guts to bite people themselves."

August Strindberg, 1895

GOING TO THE DOGS

I was distracted from the pressing duties of my office by a threatened calamity. My self-assessment of how I wanted to be perceived was captured in one of my favorite press accounts. The article, written by Geoffrey Chapman, appeared in the February 26, 1973, *Bennington Banner*, and was headlined "Cheney Vows Unpolitical Pursuit of Top Law Office." In the story, Mr. Chapman reported that I saw my job principally as problem solving, a characterization I agreed with. I'd said something to the effect that the political process involved getting beyond personal biases, focusing on the fundamental matters of disagreement, then getting parties to work together toward a solution. The article stated "Cheney, the young man from Montpelier who finessed a boyish smile and quiet demeanor against the odds to become Vermont's new attorney general, wears his new job like a comfortable old slipper . . . Cheney produced a political surprise when his low-key, ground-zero budget campaign beat out four formidable opponents."

I was then quoted: "I see a lot of balderdash in politics. I'm not a very good simplifier. I see the complexities of an issue and I feel intellectually dishonest if I try to simplify them. To solve problems you have to recognize that they are complex." This did not convey accurately what I intended. To solve complex problems you need to break them down into their component parts, find common ground, and modify as necessary to get a working consensus for a path to solution.

The article concluded with a photo and this revelation about me and Hector: "Usually arriving at work at about 9 a.m., often accompanied by his middle-aged black Labrador, Hector, Cheney's dress is as deceptive as his smile. Behind the informality of both works an ordered quick-paced intelligence and few obvious uncertainties about its goals."

Flattering as the article was, coming so soon after my inauguration (and ignoring that it seemed to say my clothing arrived at 9:00 a.m.), it created a bit of a problem. Irving Bates, the state buildings commissioner, sent me a letter noting that state regulations did not allow for dogs in government offices and therefore, I could not bring Hector to work.

Evidently, this ukase was precipitated by the *Bennington Banner* article. Bad enough to take away all my assistants, I thought, but now my dog! Hector was a good companion. He was calm and liked to sleep unless engaged in a jog or chasing a tennis ball. He was frequently a calming presence, and an excellent subject for ice-breaking conversations when excited constituents entered the office—and also for me, when I took time out to scratch his tummy.

As I pondered how to deal with Mr. Bates's request, I decided humor would be the best approach. Attorneys general are frequently called upon to issue opinions on various issues of state concern, opinions that are published annually as official records. Time for an attorney general's opinion, I thought. So I did some legal research. The best legal discussion I could find about dogs was contained in Note: *Man, His Dog and Birth Control*, 70 Yale Law Journal 1205 (1961), a tongue-in-cheek article arguing that a legislature could not restrict dogs from having abortions because punishment cannot be imposed on individuals incapable of understanding the nature and quality of the act prescribed. Although Bates's action banishing dogs from state buildings might allow me, as the owner of the dog to be punished, it would also punish Hector. That would be unconstitutional, because a long line of important cases had decided that dogs are not simply pieces of property controlled by the owner, but have some rights. I noted Chief Justice Appleton of the Maine Supreme Court, writing in *State v. Harriman* 75 Me 562 (1884), had this to say about dogs: "From the time of the pyramids to the present day, from the frozen pole to the torrid zone, wherever man has been there has been his dog." Hector, I argued, had prior distinguished governmental service in the Department of Education and the State's Attorney's office, and had appeared before several courts. The benefits of this service could not legally be taken away from him, any more than a dog could be refused an abortion, because he was not competent to understand why he should be so punished. The footnotes to the Yale article cited several cases on the importance of dogs, showing they could not be convicted of crimes and were not mere property, but were important contributors to human endeavors:

1. See e.g. McNaughten's case, 10CL 7 Fin 200 (H.L. 1843), but cf Durham v. United States 214 F.2d 862 (DC Cit 1954) (conviction possible unless mental disease or defect present) and the paucity of dog psychiatrists would make it difficult to obtain expert testimony in a Durham jurisdiction. True it is said that in 1954 a dog was found guilty in a court of law in Leyden, Holland, executed by hanging before a cheering populace and drawn and quartered. But Holland is a civil-law jurisdiction.

2. Rightfully the dog as a companion is most affectionately regarded by all persons who truly estimate loyalty and friendship as factors in smoothing the path of this world's existence. Shadow v. Barnette 217 Ky 207 (1927). "Dogs are not outlaws and have some rights" Wojewoda v. Rybarczyk 246 Mich 641 (1929). The association between man and his dog has historically been intimate and of great value. See Citizens Rapid Transit Co v. Drew 100 Tenn 317 (1898) (trolley ran over dog lying on the track while looking at birds flying overhead).

3. When we call to mind the small spaniel that saved the life of William of Orange and thus probably changed the course of modern history...and the faithful St. Bernards, which rescue travelers caught in storms in the Alps, the claim that the nature of the dog is essentially base...will not receive ready assent. Mullaly v. People 96 N.Y. 365 (1881).

I concluded that allowing Hector to stay in the office might possibly have statewide benefits because, before I became attorney general, the office had the reputation in some quarters of issuing asinine opinions, thus it should be obvious that canine ones would be an improvement. I declared there was a doggone chance that Bates's regulation would be declared unconstitutional, citing my own letter as attorney general opinion No 197-3 as authority.

The opinion was released to the press immediately upon being hand delivered to Mr. Bates, giving relief to many who were stressed by more serious legislative concerns. The *Times Argus* headlined the story with "Doggone It, Solons Kept Busy by Hector." The article detailed the fun the legislature had by attempting to pass a resolution that would allow Hector to remain in the AG's office. The House Natural Resources Committee sent it to the Appropriations Committee on the theory that it had jurisdiction to create and fund new positions in state government, and the Appropriations Committee returned it to Natural Resources as it referred to possible pollution, which then sent it to the Judiciary Committee as a legal matter, which the Speaker of the House ruled were as out of order as the dog. Finally, a floor motion was made to order the resolution to lie, which failed with sixty ayes and seventy-seven nays.

And there matters stood until, soon thereafter, I was called to a meeting with Gov. Salmon in his office on the Pavilion's fifth floor. Ushered in, I found the governor seated at his desk surrounded by stern looking people. The governor then said in a serious tone, "Mister attorney general, better look down." And there in the middle of the floor was a plastic dog turd, which among howls of laughter, I quickly scooped up. Hector, however, was allowed to remain. Some of my allies reprimanded me for peaking too soon. On the other hand, the exchange exemplified the wisdom in the adage "You have to be funny if you want to be taken seriously." The episode was a honeymoon for a new politician.

The legislative issues not only involved dogs—the state fair sought permission to exhibit a bear. Lieutenant Governor John S. Burgess and I

were required to examine the critic at issue, then located—and chained—at the statehouse entrance, resulting in one of my favorite photos.

I couldn't escape the effect of dogs in my legal career. Years later, when I returned to private law practice and defended people accused of crimes, I found that dogs could be a real asset. My client, Randy, was driving home down in the Mad River Valley on New Year's Eve—actually morning—around 1:00 a.m. It was minus five degrees at the time. The deputy sheriff on patrol saw him weaving a bit and put on the blue lights. Randy pulled off into his own driveway about a mile after the blue lights came on.

"Probably drunk" was a reasonable guess any cop would have made. But there was more to the story. Randy exited his truck as the deputy pulled in with his headlights and spotter light shining. Randy stopped by the hood of his truck to face the police car with its lights still flashing, and the deputy stepped from his cruiser. The officer had a large dog with him, who came to his side. The deputy then pulled his gun, aimed it at Randy, and shouted to order him to turn around and put his hands on the hood of his truck.

"Call off your dog!" Randy yelled.

"Turn around, put your hands on the hood!" the deputy shouted.

"Call off your dog!"

"Turn around!" the deputy shouted, while waving his gun, the dog barking. This went on for too long. Randy told me what happened next: He said to himself, "Oh, fuck it, it's cold, I'm going inside," and started down the path, went maybe five yards when the dog rushed him, knocked him to the ground, and put a hard bite on his crotch, about an inch from his testicles. Randy, now full of adrenaline and triggered by terror, picked up the eighty-pound

151

dog and threw him into the woods. The deputy then attacked Randy with his baton, striking him and causing Randy to pick up a nearby stick and flail at the deputy. Eventually, the deputy got the upper hand, handcuffed Randy, got help, and made his arrest. Randy was charged with drunk driving, assault on an officer, and cruelty to the dog.

At *voir dire* I was clever enough to ask potential jurors if any were afraid of dogs. Several, mostly women, said they were. I left it at that. Then we attorneys did the usual questions about believing cops or not, and any bias for or against cops, and then whether they were opposed to drinking on New Year's Eve— all standard stuff. I tried to suggest that Randy hadn't had much to drink, that the problem was the dog, because he was afraid of it, and that the deputy had attacked him with the baton and he'd fought back in self-defense. But the trial wasn't going well for me. The deputy testified at length about how well-trained his dog was, particularly as he was a family pet who slept on the bed, was great with his kids, and especially that he was not aggressive. The dog, he testified, was trained only to intervene to protect him in case an offender tried to attack.

He implied to the jury that they could be assured he and the dog were not the aggressors, but that Randy was. Desperate, I subpoenaed the dog. No one objected, so the judge okayed it. I was just screwing around, thought some juror might be scared and that might help my client; but I'd never met the dog, asked it to shake, or really knew anything about it.

The deputy brought the dog on a leash, paraded him around the courtroom giving him various commands—sit, stay, lie down, and roll over. The dog performed well, apparently well-controlled. Then the deputy brought him up to the jury box, so the jurors could get a good look at him. The animal sat dutifully about two feet in front of the jury box. Only the jurors in the front row could see him from that location. The rear row, and some in the front row, suddenly stood to get a better look. And as soon as the jurors stood, the dog went nuts, letting out a blood-curdling snarl and lunging for the jurors over the front partition of the jury box. They looked terrified, even though the deputy was pulling back on the leash. The deputy blurted to the jurors "You looked at him wrong!"

"I guess so!" I thought. Anyhow, the jury found Randy guilty of drunk driving, but acquitted him on the more serious charges of assaulting a police officer and a dog. I chalked up my courtroom maneuver to dumb luck as a lawyer, but Randy was impressed. I congratulated Randy, reminded him to be careful on the road, and thought to myself, if he ever wanted a pet, he should consider a cat.

Yes, alas, it's true—I have yet another dog story to tell. Years after the events just described, Hector had passed on and I'd opened a law office on North State Street in Montpelier. I frequently walked from the south of town to the office with my two Rat Terriers. One day, as I passed the Pavilion and came to the Vermont Supreme Court building, I was thinking about a pending case I expected to be decided soon involving a fraudulent scheme for forcing consumers to arbitrate any claims they might have against a home inspector who failed to discover serious flaws. The contract specified that the consumer must pay a $1,200 arbitration fee to select an arbitrator from the home inspector's association, and pay the inspector's attorney's fees if they lost. I had argued the case and understood Justice Marilyn Skoglund would probably write the opinion. She and I had frequent and, I believed, mutually respected contact. I really wanted to win this case.

As I started across the statehouse lawn, I saw Justice Skoglund with her dog. One of my dogs stopped to poop—coincidently, so did Justice Skoglund's dog. As we each reached down to clean up after our dogs, we glanced at each other and broke into laughter. We nodded politely and went about our day's work. Only in Vermont, I thought, would the judge and counsel be picking up dog shit together between the legislature that wrote the law and the court that would interpret it, while awaiting a decision. Vermont is a great place to work. The case came out just fine.

CHAPTER 15

"There oughta be a law."

Harry Shorten & Al Fagaly, 1940

THERE OUGHTA BE A LAW

Once the important duties of securing a place for Hector and planning how a lawsuit with a budget larger than that of the entire office would be conducted were settled, it was time to turn to the real job every attorney general faces: how to get re-elected. You might think an attorney general would spend most of his time before black-robed justices in an austere court of law, or at least huddled in a book-lined office with fellow lawyers working up strategies to win the next big case, but that was not really my experience. Instead, it was necessary to initiate actions the people who elected you would want taken, often over the objections of people opposed. Opportunities for an attorney general to act are of two kinds: incoming issues—those that come to his attention because they are inherent in the office, such as resolving disputes between different executive officers concerning what course the law requires, or defending suits against the State; and outgoing—those initiated by the attorney general to carry out policies he wishes to advance. The incoming issues are resolved either by issuing formal "Opinions" (discussed later) or litigation, both civil and criminal. Outgoing issues are resolved by proposing and lobbying for legislation, or initiating lawsuits in causes the attorney general has a personal interest in.

Litigation is a powerful policy tool. In my tenure, the suit against New York and International Paper Co. absorbed most of the talent and time available for proactive civil litigation, with one important exception. It is common for the attorney general of one state to initiate a civil suit against identified wrong doers—for example, consumer fraud cases in which the product causes great harm to the public. An attorney general of one state with a large staff seeking electoral support may initiate such a suit and invite other state attorneys general to join as plaintiffs, to the glory of all concerned. The joining attorney general often has little work to do other than reading suit papers, occasionally suppling supporting local data to the parent state, and monitoring events for political heresy. Joining these suits allows an attorney general to demonstrate social consciousness, with the added benefit of producing electoral advantage as well as large damage awards for the benefit of his state—the recent multistate suits against Volkswagen and the Trump Administration are contemporary examples of such cases. I joined several such suits, expecting to earn the anticipated benefits, but doing so did not engage my personal energy, so I omit discussion of them.

By contrast, the public often looks to the attorney general to advance justice by proposing new laws. Surprisingly, as much to me as perhaps to anyone, I spent huge chunks of my time in the corridors and committee rooms of Vermont's historic statehouse, working on legislation I either initiated or considered important, and answering questions from lawmakers on matters both pressing and trivial. Not incidentally, some of these problems, and their proposed solutions, fulfilled campaign promises. My work with the education department had been important preparation for this. Since Vermont has two-year terms of office for legislators and executive branch offices, an office holder has a short time to produce results. The first year is generally one of preparation, drafting provisions, and cultivating allies. The year following inauguration is when the real effort to seek passage of laws to implement promises occurs. Necessarily, the attorney general must spend a considerable amount of time in the statehouse, as well as attending to other simultaneous duties. In addition, problems that were not the subject of any campaign debate or promise frequently arise that demand legislative solutions.

155

Vermont's statehouse is an inspiring and, admittedly, fun place to be. Causes, personalities, and ambition are a lively mix. The statehouse, a massive, granite structure, is Vermont's architectural echo of a building created by fifth-century BC Athenians as a temple to Athena in celebration of human and godly creativity. It is one of the oldest and best preserved of our nation's state capitols. The first structure on the site was built around 1808. The second structure, mostly destroyed by fire, was replaced by the current building in 1857. After nearly 160 years, it remains an icon in Montpelier (the smallest capital city in America), with a wooden statue of Ceres, the goddess of agriculture, looking out from atop the golden dome. Its House and Senate chambers, the oldest active legislative halls in the United States, have preserved their original interiors. It is also a monument to Vermont's incredible effort and casualties incurred during the Civil War. It speaks of large issues and strength; a bust of Abraham Lincoln greets visitors on the first floor, and a painting of George Washington dominates the House of Representatives on the second floor. The Cedar Creek Room, adjacent to the House chamber, is a large reception room featuring an enormous painting by Julian Scott, 1874. The painting nearly fills the south wall and depicts the Battle of Cedar Creek, with portraits of Civil War generals looking out to the battlefield, fought on October 19, 1864, in western Virginia, in which Union troops, especially indomitable Vermonters, turned back a Confederate surprise attack threatening a crushing defeat of Union forces. The painting highlights the contributions of Vermont troops in the battle. The statehouse has a large front lawn, perfect for protest demonstrations, pick-up touch football, dog walking, ice skating, or sunbathing. The statehouse reflects Theodore Roosevelt's observation that the state itself was hewed out of the wilderness by the character of a determined people, as their descendants hewed out the granite to build it. Over the years I worked there, I came to appreciate that it was built so strongly, not only to defy any natural calamity but also to hold up the many crazy ideas that circulate within it, perhaps also as a fortress against the crazy ideas from outside, like slavery, discrimination against gay people, and environmental destruction.

A courthouse, as I've described, is built in theory to determine the truth between differing contentions of fact. By contrast, the statehouse was built to resolve disputes about opinions. Opinions have been characterized as the laziest form of human thought, requiring no special knowledge or study as to what is good for the general population, and once formed, may then become as hard as steel. The legislature is a blast furnace that smelts opinions. As New

York Judge Gordon Tucker observed in 1886, "No man's life, liberty, or property are safe while the legislature is in session." The legislature is dedicated to the proposition that presentation of facts—now called data, cogent argument, friendship, loyalty to others, political party, and possibly compromise can promote public welfare. Hence, proposing legislation requires not only talking to a lot of people to move them to adopt a congenial opinion to be expressed in law, but also to be agile in detecting defections, promoting new adherents, and being resourceful in helping allies, if possible, to advance their opinions about other subjects. It all takes a lot of time and perhaps skill. Although the attorney general is called on to give advice on many legislative issues, the ones I personally wrote are described in what follows.

Crimes

During the 1972 election campaign, I emphasized that criminal law was archaic and unjust. I argued "law and order" should start with clear legislation to aid police or prosecutors in convicting people of clearly defined offenses. I formed this opinion based on my experience as a prosecutor. I was frustrated that many crimes were defined by common law judicial decisions in cases over time, rather than by the legislature. A consequence was that different judicial cases often ruled different facts that must be proven for a conviction. Other crimes were judicially defined in broad concepts rather than precise definitions. For example, a common law conspiracy, a judge-made crime, was defined as group action that is "oppressive, immoral, or wrongfully prejudicial to others." Such broad subjective phrases, rather than specific factual situations, invited lengthy arguments as to what was prohibited.

Other crimes, however, are defined by specific legislation which sets out the conduct declared to be unlawful. Although such definitions have often been an improvement in clarity, they, too, were often unclear, having been written in archaic language that was then interpreted by judges over time. Another problem is that legislation frequently defined crimes in relation to the type of property involved, rather than underlying wrong to be corrected. My favorite crime, for example, was entitled, "Painting and Disguising Horses." The prohibited conduct was clear, however, the evil to be prevented was fraud in an important consumer transaction—the law could be written to broaden its application.

Over time, the legislature had created several species of burglary crimes to criminalize different kinds of property that was stolen, times of day of the offense, and different places from which it was stolen. As a result, different penalties for each species of burglary might be specified. Instead, I thought penalties should be ranked in order of magnitude of harm to the victim. An overriding concern was that no consistent ordering of the severity of authorized penalty existed. The legislature tended to create "designer crimes" (like deceptively painting horses) on an *ad hoc* basis as the hue and cry over some horrible event moved the legislature to criminalize it. I saw an opportunity to structure criminal law so that penalties would be consistent with the harm inflicted on victims. Restoring capital punishment after the U.S. Supreme Court invalidated many state's laws in 1972 did not seem to be a smoldering issue, nor one I wanted to take up.

Soon after being elected, I created a Criminal Law Revision Commission composed of representatives of the state's attorneys, the newly created defender general, the Vermont Bar Association, police, and members of the legislature. A law professor, Sanford Fox, who'd authored comprehensive revision laws in other states, was retained as draftsman and reporter. The commission diligently reviewed every judicially or legislatively defined criminal offense in order to determine whether the definition should be clarified, or whether the offense should be eliminated or perhaps included in a broader character of crime. All offenses were then placed in a uniform ladder of punishments, ranked in order of harm to society or the victim. This comprehensive revision was prepared and submitted to the January 1974 legislature. The bill, with many changes recommended by the House Judiciary Committee, was passed by the House of Representatives and sent to the Senate. The commission decided to do nothing in amending the capital punishment law to conform to recent U.S. Senate standards, and thereby prevented capital punishment in the state.

Ahh, the Senate—"there's the rub" I reflected, alluding to Hamlet's dilemma in the famous "To be or not to be" speech. The rub here also was the same, "to be or not to be," but was discussed under the term "Capital Punishment." The conundrum of capital punishment is comprehensively explored by Scott Turow in his book, *Ultimate Punishment* (2003), which examines the arguments for and against it. Turow himself says he is "agnostic," meaning he would evaluate each case as it arises. In spite of many arguments about which reasonable people can differ, I felt any person in public life must simply make up his or her own mind: you must either be for it or against it, because it is impossible to balance all the pros and cons of individual cases in light of all the reasons supporting or rejecting death sentences. Unlike the next of kin of people killed in any of the horrible accidents that occur regularly in our chaotic society, surviving families of murder victims have a different burden. In addition to the horrific facts of each case is an additional horror that a living human being intentionally, as Turow says, ripped from the survivors of the victim an irreplaceable, precious life. Arguably, the state had the same responsibility as any public servant when it came to the question of killing a human being. Unfortunately, the equation is seldom precise and innocent people may be convicted for many reasons: police and prosecutors may seek to be heroes; ambiguous circumstances occur; facts are often disputed; scientific error intending to show guilt may occur; and there may be juror bias against the perpetrator or victim for reasons of race, gender, or other factors inherent in the accused. No one has demonstrated that the death penalty deters murder. There also is a question whether the state, acting in a democracy with the purpose of making lives better for its citizens, should even have a policy to kill people. If capital punishment is permitted, it is necessary to believe the criminal justice system functions perfectly in all cases, always creating just results; otherwise, every case simply requires re-argument as to the wisdom of having a death sentence. I became opposed to capital punishment. No representative in the House sought to amend the law to reinstate it. The bill's journey through the House was therefore a pleasant one.

In the Senate, the bill passed through the Judiciary Committee intact and arrived on the floor for passage. I hoped this bill, and the thought and hard work that went into it, would pass and improve the administration of justice. But it was not to be. On the Senate floor, pro-capital punishment proposals of amendment arose and familiar arguments surfaced with familiar responses. The debate went on far into the afternoon on the day when time was running out for bills to be passed. The Senate recessed for dinner, then reconvened. The Judiciary Chairman, T. Garry Buckley, who appeared to have enjoyed the liquid part of dinner, put up a spirited effort to pass the bill. I sat with the spectators on the Senate floor, listening as the debate fluctuated. Buckley, in a last desperate attempt to save the bill, offered an amendment to the pro-capital punishment proposal, saying he would accept it, but for fear of convicting the innocent, it would have to have a provision that three eye witnesses to the murder must testify to support the death penalty. Of course, the impracticality of this led to its defeat. I passed Buckley a note, "Let's get out of here. Pull the bill, I don't want it with capital punishment in it. It's better to give up several small improvements in justice than to enact one really bad one." Buckley agreed. The bill was withdrawn. The episode became known as "The Three Eyed Witness" debate. It signaled that needed reform, the product of hard, conscientious work, would have to be done one bill at a time—for example, assaults and burglaries as stand-alone bills—so the death provision would not kill the entire effort.

Unexpectedly for me, capital punishment again reared its head that year, reappearing at that summer's National Association of Attorneys General (NAAG) conference in Idaho. I attended with my older brother, Eric, who was a professor of geology at the University of Washington. The NAAG conference is an opportunity to meet other attorneys general and learn of trends in legislation or administration, the currents in law enforcement, or strategies for riding political winds. There is a lot of swagger at these events, as attorneys general from larger states strive to be important. For that reason, the NAAG is commonly referred to by the press corps as the National Aspiring Governors Conference. The conference can be used by participants to curry press favor for particular ideas or recognition. I casually introduced Eric to other AGs, or their staff, as my staff geologist, saying he was funded under Title 8 of the "Aiken-Hawley Act"—an entirely fictitious law and fact, which I named after George Aiken, Vermont's nationally recognized senator. Jealous AGs sent staff members to inquire how they could fund a staff geologist, and expressed curiosity about the "Aiken-Hawley Act." When told it was a joke, the fun abated, but I was amused to see the dreams of others to have increased prestige arise and disappear.

Each NAAG conference schedules an event in which all AGs in attendance can meet to propose and vote on resolutions. At the Idaho conference, an attorney general from a large midwestern state circulated a petition urging support for capital punishment as a national policy. The AGs were all seated at one large, round table. I went around the room and quietly asked each AG how many death-row inmates there were in his state (there were no women AGs at that time). I came up with an estimate that there were at least 500 death-row inmates in states represented at the conference. When the resolution came up, I identified myself as being from a small state that did not have capital punishment. I stated that I could not support a resolution to kill over 500 people convicted of crimes I knew nothing about, on evidence I had no knowledge of. I urged rejection of the proposed resolution. It was defeated.

After that satisfying experience, I joined a welcomed scheduled cruise on beautiful Lake Coeur d'Alene, on a large pontoon boat. A convivial crowd assembled on the boat on that wonderful summer afternoon. Drinks and food were provided (possibly by some corporate sponsor). The mood was upbeat, with music playing on deck circulated over the loudspeaker. As the cruise slipped along the lake, I was standing near the bow conversing with Eric and a staff member of another AG when the AG who'd sponsored the capital punishment resolution approached. He had, as I recall, two other men with him. The AG came close to me and said in an angry voice, loud enough to be heard by his companions, "Why did a little shit like you from a little state like Vermont think he should mess with a big important national issue?" I glanced briefly towards the water—it looked warm and inviting—and glanced over to Eric, who looked appalled. Everyone was silent. Then, without further comment, the AG's companions tugged his sleeve and they walked away. Thereafter, the cruise proceeded pleasantly without further controversy. I thought, "There is another reason to oppose capital punishment. It seems to provoke aggression."

Access to Public Documents

I also authored a bill, which became law, to open government records to the public. This time, Richard M. Nixon, thirty-seventh president of the United States, was the precipitating factor. From the time I was elected in 1972, and accelerating during Nixon's time in office as the Watergate scandal unfolded, the national news was pungent with stories of deceit in government and attempts to cover up official actions. Before Watergate became a critical issue, in 1972 the citizens' group Common Cause brought suit against the Committee to Re-elect the President, seeking disclosure of the names of donors of millions of dollars to his 1968 campaign. Nixon resisted, but eventually the civil court ordered the president's secretary, Rose Mary Woods, to disclose the donors list. Its production, eventually dubbed "Rose Mary's Baby," revealed that over six million in cash had been accumulated through illegal donations to a Nixon slush fund. Many donors were then prosecuted for illegal campaign contributions. On April 30, 1973, senior Nixon aides, H. R. Haldeman and John Ehrlichman, resigned because of their complicity in the Watergate burglary, refusing to give up pertinent records of their interaction with

Nixon. On May 18, 1973, Archibald Cox was appointed special prosecutor, and on October 20, 1973, Nixon fired him and other investigators in what became known as the "Saturday Night Massacre." In July 1974, the Supreme Court rejected Nixon's claim of executive privilege, ruling that Nixon must surrender the "smoking gun" tapes detailing his knowledge and planning of the Watergate burglary. The drumbeat of corruption by Republican office holders and their attempts to conceal information filled the news.

These events generated a growing public perception that politicians—that is to say, particularly Republican politicians—were evildoers who used public office for illicit purposes and tried to hide their crimes. As a consequence, demands that government files be open and exposed to the antiseptic qualities of sunshine grew in volume and frequency. Public demand for government documents to be open to the public was rising at the same rate as disgust with Republican leadership. I couldn't do anything about the national scene, but saw an opportunity to show that Vermont was different. I didn't have any staff people to draft legislation, so I personally searched for examples of state laws, or proposals for model laws by interest groups, that required government records to be open to the public, and found several sources I could cannibalize into a proposal suitable for Vermont. I combined them into what became Vermont's first access-to-public-records law. Its policy statement read:

> It is the policy of this subchapter to provide for free and open examination of records consistent with Chapter I, Article 6 of the Vermont Constitution. Officers of government are trustees and servants of the people and it is in the public interest to enable any person to review and criticize their decisions even though such examination may cause inconvenience or embarrassment. All people however, have a right to privacy in their personal and economic pursuits, which ought to be protected unless specific information is needed to review the action of a governmental officer.

I felt this statement and the law's provisions would be a constructive response to public malaise over Watergate and the growing public demand for openness and honesty in government. The law included a definition of "public record" or "public document" which listed with particularity some sixteen classes of documents that were exempt, including: documents declared by law to be confidential, juvenile or educational records, tax returns, medical information, criminal investigations, litigation discovery, and "records concerning formulation of policy where such would constitute a clear invasion of privacy" (the so-called exemption to permit submission of what prove to be stupid ideas to those in charge without fear of later ridicule). Today, these simple exceptions have expanded into forty-two exemptions, as special needs for secrecy won legislative support. The proposal was filed as a bill in 1974, failed of passage, but was resubmitted in 1975, when I was out of office. It was approved with amendments in 1976.

Mac's Party

An unanticipated crisis in 1973 was a plan by one landowner of several open acres in the Northeast Kingdom to hold a reprise of the Woodstock Festival. The event came to be called "Mac's Party." Advertisements for the event invited the general public to picnic, "party," camp out, and listen to music. There were no reliable estimates of the number of possible participants, but law enforcement, as well as neighbors, were concerned. Vermont had no law regulating such an event, such as requiring sanitation, trash control, noise limits, illegal activities, or traffic. I went to the proposed areas with Mac and state police officers but was unsuccessful in getting any specific details of how many people to expect. I considered seeking an injunction ordering regulatory control, but abandoned the idea since I lacked facts to justify an injunction. I doubted mere speculation would be enough to overcome a judge's disposition to allow a landowner to use his land peacefully. Instead, a robust police presence was provided. In the event, the party was a small echo of the Woodstock Festival, with the unwelcome exception that a person did get shot. Criticism of official inaction naturally arose.

My response was to personally draft and submit for enactment a law regulating such events in the future. Had it been in place, the worst of Mac's party could have been prevented. I reasoned it was always good to close the barn door against the possibility of unknown horses escaping later.

The Brookfield Massacre

"This is really nuts," I thought as I reviewed the list of cases pending before the state supreme court (this was before WTF was coined). There, before my wondering eyes, was a case entitled *State of Vermont Agency of Environmental Conservation vs. State of Vermont Department of Transportation.* "What the hell is going on here?" I asked myself. "How can one state agency sue another state agency through their respective lawyers (probably titled "Assistant Attorney General") without the knowledge and consent of the attorney general who, by law, represented the state in all lawsuits?" Even more fundamentally, how could the state sue itself? Answer: it could not. I called Governor Salmon.

"Tom," I asked, "do you know anything about the environmental agency suing the highway department? I just read that is exactly what's going on in the supreme court's pending docket list." The governor promised to get back to me.

Not long after that call, I got the story from the environmental agency, as directed by Governor Salmon. The dispute between the two agencies arose in the town of Brookfield, population of about 1,200. Beautiful as Vermont's rural towns are, it would be hard to find one more breathtaking than Brookfield. It is reached on gravel roads from both north and south that run along a ridge providing stunning mountain views. Sunset Lake borders the west side of the village, with forests, hills, and small houses to the east. Highway 65 spans Sunset Lake on the famous floating bridge, which is supported by pontoons. At the intersection of Ridge Road and Highway 65, just south of the bridge, the highway department thought it prudent to improve sight distances at the intersection by taking out several large, beautiful trees that spanned Ridge Road. Removal of the trees, the department insisted, would allow faster and safer driving. Local residents were outraged over the destruction of their sylvan environment to accommodate speeding tourists.

Further research revealed the Brookfield issue was just one such highway project, with similar ones festering in thirteen other Vermont towns. Governor Salmon dubbed the problem "The Brookfield Massacre" as the volume of protest over such actions by the highway department gained decibels—all similar projects had been contested by local selectboards or environmentalists.

This was the precise situation I had exploited in Connecticut, in the Save The Park movement, that saved many parks from highway depredations. The Vermont legal issue arose because the highway department insisted Vermont's new land-use law, Act 250, did not require environmental review of projects pending before passage of the law. Governor Salmon, Environmental Conservation Secretary Martin Johnson, Highway Commissioner John Gray, and I worked out a settlement by which the environmental agency could require the highway department to respond to its concerns in thirteen exempt projects, but would not be required to obtain Act 250 permits unless so ordered by the governor. Since a state agency cannot contract with another state agency any more than they can sue one another, the settlement was denominated a "Memorandum of Understanding" and was thereafter considered to govern relationships unless revoked or modified by the governor.

I called the settlement "a landmark in intra-governmental relations." Privately I thought, it's all part of a long ongoing fight between oil interests, cars, and the environment, requiring constant vigilance to protect the earth. I was happy to have been involved in this fight. Unfortunately, greater massacres occur on a daily basis all over the country, with only futile democratic control or compromise.

CHAPTER 16

"Truth is one forever absolute, but opinion is truth filtered through the moods, the blood, the disposition of the spectator."

Wendell Phillips, 1859

OPINIONS

Vermont Law requires the attorney general to give advice to state government officials. It provides: The Attorney General shall advise the elective and appointive State officers on questions of law relating to their official duties and shall furnish a written opinion on such matters, when so requested.

The most dramatic event requiring an opinion from me was the economic turmoil caused by the Arab-dominated Organization of Petroleum Exporting Countries' (OPEC) oil embargo in October 1973, which lasted into 1974. The Arab oil exporting countries retaliated against the United States because it had furnished assistance to Israel during the Arab-Israeli War. OPEC embargoed exports of oil to the U.S. causing not only acute shortages of gasoline, but also price rises of about 400 percent. Chaos erupted. An economy car got about eighteen miles to the gallon, but it was almost impossible to find any gas to buy. Long lines grew at the pumps as people waited to buy what little was available, and then were only able to purchase a few gallons. People couldn't get to work. There was a combination of shock and disbelief as the supply of gas ran dry. By December 1973, newspapers in Vermont reported stations empty of gas and no relief in sight. Violence was imminent and threats of harm were common. More common were many schemes of discrimination as desperate people sought fuel. Some gas stations wouldn't sell gas to people unless they'd done work on their car, or unless they were a known customer. People insisted the station where they commonly bought gas was "Their Station" and others should be refused service. People with out-of-state plates were often not allowed to buy gas. Plans were proposed for limiting sales to every other day, depending on whether your license plate number ended in an odd or even number. Even then, the stations might stay open for only a few hours. People were scared and angry. A collapse of commerce seemed imminent as the lines waiting for fuel lengthened. There were calls for "government" to do something. Governor Salmon's Special Assistant for Energy Affairs asked for an opinion as to whether it was proper to refuse to deal with out-of-staters.

Armed with the pen rather than the sword, and with the help of the assistant attorneys general in the Consumer Fraud Division, in December of 1973, I wrote a four-page opinion based on the Federal Trade Commission Act (FTC) and Vermont's consumer protection laws, that a refusal to sell gas to out-of-staters would be unlawful (No 184). The opinion cited: Vermont law, which declared "Unfair methods of competition in commerce and *unfair or deceptive practices in commerce are hereby declared unlawful*"(emphasis mine); and a U.S. Supreme Court case interpreting the FTC in which the court approved a Federal Trade Commission's statement that: The wide variety of decisions interpreting the elusive concept of unfairness at least makes it clear that method of selling violates (the Act) if it is exploitive or inequitable and if, in addition to being morally objectionable, it is seriously detrimental to consumers or others.

The opinion concluded that discrimination against out-of-staters would be unlawful and that my office would prosecute such cases. The broad reading of the Federal Act to include actions that were morally objectionable was broad enough to condemn virtually all the schemes that had arisen to favor some people over others. I also stated I would send a copy of my opinion to all state's attorneys, with advice to prosecute unfair sales methods and discrimination. State's attorneys prosecute crimes; I knew they do not take civil actions to curtail "unlawful" consumer behavior. Still, I wanted to plant the seed of an idea in people's minds that discriminating practices in the sale of fuel might provoke legal repercussions.

Newspapers throughout the state published the substance of the opinion, adding that the governor was urging people to comply with the no-discrimination policy. To my surprise and delight, the opinion seemed to calm people down. People could readily appreciate that having rules and practices requiring fairness and equitable allocation of scarce resources was better than a free-for-all scramble for gas. Readers may be interested to learn that, in 2005, the legislature passed a law prohibiting "price gouging" in retail fuel sales, defined as a gross disparity in price compared to the distributor's price—an example, no doubt, of the swift response of government to economic exploitation.

Attorneys generals' opinions are often belittled, criticized, or ignored. In an opinion by long-time Associate Justice John A. Dooley, the Vermont Supreme Court ruled: "The opinions of the Attorney General are . . . merely advisory opinions for the benefit of state officers. They have no binding effect in this court." Another view of the significance of an attorney general's opinion was stated by Paul A. Gilles, an attorney and frequent writer on Vermont history, who observed "what the State's highest-ranking lawyer thinks is not really precedent binding on any court in the sense that a judgment is, but the General Assembly certainly listens to what the Attorney General thinks, and governors proceed at their risk in ignoring the advice of the one who will defend their decisions when challenged." The Gas Embargo opinion was unique in its effect, not because it was brilliantly written (which, of course, it was), or because it had the force of law, but because in the context in which it was rendered, it provided a partial solution to a political and economic crisis. It provided a legal basis for fuel sellers and customers in line for gas to expect to be treated fairly when, in the absence of law, there would otherwise be chaos.

The function of an attorney general's opinion is usually not so dramatic. The principal opinion writer was Louis Peck, who held the title of Assistant Attorney General for Government Affairs. This is the only position in the attorney general's office that is in the civil service; therefore, the incumbent does not serve at the pleasure of the attorney general. The position was created to allow guidance to the state government to be free from overt political direction. Historically, the incumbent is highly regarded as a non-partisan advisor. Louis Peck was later appointed to be a justice of the supreme court for that reason. Traditionally, Peck was assigned to write and sign opinions resolving disputes between agencies of state government or between municipalities and the state. He also supervised and edited opinion letters. I would personally review, sometimes cursorily, each opinion, signing only the few I wanted to emphasize as my statement as to how some topical issues of concern ought to be resolved. Most were drafted and signed by assistant attorneys general who dealt with arcane arguments between state agencies. If I approved, the opinion would be released. I enjoyed this aspect of the job. It educated me about what was going on in state government, helped me get to know the abilities of assistants, and often produced interesting debates. The opinions settled many issues without time-consuming and expensive litigation, and were undoubtedly a benign governmental force.

Status of Women

By 1974 the rising tide of advocacy for women's equality had led to more female lawyers and legal protection against discrimination; and with these events came social changes reforming customs of male domination. President Kennedy had urged every state to create a commission on the status of women. Governor Philip Hoff had done so in 1964, creating the Governor's Commission on the Status of Women, but it was slow to get started. The only female assistant attorney general, Phoebe Morse, was assigned to the commission as her client agency. She brought two interconnected issues to me for resolution. The first was the custom which seemed to compel women to change their surname to that of their husband when they married. The second was a corollary to the first: if there were a divorce, the woman would have to petition the court to have her maiden name restored. No law required either action. Many women found these archaic customs a demeaning and insulting relic of another age.

Personally, I recalled my mother's pain that none of her children became acquainted with the Swenson family, as though her marriage to a Cheney had divorced her from her birth family. As I aged, I learned more about the Swensons, who seemed a fascinating, even brilliant family that I never got to know for this reason.

The divorce custom was particularly vulnerable. If a woman petitioned the court to "allow" her to take back her maiden name, the request was invariably granted. Nevertheless, without a court order, the bureaucracy would not make the change. For example, in dealing with the Department of Motor Vehicles, or town clerks in charge of voter lists, women understandably asked "Why can't I be who I want to be?" and "What right does a man have to tell me what my name is?" Good questions, I thought. I suggested to Phoebe that she ask the chairperson of the Governor's Commission on Women to request an attorney general's opinion on what was required. Surprisingly, the request came, and I assigned Phoebe Morse to write the opinion. I knew it was an issue she cared deeply about and would come up with a compelling opinion to reverse ancient practices, and that it would be followed.

The resulting opinion, which I personally signed, was a *tour de force* on the subject of people's names. It started by pointing out that Vermont Statutes provided for the state to be governed by common law, meaning historic judge made law, if no statute altered it. At common law, people were free to choose any name they wanted, so long as the purpose was not to commit fraud. Morse then analyzed several statutes as they applied to issues of governmental record keeping, such as voting, land titles, and motor vehicle registration, where consistent naming is helpful. The opinion demonstrated that none of these statutes overruled the common law. The opinion concluded that a woman could choose any name she wanted at the time of her marriage or divorce, so long as there was no intention to defraud. Before long, various administrative agencies and the courts accepted that interpretation and devised ways to legitimize their records. Thus, the opinion became the law of Vermont (Opinion 179).

Gerrymandering

The U.S. Constitution requires a census to occur every ten years. Vermont law requires the legislature to be reapportioned in the next biennial session following the census. That duty was undertaken in 1973, after a series of U.S. Supreme Court decisions on the subject. The president of the Vermont Senate, where multi-member districts were customary, asked for an attorney general's opinion as to whether (1) multi-member districts were permissible if they did not produce the same ratio of people to a senator as would occur in a single-member district; (2) how much population deviation was permissible; and (3) what factors were constitutionally permissible in creating districts that were not of equal population. This request was assigned to Louis Peck, the most non-political person in the office. He dealt with these thorny questions in an eight-page opinion to the effect that multi-member districts were permissible, provided they did not discriminate on the basis of race or other identifiable minorities, equal population per legislator was a good-faith goal with substantial deviations prohibited, and a list of general factors involving the functioning of government. This guidance was useful forming the litigation that followed, which I personally participated in. The court supervised districting to prevent gerrymandering. It was a grueling process, principally because incumbents sought to protect their seats, but I think in the end it was fairly done (Opinion 27, page 168). The process was also typically Vermont, because the supreme court, not the legislature, was the final step in setting districts.

Voter Qualifications

Vermont experienced substantial immigration in the 1960s, referred to by some as "Hippies, Freaks, and Radicals." Both immigration and reapportionment created issues of potential advantage or disadvantage to substantial groups of residents concerning who could vote. Vermont law at the time required a 180-day residency to be qualified to vote in a municipal election, and a ninety-day residency to vote in a union school district election. Federal courts had struck down durational residency requirements saying, in essence, that states must instead devise a way to determine if people seeking to vote were bona fide residents of the state or town or union school district as the case might be. I wrote and personally signed opinions holding that state or municipal durational residency laws were unconstitutional, and urged municipal clerks to ignore them and to update their voter lists with hearings held at not more than thirty days or less than three days before an election (Opinions 34 and 36).

The opinions I selected for comment in this chapter are intended to be illustrative of the work of the office, and of course, are of personal interest to me. For those interested in the issues and conflicts of the time, the *Biennial Report of the Attorney General, June 30, 1974*, is a treasure trove. Over 200 opinions were issued during my time in office. Modesty requires I advise the reader that this may not be the place to look for authoritative resolution of those issues. Sympathy requires that I warn readers that reading and understanding them all would be a crushing and tedious task. Pride leads me to believe that many conflicts were resolved by these opinions, helping to produce a peaceful community and well-functioning government.

CHAPTER 17

"Down in the valley, valley so low,
Hang your head over, hear the wind blow. . .

. . . Write me a letter, send it by mail,
Send it in care of Birmingham jail.

Into the past, love, wanders my mind,
Sad recollections are all that I find."

Richard Dyer-Bennet "Down In The Valley", 1955

THREE BAD COPS – THE ST. ALBANS MASSACRE

An ill wind was blowing during 1974, the second year of my term as attorney general. The year was a combustible mixture of national misdeeds by President Nixon as a result of the Watergate affair, local corruption in the St. Albans police prosecution of drug crimes in that city, and the State Police Commissioner lying to me. Aside from Watergate, it all happened in St. Albans, where former State Police Officer Paul Lawrence, hired as a part-time officer by the city, faked drug buys from innocent "hippies." In St. Albans that year, the collective impact of the "drug problem" and economic recession created malaise. Bad cops exploited the situation and were assisted in doing so by prosecuting attorneys, including Assistant Attorney General William

Keefe. The full story of what came to be known as the Lawrence Affair is ably told in Hamilton Davis's book, *Mocking Justice: America's Biggest Drug Scandal* (Crown Publishers 1978).

This chapter deals with events that I took part in prior to Lawrence's arrest. It is written with assistance of background factual information, unknown to me at the time, derived from Davis's excellent report in *Mocking Justice*. I have profoundly sad recollections of that time, and blame myself for occasional naivete and failure to both diagnose the evil involved and to take action in rooting it out.

In the late 1960s, the economic backbone of St. Albans and the surrounding area was the Central Vermont Railroad, which provided many jobs and much economic vitality to the area. The railroad was owned by the Canadian National Railroad. Sometime in the early 1970s, the Canadians decided to move most of their management and repair jobs to Montreal. Suddenly, many jobs, as well as the crux of community leadership, were lost. At the same time, young people, characterized by the "political class" there and elsewhere as "hippies, freaks, and radicals," moved into the area seeking freedom from urban life and hopeful of the prospect of avoiding the draft. They brought with them drug use and suspicions of promiscuous sex. This immigration provided many benefits to the area, as well as the state, but conservatives principally saw the disruptive aspects.

In 1969, Merle Haggard's popular song, "Okie from Muskogee," was the voice of the counterculture, reflecting the attitude that made the Lawrence affair possible.

> "We don't smoke marijuana in Muskogee
> We don't take our trips on LSD
> We don't burn our draft cards down on Main Street
> 'Cause we like living right, and being free."

The hit movie, *Easy Rider*, starring Peter Fonda, in which two free-spirited, drug-using, motorcycle-riding "hippies" were shotgunned off the road by aggressive locals, told a tale of the repressive culture incubating in many areas.

To combat this perceived cultural and health threat, the St. Albans City Council turned to their police department. In August 1973, the council, over the opposition of some, directed their police chief to hire Paul Lawrence, the former state police officer. Lawrence had a questionable reputation for honesty,

174

but also a reputation of being a great undercover drug cop who could make drug buys and produce arrests. By late October, 1973, Lawrence claimed to have made many drug buys, and prepared affidavits detailing his activity that could be used to establish probable cause for at least thirty arrests for drug offenses. He was ready for a round-up raid whenever State's Attorney Mike McGinn was ready for it. Such a raid could be expected to do two things: assure the community that McGinn was "tough on drugs," but it would also "blow the cover of a narc," as those arrested, as well as the legal system, would spread word of Lawrence's identity, thereby alerting potential offenders to avoid him in the future. In the end, it failed to do either.

At least thirty people were arrested in the October raid, but as the cases were about to come to trial in December 1973, McGinn resigned. Ronald Kilburn was appointed to succeed him, promising there would be "no softening" of the anti-drug campaign, and suggesting five-year jail terms for possession of marijuana. But Kilburn had a conflict of interest in many of the cases, because his former law firm had previously represented some of the defendants. To fill in for the disqualified Kilburn, I sent Assistant Attorney General Bill Keefe, the only assistant attorney general at the time in the criminal division, to St. Albans to prosecute the individuals that Kilburn was unable to. Keefe had been with the attorney general's office a long time. I regarded the assignment as routine processing of legitimate undercover drug cases. I had only met Keefe once before, during the Colby trial years earlier, as related in Chapter 7.

I was somewhat aware that a vigorous drug war was being prosecuted in St. Albans, but I had no details or briefings by Keefe. My involvement in the St. Albans drug war was dramatically ratcheted up in February 1974, when another raid took place in St. Albans based on Lawrence's charges. Soon thereafter, a group of five lawyers, representing defendants charged with drug crimes as a result of Lawrence's sworn affidavits, asked to meet with me. Several of these attorneys had supported my campaign for attorney general in 1972. So had Ron Kilburn. I respected them all and readily agreed to the meeting. I expected them, as good defense attorneys, to vigorously proclaim the innocence of their clients, as they were bound to do. However, I regarded all lawyers as officers of the court who were interested broadly in justice. Before the advent of the Public Defender system, defense lawyers were all in private practice, active in the political life of their communities, and interested not only in doing their best for their clients, but also in what was best for the community. I was disposed to listen and learn, and asked Bill Keefe to sit in on the meeting.

The delegation of five lawyers, dressed for a court appearance in suits and ties with shined shoes, appeared at my office at the appointed time. I greeted them and showed them to the conference room. Bill Keefe (and Hector) joined us. The conference room had photographs of past attorneys general on the wall, but was otherwise spare, with a table that could sit four to a side and a bookcase of Vermont Statutes and Reports. There was a window high on the wall that offered no view of the outside. The visitors took one side of the table, I and Keefe the other. Hector curled up behind me. Jim Levy, a young, idealistic lawyer who had supported me in the election, opened the discussion, leaning forward slightly with his hands on the table, using them for an occasional gesture for emphasis. His companions nodded in agreement, adding a few details but otherwise were silent. My previous experience of the futility of fighting the drug war, coupled with my belief that it was initiated in part to stifle dissent, inclined me to listen carefully to what the defense lawyers had to say. Although I cannot remember the precise conversation, I do remember the substance of what was said. In essence:

"Kim," Levy began, "I believe we have a really bad cop here, and I'd like to tell you why I believe this." The other lawyers nodded in agreement.

"Go ahead, Jim."

"Have you seen the Champlain Security background report on Lawrence?" Levy asked. He went on to explain that lawyers representing many of the accused had persuaded the defender general to pay for an investigation into Lawrence's background. "The report shows Lawrence engaged in many questionable activities while working with state police, and that probably he was fired by the state police. He also engaged in apparent dishonest behavior when he was the Vergennes Police Chief."

I told Levy I hadn't seen the report and asked for a copy. Levy produced it and laid it on the table. It was fifteen pages of single-space type, so I asked Levy for the high points.

"There's a lot in it," he began. "Lawrence started as a Burlington cop in 1966, and quit in 1967 to become a state trooper. In 1971 he resigned to take a civilian job. His stated reason for quitting was that he'd been reassigned to work in another part of the state and didn't like it. The report suggested the real reason he quit was an investigation into a bizarre incident he was involved in while acting as an undercover officer in the Rutland area. The report stated that one night, he had been investigating a burglary at a laboratory. He was alone. He fired shots into the building, calling the dispatcher on his radio to report he had encountered burglars and after a brief gun fight they had fled. State police investigators were highly skeptical of his story. Lawrence was never formally accused of wrongdoing or disciplined. Instead, as frequently happens in the state police, the commissioner reassigned him to an undesirable location as punishment. Lawrence claims he was dissatisfied with being reassigned, so he quit. Probably, it was the result his superiors wanted." Levy looked at me as though he'd made an irrefutable reason to distrust Lawrence.

"Okay, Jim, what else do you have," I asked.

He replied, "Probably of most interest to you is that, while working as state police officer, he did some undercover work in Windham County when Jerry Diamond was state's attorney. Diamond caught him lying about making two busts on the same date, which were miles apart and couldn't have happened. Diamond refused to prosecute any more of his cases. Next, Lawrence became chief of police in Vergennes, but was suspected of misusing his expense allowance and forced to resign. Before he resigned, Addison County State's Attorney John Deppman, who, like Diamond, doubted Lawrence's honesty, also refused to allow Chief Lawrence to make arrests without clearing each case with him first."

I thanked Levy for bringing the report to my attention and asked him if there was anything else he wanted to say. "Well, Kim," he responded, "there is one additional really interesting point. In November of last year, we took a photo of Lawrence at a Liquor Board hearing. It was good photo that showed his face clearly. It was published in connection with the Liquor Board story in the local newspaper, the *St. Albans Messenger*, accompanied by a story about local drug arrests. Even though Lawrence had his face all over town and was exposed as the narc responsible for many arrests, he continued to make cases. That doesn't make sense. By then, all drug users would know who he was and wouldn't have anything to do with him. That's usually what happens when a narc in a particular area is outed."

"Is there more?"

"Those are the high points about Lawrence," Levy paused, then continued. "Oh, Kim, I think you know we had seventeen of our clients polygraphed and eleven came back innocent."

"Yes, Bill told me about that. But as you know, polygraphs, like any other truth-finding device—like torture, are subject to their own peculiar errors and

debate among experts. But I agree, it is a circumstance we need to consider."
This circumstance concerned me more than I let on. The test results found
some people guilty but many innocent. The polygraph operator appeared
reputable. Such tests were commonly used by police agencies as an indicator
of truth, even if not absolute. But eleven innocent findings were unusual.

"Well, let me finish up then," Levy continued. "We have problems with
Judge Gregg, you know; he's presiding over all these cases. He shuts down any
meaningful cross-examination relating to Lawrence's unsavory background
when we try to attack him. Gregg's really prosecution-oriented, we haven't
had a fair trial yet. Worse, of the four trials we had, six of the jurors served on
each trial—it's a goddamned circus."

"I can see why you're concerned," I replied. What I thought was that Judge
Carl Gregg may well have been legally correct in his rulings. The incidents
mentioned in the Champlain Security report, that Jim Levy felt would sink
Lawrence in a jury trial, would not be admissible in evidence. Rule 603 of the
evidence rules does not permit random character assassination of a witness.
The rule clearly states, "Specific instance of the conduct of witness for the
purpose of attacking or supporting his credibility, other than conviction of
a crime as provided in Rule 609, may not be proved by extrinsic evidence."
Extrinsic evidence would be testimony about the incidents in the Champlain
Report. The reason for the rule is that proof regarding any of these incidents
would require a trial-within-a-trial, that is, evidence that each occurred with
the opportunity to contest the truth of the claim. Possibly cross-examination
of Lawrence about each incident could be allowed, but the judge would have
to determine that it had a direct bearing on Lawrence's truthfulness, and was
not just questionable behavior.

"Yeah, I know," Levy responded. "Judge Gregg shot us down on trying to
discredit Lawrence based on stuff in the report."

"Did you try to show that the timings of Lawrence's buys were not
consistent with your clients' availability?" I asked.

"No, we couldn't. On the cases that were tried, Kim, these claimed buys
were often made months or weeks before the arrest. Our clients weren't people
who kept diaries of their whereabouts, like a lawyer billing his time, every day.
For Chrissake, I can't remember what I did and where I was last week. These
guys were not that bright, they couldn't remember a whole lot—some of them
certainly used drugs. They weren't really clear about where they were and who
they were with months ago. We simply didn't have the means to contradict

Lawrence on such things."

"Okay, Jim. I think I've got the picture. Let me look into this and see what, if anything, I can do." I was deeply concerned about what I'd heard. Even though the facts in the Champlain report might not be admissible in evidence, Lawrence appeared to be a bad cop. Most upsetting were the incidents in which two state's attorneys refused to prosecute Lawrence's cases. The ability of a prosecutor to decline prosecution was one of the real safeguards in the system. Even though such refusals could be a function of personal unfounded suspicion or personality issues, they were an essential part of the justice system. Often, it is impossible to know the truth of an allegation; but if something doesn't seem right, the state's attorney must act accordingly. In addition, I had successfully moderated drug hysteria in Washington County while state's attorney, and was concerned about social pressures leading to a rush to judgement. I also had personal experience with state police exposing wrongdoing by other police, knew a trooper was on the scene, and hoped any wrongdoing by St. Albans police would be exposed.

It seemed likely that state police presence would be a check on a locally hired cop, if only to assert their dominance, as had happened to bring down Sheriff Mayo in the deer jacking case. This seemed particularly likely in the case of Lawrence, who had in effect been fired by the state police, and had been unemployed before being hired for special duty in St. Albans. However, Bill Keefe was the officer on the ground, so to speak, who vouched for Lawrence. Truth is an elusive commodity. Skepticism is a virtue. The meeting broke up with no promises being made.

Keefe had not been invited to say anything; the lawyers had probably heard it all before. He went to his office; I followed him, closed the door, and sat a couple feet away, looking him squarely in the face. "Why didn't you give me the Champlain Security report, Bill?" I started.

"Kim," he replied, "I thought it was vague garbage; there certainly was no smoking gun there."

"Yeah, but you should have given it to me—I don't like surprises."

"Okay, sorry, but damn it—it really doesn't prove anything. I went all over it with Ronnie Kilburn. Then we met with Lawrence and went over every detail in the report with him point by point. We laid it to him. He gave credible responses. I wouldn't put a guy like that on the stand until I had done my own cross-examination of him. I needed to be sure he was okay, and I thought he was. Anyhow, none of that stuff was admissible evidence; it was just character assassination, as Judge Gregg ruled. Seems to me, Judge Gregg was arguably correct in his rulings about not allowing Levy and the others to cross-examine on incidents in the report. Kilburn agreed with me that Lawrence was clean."

"Were any of his buys corroborated by others?" I asked.

"Usually not. Most of the cases relied on Lawrence's testimony alone." Keefe went on to argue that uncontrolled buys were not unusual in undercover work. He gave his opinion that the defense lawyers representing a bunch of hippie druggies were typical of the whining defense bar. He said he'd gone over all these allegations with Lawrence personally. "I believe him," Keefe concluded. "There's a real problem in St. Albans. State's Attorney Kilburn and I have gone over all this; we believe Lawrence."

I summed up with Keefe by pointing out that belief was not proof and that we've all been fooled from time to time. I emphasized that the whole basis of our justice system was that truth would emerge in an adversary system where each side gets a fair shot at the jury. I thought it was worth a try and told him what I wanted him to do: (1) any time the defense asked for a change of venue, I wanted him to agree to it. Get these cases out of St. Albans and away from Judge Gregg. I wanted jurors from outside that community, and perhaps they and another judge would see things differently; and (2) I wanted him to find the best polygraph person he could, to polygraph Lawrence and the defendants. I knew state police would resist giving one of their own a poly, but Lawrence was a part-time employee of the St. Albans PD. I didn't know if St. Albans PD or Lawrence would agree to a test—I'd heard some officers didn't think highly of Lawrence—but I wanted to know if he refused, and I'd figure out what to do if so.

When I finished with Keefe, I knew there was only one sure way to learn the truth. If Lawrence was dirty, it would be necessary to catch him in the act of making a false buy. Possibly Keefe and Kilburn could insist that the St. Albans police department corroborate Lawrence's buys by following him closely enough to verify that each buy he made really happened, or that Lawrence be searched by other officers to make sure he had no drugs on him, then search him after an alleged buy to prove he'd acquired drugs from the suspect. Such operational security measures like these would take time and training, as well as enthusiastic support. I doubted these measures would materialize in a community enamored by evident success in the drug war and concluded that catching Lawrence in the act was the most promising way to proceed.

Soon after these meetings, I believe in February 1974, I called State Police Commissioner Edward W. Corcoran, who'd been commissioner since 1970. I'd not had any substantive relationship with him, but told him I wanted the state police to have an undercover officer attempt to get Lawrence to make a fake buy from him. That would be the only sure way to determine if Lawrence was dirty. Corcoran agreed the effort was warranted and said he'd do it. I followed up the phone call with a letter requesting this investigation. Corcoran responded in writing that he would do so.

I later held a meeting in the attorney general's office with Corcoran and Major Glenn Davis, Jr. to discuss this project. The meeting confirmed that the plan would be implemented as soon as possible. I talked with Corcoran at least three times thereafter and was assured by him that he was working to get an undercover person for the job. He said he'd discussed the issue with the Maine State Police, who would cooperate; however, it would take some time, as it would be necessary to provide the agent with false identification papers to protect his anonymity, and to assign a person to the job. Corcoran did not give a start date.

I did not tell Keefe, or the defense bar, about this plan, as secrecy was necessary for its success. Unknown to me at the time, but certainly known by Corcoran, during the time when Lawrence was a state trooper, two state's attorneys had refused to prosecute cases brought by him because he falsely claimed he'd made drug buys when evidence proved otherwise. Keefe never reported to me on what he'd been instructed to do, and I naively assumed no news was good news. I also believed that Corcoran would do what he said he would, but it would take time to plan a fool-proof operation.

In mid-May, Keefe told me that St. Albans PD and Burlington PD had arranged a "narc" swap. Lawrence was going to work in Burlington, while the Burlington "narc," David Demag, went to St. Albans. No specific date was set. I was pleased with this news because it meant another police organization, the Burlington Police, would be in a position to keep an eye on Lawrence. In early July, I called Captain Richard Beaulieu, the head of Burlington's drug unit, to alert him that a state police undercover agent might be working in Burlington where Lawrence was. I told Beaulieu the state police had been ordered to get an undercover officer to check out Lawrence, and I was concerned that Burlington might be doing the same thing. Beaulieu was concerned—if the state police were trying to unmask Lawrence, there may be a looming conflict between two undercover officers that would sink both efforts. Someone could get hurt that way, I agreed. I asked him to speak with Major Davis to get details of the state police operation. Hearing nothing further, I assumed all was well and dueling operations to expose Lawrence would not collide. I assumed State's Attorney Leahy and the Burlington police were working on a plan to expose Lawrence.

Unknown to me, several Burlington undercover officers had become suspicious of Lawrence. Among other things, they found it incredible that Lawrence was so successful in making buys when they found it difficult to do so. Not only were they concerned that a dishonest cop might be working in the city, they were offended by Lawrence's reputation as a "Super Cop," as stated in an article by long-time United Press International reporter and freelancer, Rod Clarke, when in spite of their hard and honest work, public opinion seemed to be that they were incompetent. Unlike events in St. Albans, they compared notes with each other, revealing that the dates, places, and times of the buys Lawrence swore he'd made were often not verifiable or were easily contradicted. They reported to State's Attorney Leahy several of these inconsistencies or instances where Lawrence's description of buys could not have occurred as he stated.

Leahy agreed to find an undercover decoy. As ably reported by Davis in *Mocking Justice*, Leahy quickly arranged for a reliable decoy officer, Michael Schwartz, to be sent to Burlington from New York to assist. The plan was to tell Lawrence that Schwartz, whom Burlington police would refer to as "The Rabbi," was a drug pusher from another state who narcotics officers knew came to Burlington periodically to sell drugs, usually heroin, but were unable to make a case against him. A fake file on The Rabbi was created, complete with a photo of Schwartz. The expectation was that Lawrence would contact The Rabbi and claim to have made a buy from him.

Arrangements were made for Burlington police officers to take a room in the Huntington Hotel, where they had a good view of City Hall Park. Other officers strip-searched Schwartz to prove he had no drugs with him, and arranged a surveillance of him as he went to the park. Lawrence, who was writing police reports at the police station, was shown a photo of The Rabbi by a Burlington officer and told he was a known heroin dealer who was seen recently at City Hall Park. Lawrence was interested. He left the station at 12:10 p.m. At 12:25, Schwartz was in the park, moving from park bench to park bench. He reported by radio that he saw what turned out to be

Lawrence's car slowly drive by. The driver stared carefully at him, didn't stop, then drove away. Just before 1:00 p.m., Lawrence came back to the police station and announced he'd just bought a spoon of heroin from The Rabbi for thirty bucks. He fished in his pocket and brought out the drugs, which he turned over to Burlington custody. Lawrence corroborated his story by referencing the file photo in the fake file. Burlington officers knew Lawrence had not even talked to or met The Rabbi. The entire buy was a fraud.

On July 10, 1974, Lawrence was arrested for perjury by Burlington Police. Incredibly, though Lawrence had not even been in physical contact with Schwartz, he assumed his testimony would be believed. The enormity of Lawrence's crime instantly put into question the entirety of the St. Albans prosecutions. Later investigation by the Giroux Commission, appointed by the governor, established that at least seven buys claimed to have been made by Lawrence, like the one involving The Rabbi, never took place. Many others were also found to be fraudulent.

By coincidence, I was campaigning for re-election in towns south of Burlington when I heard the news of Lawrence's arrest. I cut my schedule, called Leahy, and asked to see him in Burlington as I headed home. He enthusiastically agreed. I met him in the state's attorney's office and he led me to his private office, away from his fawning staff, who were obviously enjoying the prospect of the meeting. Patrick was on an emotional high. He was running for U.S. Senate and was as excited as an Olympic Gold-Medalist, for which I did not criticize him—I would have felt the same way. I tried to say how happy I was for the good of the state and for law enforcement, but Patrick would have none of it. He wanted me to know what a great job he had done. While my praise for law enforcement was true, I was a trifle insincere given how the event would affect us both politically. I have always admired Patrick and still do. I saw him as a mentor, but that day I had to reach deeply into my role as champion of justice to assuage my disgust with him for beating me and the state police to the punch. Later, I could see the Lawrence matter and how it worked out as evidence of fortuitous events that affect political aspirations.

I interrogated Bill Keefe about whether he had carried out my instructions. Bill admitted he never tried to get Lawrence to take a polygraph, although he did have some of the defendants polygraphed by someone with compromised credentials, who found them all guilty. He never consented to a change of venue. I think he might have agreed with one St. Albans councilman who remarked that Lawrence may have arrested people innocent of drug offenses, but he had nonetheless arrested the right people.

Soon after the arrest, Lamoille County Deputy Sheriff James A. King told State's Attorney Kilburn that he, King, had searched a table drawer at the site of one raid and found it empty, only to have Lawrence show up moments later and say he'd found a glassine envelope containing heroin in the drawer. King stated he told Vermont State Police Corporal Stanley Merriam, the lead state police officer in St. Albans, about this, and went on to say that Merriam told King to "shut your mouth, you'll cause a big stink right now," that King was merely a part-time deputy, and he, Merriam, was a full-time professional, thoroughly experienced in drug work, who knew what he was doing. King obeyed Merriam.

I ordered Keefe to hold an inquest as soon as possible to investigate this circumstance, as well as any other pertinent issue. An inquest is similar to a grand jury investigation. Results or testimony are confidential by law, however, a judge presides to ensure fairness. Witnesses and records can be subpoenaed under oath. Both King and Merriam testified. King repeated his story, while Merriam denied it. I then asked Corcoran to polygraph both men, which he promptly arranged to take place on August 1, 1974. The tests were conducted by a highly-regarded operator recruited from the Maine State Police. King passed, Merriam failed.

On August 12, James L. Morse, then an assistant attorney general and later a supreme court justice, advised me after careful legal research that Merriam could not be successfully prosecuted for obstruction of justice.

I tried to conduct a thorough investigation into what went wrong in St. Albans law enforcement, but it became clear the attorney general's office was compromised because of the participation of Keefe. Further, Lawrence's arrest highlighted the likelihood that many innocent people had been convicted and Governor Salmon would be called upon to determine if pardons should be granted. Accordingly, I did not investigate.

Approximately eighteen months later, in March 1976, Governor Salmon appointed a commission to review all Lawrence's convictions and make recommendations regarding pardons. The chairman of the commission was Father Raymond Giroux, chair of the State Parole Board, assisted by Court Administrator Michael Krell and Paul Landler, a "citizen" appointee. Governor Salmon also appointed attorney Robert Gensburg (the former state's attorney who resigned after the tour of Windsor prison in 1969) as special investigator, assisted by Robert Army, the best detective the state police had. I knew and admired Gensburg. I'd also worked with Robert Army and found him an excellent investigator. The Giroux Commission, (which I describe in more detail in the epilogue), produced a complete report of the Lawrence Affair, with a scathing indictment of the prosecutors and the State and St. Albans Police Departments. The report recommended pardons be issued to seventy-one individuals and an upholding of twelve convictions. The governor accepted and acted on those recommendations. Notwithstanding the pardons, many individuals suffered lifetime, excruciating emotional upset as the result of being labeled a criminal by a corrupt legal system.

One aspect of that investigation not pertinent to the pardon issue, but critical to the issue of "bad cops," was brought up by Robert Army who became lead fact gatherer for the report. He'd done excellent work for me when I was state's attorney, and was a diligent investigator who followed the facts. In the course of his work, Army discovered a copy of my letter to Corcoran, directing him to have an undercover agent investigate Lawrence. Army gave me a copy of the letter but, demoralized by my election loss in 1974, I thought this old news was no longer important to anybody. Before leaving office, I'd suspected the state police intentionally disobeyed my directions, but saw no point in pursuing the issue. In 2019, while researching state archives in preparation for this memoir, I found a copy of a recorded interview Army conducted with the director of the state police, Major Glenn Davis. Davis recalled meeting with me and Colonel Corcoran on May 28, 1974, and acknowledged that he and Commissioner Corcoran agreed with my request to set up an undercover investigation of Lawrence, whereby Vermont State Police would obtain the services of a Maine State Police officer. I recall the meeting as taking place at least two months before that. In that interview, Davis stated administrative arrangements took some time, but the officer was ready to start work on July 13, 1974, the Monday following the Friday arrest of Lawrence. I seriously doubt that was the truth.

In 2019, in preparation for this memoir, I called investigator Army who was in Florida suffering from cancer. He told me that, following his interview with Davis, he searched Vermont State Police records for evidence to confirm the state police had actually engaged an undercover agent who was due to begin work in July, but found no such records. He also investigated Maine State Police records, finding no record there of such an arrangement. Davis's testimony was false. Gensburg made no reference to this incident in the Giroux Report. I believed Army: Davis's and Corcoran's promises to me that they would investigate Lawrence were a lie. In writing this memoir, I searched for all records in the attorney general's office and the state police archives, that would verify this conclusion, but all records of that time, in either office, have been lost or destroyed. If Corcoran and Davis had acted as I directed, it appears certain Lawrence would have been exposed much sooner, and many innocent people would have been spared being falsely arrested. Lawrence was reckless and would have been easily unmasked, as demonstrated by what happened in Burlington—"The Rabbi" exposure took place in one day. My belief in the mendacity of state police commanders is buttressed by Robert Gensburg's statement on page 202 of the Giroux Report:

"There is at least, as far as I could tell, a very substantial question at the outset that the Vermont State Police were seriously in cahoots with Lawrence or their lab which enabled Lawrence to operate in the fashion that he did."

At the time of Lawrence's arrest, my campaign for re-election as Republican Attorney General, and Pat Leahy's Democratic campaign for U.S Senate, were in full swing. I was delighted to know that Lawrence had been busted, but unhappy that Leahy had beaten me to the punch and would be given credit for it, while I would be blamed for doing nothing. Leahy had the cooperation of the police who reported to him, while I did not.

Over time, as I processed the Lawrence story, I concluded that most people thought the Paul Lawrence calamity was the work of one bad cop that wouldn't happen again, but really there were at least three bad cops, and it took all of them to create such egregious injustice. Lawrence for sure, but there also was Stanley Merriam, who knew Lawrence was framing innocent people and covered it up. Then there were Commissioner Corcoran and Glenn Davis, who promised to investigate effectively but never did, and then lied about it.

The public looks to police to solve distressing social issues. They respond as best they can, often accompanied by withering criticism, creating a culture where police officers feel everyone is against them. Lawrence looked like the answer to perceived problems in St. Albans—multiple drug arrests of counter-culture individuals would strengthen the narrative that repression was a practical strategy. Certainly, the police did not want to undercut that narrative, for fear of being seen as part of the problem and jeopardizing funding. I believe that attitude included the judge and prosecutors. In my time in law enforcement, until this event, I believed law enforcement in Vermont functioned in a world of integrity. In spite of the Lawrence events, I still do—with this addition. In the epilogue, I will relate the long and painful story of Vermont State Police history growing out of the Lawrence affair, which demonstrates police mendacity is a risk, and the difficulty in uncovering it. A transparent political process, accompanied by vigorous journalism or the threat of it, allowing the sun to shine into dark places, and a governor willing to act decisively, are an essential bulwark for integrity.

CHAPTER 18

". . . if the good people in their wisdom shall see fit to keep me in the background, I have been too familiar with disappointments to be very much chagrined."

Abraham Lincoln, 1832

1974 ELECTION

President Richard Nixon had been slowly twisting in agony from 1972 until he resigned the presidency on August 8, 1974. The hot, fierce wind created by *Washington Post* reporters Bob Woodward and Carl Bernstein fanned the flames in the fuel stacked around the stake to which Nixon was tied, and the flames were growing hotter. They would consume not only Nixon but also the leadership of the Republican party. "Deep Throat," the reporters' secret source (later revealed to be Mark Felt, associate director of the FBI), helped guide them in their stories that gradually exposed Republican criminal conduct and Nixon's illegal coverup. The fire was also fanned by Republican lies, evasions, and missteps. Even the U.S. Supreme Court had had enough. It ordered the release of the "smoking gun" tapes—conversations Nixon secretly recorded in the Oval Office. These talks with political aides established Nixon's venality beyond doubt. His own statement that "I AM NOT A CROOK!" became laughable. And all Republicans were thereby tarnished.

At the same time, in Vermont, a young lawyer and legislator from Brattleboro, Thomas Salmon, was capitalizing on Vermonters' disaffection with the GOP and their alarm about what was happening to their landscape. Salmon had been elected governor, articulating one powerful idea: that the beauty of Vermont was threatened by rampant development, which he could stop. Outgoing Governor Dean C. Davis and Attorney General James Jeffords, both Republicans, had been successful in passing Vermont's first and only land-use development law, known as Act 250, in 1970. Salmon embraced it but wanted to push ahead with additional regulations. Act 250 was a complex law requiring establishment of district commissions to decide whether local development projects complied with state law. Rampant development continued in environmentally sensitive areas while the law was still in its infancy. Salmon seized on the dismay of many Vermonters during his campaign, proposing a capital gains tax to be levied on developers. In his 1973 inaugural address he reminded lawmakers of his promise:

> "In recent months I put before the people of our State an underlying theme entitled 'Vermont for Vermonters.' By this theme I did not mean that we are a state made up of recluses. I tried to give voice the alarm of most Vermonters as they witness the wholesale assault on our land from without. Our neighbors [other states] unable to resist the promise of development have been shortsighted on the problems development brings. They are now paying the Price . . .

> . . . Let us tell the developers who are not interested in profiting Vermont, but making Vermont profit them, what I told them six months ago: 'We are not going to change our laws . . . They are going to have to change their ways.' Let us tell them, and let us tell the rest of the country right here and now: 'Vermont is not for sale!!'"

Salmon's campaign theme benefited from one additional, even more compelling idea—the bad guys, the out-of-state developers threatening Vermont, not the Vermont taxpayers, would pay the bill for change under a proposed new capital gains tax. Voila! A popular tax. His personal energy and charm were a great asset to his campaign. I admired this political hat trick.

As for my race, I had no villain to castigate and make pay. I was the other side of the coin. I thought I had the third goal to get a hat trick: energy and charm, but the others were missing. I was concerned that, as a Republican office holder, I'd have to prove "I AM NOT A CROOK" to be re-elected. How does one do that when it was not he or she who was accused? Then, on September 8, 1974, two months before Vermont's general elections, President Gerald Ford pardoned Nixon and the roof of my campaign collapsed. Public outrage was immediate and growing, day-by-day, suggesting that all Republicans were dishonest, self-dealing, hypocritical, and unconcerned about justice. The power of this idea was evidenced by the fact that Jimmy Carter, a good, decent man, defeated Ford, another good, decent man, in the presidential election of 1976.

When the campaign began, I faced no opposition from my own party, and was renominated in the primary on September 11. The Democrats nominated Michael Jerome Diamond, then Windham County State's Attorney. There was a third party in Vermont back then, Liberty Union, and it nominated legal aid attorney Nancy Kaufman.

The Liberty Union Party was a 1970 creation of mostly disaffected young people, urban transplants, and Vietnam War foes who wanted radical economic change. Bernie Sanders was a member back in 1974, before he became mayor of Burlington, then congressman, and now a U.S. senator and presidential candidate. One could count on Liberty Union to win single-digit support in statewide elections. Kaufman was an aggressive and principled advocate for her clients, but she and her party had little traction with the electorate.

I had reason to be hopeful, and thought at one point I was overcoming the prevailing anti-Republican bias, largely because Vermont's most trusted pollster, Vincent Naramore, had numbers to suggest that. The Vermont College professor, usually the sole pollster in those days, released results of a survey taken from September 24-25, showing me with 46-percent support. Diamond had only 19 percent, and Kaufman was in the single digits, along with a smattering of others. The survey also showed Richard Mallary, the Republican congressman running for U.S. Senate against Patrick Leahy, was ahead, 43 percent to Leahy's 29 percent. The election was only six weeks away, but for Republicans, the political malignancy created by the Nixon pardon was metastasizing. Both Mallary and I would lose.

Because "justice" was foremost in voter's minds, the attorney general campaign excited particular attention. Diamond and I were both highly regarded. On September 12, Diamond's hometown newspaper, *The Brattleboro Reformer,* editorialized:

> The forthcoming battle between Diamond and Cheney for the Attorney General's post could be the most constructive of this political year. Cheney's personal honesty and integrity are a refreshing breeze on the Republican scene. They are both good men, and Vermonters are lucky to have them seeking political office. It's a pity they have to oppose each other.

What was Diamond like? I doubt any characterization of one candidate by his foe in a hard-fought race can be unbiased, but that said, I didn't like him. I thought of him as a tightly wound individual who met conventional standards of acceptance—he made a good presentation. He dressed impeccably on the campaign trail, appeared athletic, and his voice was not commanding, but he was aggressive in a sort of high-pitched way. He is ten years younger than I. And Diamond, like so many—including me—had immigrated to Vermont. He came from Tennessee after law school, to clerk for a US District Court judge, and in short time developed an appreciation for Vermont values and traditions. He was a vigorous campaigner with enthusiastic supporters.

I also thought he was deceitful during the campaign, but that, unfortunately, was not a judgment shared by the electorate who seemed eager to hear what they wanted to hear. At one rally in Middlebury, he charged that a court had declared all the state's environmental regulations invalid, and that I did nothing about it. I was stunned. I had no rebuttal. Damn, I thought, someone screwed up in my office and didn't have the nerve to tell me. I was silent, fearful of saying something false and confused by the breadth of the charge. On investigation, I found the accusation to be totally false, and said so, but he refused to backtrack or even acknowledge that there was no such case, or say where he'd gotten such information.

Inflation was taking a toll. Prices at grocery stores were rising rapidly, and consumers were suffering and getting ticked. So Diamond invented a new crime, some other ill-defined reprehensible behavior he called "repricing." He castigated supermarkets for raising prices of items they'd recently placed on the shelves. He implied that I was inept for not stopping it, and that I didn't support the needs of consumers. It was nonsense, but served his purpose to pose as the consumers' champion. Such pricing did not violate any law, nor was it a violation of any consumer fraud legislation, nor did he propose any law to stop it. In 2005 the legislature added "predatory pricing" as a behavior violating consumer protection laws, defining it as an act intending to harm competition. Diamond's claims were a cheap shot, which I pointed out to the media. He dropped it; he'd made a point, making noise appearing to herald a budding consumer protector. It was dishonest. I let it go. I saw no gain in making a personal attack, but I realized such maneuvers helped portray him as an aggressive personality who was looking out for the common man and woman. Unfortunately, in the political world there are no referees, except the voters; so often there is little one can do but rely on their good judgment and the integrity and smarts of the journalists covering the race.

Neither Diamond nor I had much money for radio or TV ads, so we both fought for publicity through newspaper accounts and direct mail. I was, however, able to finance a few thirty-second TV spots, spending a total of $8,300 ($43,260 in 2020 dollars), to Diamond's $9,300 ($48,500 in 2020 dollars). My ads were intentionally simple. I was shown in a bright light, sitting on a stool before a dark background, staring directly into the camera and talking about the necessity for honesty and purpose. In other media and in stump talks, I did address the pardon issue linking the decision to pardon Nixon with Ford's plan to grant some form of amnesty to Vietnam War draft evaders, a trade-off meant to calm the nation. I also continued to find speaking engagements at service clubs, giving talks on such matters as the settlement of the IPC suit, the law I'd written and gotten passed for access to public documents, our regulation of Vermont Yankee Nuclear Plant, the status of consumer-fraud protection, my efforts to rewrite the entire criminal code, and a need for a workable energy policy to help Vermonters during national fuel shortages.

I went to as many public gatherings as I could, and enlisted supporters to take me around their towns to meet key people. I sought out editors of weekly newspapers for interviews, and did radio interviews at stations across the state. I generated press releases whenever I could find something new to say, and handed them out with the help of, among others, a cadre of students in the northern part of the state, who working for me (deceitfully, I claimed my remarks were often given to a gathered crowd, when in fact they were my friends). I touted my record, which I thought people would appreciate, and which, as the Naramore Poll showed, they did.

Diamond's campaign was to criticize anything I'd done and argue it could have been done better. For example, he said the IPC lawsuit was unnecessary and the lake could have been cleaned up without the high legal costs. That, of course, was not the judgment of the environmental policy makers when then-Attorney General James Jeffords initiated the lawsuit. I'd talked of planning a suit against New Hampshire to free Vermonters working in that state from having to pay income tax on income earned in New Hampshire while New Hampshire residents paid no income tax. Diamond said I waited too long to resolve the issue. I also proposed allowing variable interest rates to help homeowners obtain mortgages, and for some reason in his eyes that meant I favored the rich.

Diamond, to his credit, did not fan the flames of the drug war. He did, however, endorse a New York law called "shock probation," in which offenders would be sent for short terms to prison before being released on probation. New York had constructed special prisons in the north country where city kids could be sent to scare them into behaving. The idea made no sense in Vermont, but it did appeal to hard-liners, and it probably helped Diamond.

I seldom responded directly to Diamond's criticism, as his "getting ink" (that is, press stories) and responses from me would only invite further argument about past actions over settled issues. I didn't want to be defensive. I wanted to emphasize what I had done, and what lay ahead. Fortunately for us and the electorate, our campaign was devoid of personal attacks.

With Paul Lawrence facing trial, and investigations on hold, the Lawrence Affair moved off the front pages of political commentary. I was prohibited by professional ethics from commenting in detail about a criminal case in which my office could be involved, but I did comment on his arrest and the whole business as being a "black day for law enforcement" in Vermont, adding that I advocated pardons for anyone convicted based on Lawrence's testimony. Diamond criticized these comments for ruining Lawrence's ability to get a fair trial and ignoring the presumption of innocence. He himself had refused to prosecute any Lawrence cases.

Election night was rough for me. I went to election central in Montpelier to watch the results. It quickly became apparent—it would be close. I looked apprehensively at the Burlington vote, which was stronger Democratic than I would've liked. There were the usual cheers and groans as each area vote was tabulated, but in my case, not a lot of congratulatory back slapping. I left late, tired and despondent, and went to bed thinking I'd lost by eleven votes out of the 135,731 cast. A recount later showed I'd lost by more, with Diamond winning a plurality of 571 votes, or 47.2 percent, while I received 46.7 percent. Kaufman had about 6 percent. At the time, I felt she took votes from both Diamond and me as establishment supporters, though normally a split on the left elects candidates on the right.

To this day, I try to understand this result. I am convinced the outcome had more to do with what happened in Washington than in Vermont. In the 1972 election, 175,305 votes were cast for attorney general, while in the 1974 election, the vote total was 135,731—almost 40,000 fewer people voted that year. Even taking into account that '74 was a non-presidential election year, when typically fewer voters care to vote, this seemed a significant drop. In 1974, many people could not bring themselves to vote at all, and particularly to vote Republican. GOP incumbency was a liability. Republican Richard Mallary, a pillar in Vermont government and public service, and popular incumbent congressman, lost to Leahy.

Certainly, I lost support from many of my former supporters in the St. Albans area as a result of the Lawrence case. Possibly that was enough for me to lose the election. At least I thought so at the time. Perhaps voters there blamed me for the Lawrence debacle. I blamed myself for not pushing the commissioner hard enough to get the promised undercover agent working, even though later developments, as I relate in the epilogue, showed nothing I could have done would have moved him to keep his promise. But the overwhelming disgust about Watergate, Richard Nixon, and the subsequent pardon were a key factor. Whatever the cause, my political career was over. It began inadvertently, the result of my restlessness, ambition, lucky timing, and willingness to take a chance. And it ended abruptly, in a way I would never have expected.

Neither Diamond nor I had obtained a majority vote, so in a sense, the election was not over on election night. In such cases, when no candidate won a majority, Vermont law at the time (since repealed) required the legislature to determine the winner. Although historically the plurality winner was routinely selected, some legislators felt they were not bound to do so. This circumstance brought some suspense to the outcome, as well as an opportunity for me to fantasize about a victory until the vote on January 3, when legislators next convened. But on that date, my term as attorney general, my income, my personal energy, and my sense of self-worth temporarily evaporated. I could not muster the equanimity of Abraham Lincoln, quoted as an epigram to this chapter.

Years later, I served with Jerry Diamond on the board of the Vermont State Employees Credit Union. After defeating me, he served two terms as attorney general, lost a bid to become governor against Richard Snelling, then entered private practice, just like me. The passions of our electoral combat, and the personal animosity spawned by such, had cooled with time. The other board members of the State Employees Credit Union were well aware of our personal history, but I saw Diamond as a productive member of the board, and when I nominated him for chair, he was elected. He thanked me for the gesture, and we took it as kind of hatchet-burying ceremony. After completing his chairman's term, he nominated me for the chairmanship, and I was then elected. I also appreciate his work in publishing a critique of the state police, as noted in the epilogue.

CHAPTER 19

*"I was headed out down a long bone-white road, straight as a string
and smooth as glass and glittering and wavering in the heat and
humming under the tires like a plucked nerve. I was doing seventy-
five, but I never seemed to catch up. . . And kept on moving west. For
West is where we all plan to go some day. . . It is where you go when
you get the letter saying: Flee, all is discovered."*
Robert Penn Warren, *All the King's Men*, 1946

HEADING OUT

My defeat for reelection as attorney general hit me like a letter saying,
"Flee, all is discovered"—the words in the letter received by Jack
Burden, a character in Robert Penn Warren's 1946 novel, *All the King's Men*.
The words caused him to head out, to get in his car and drive nonstop from
Louisiana to Los Angeles and back at high speeds, with the heat, the noise,
and the flashing scenery all acting as balms to his shattered soul. The fact that
art may imitate life, or brutally depict it, was becoming increasingly apparent
to me.

Jack had been a young idealistic journalist who believed he'd reached
the top of his profession, but found himself doing work for Governor Willie
Stark, "The Boss," (modeled after Huey Long, the demonic populist political
figure of the 1930s), hired to dig up past indiscretions of Stark's opponents—
in particular, one Judge Irwin, a well-respected leader whom The Boss wanted
silenced. Jack, who didn't know who his father was, came to know personally,

admire, and receive helpful guidance from the judge. As The Boss directed, Jack investigated and uncovered an unsavory part of Irwin's past, and wrote a story showing Irwin had engaged in a huge kickback scheme. After the story broke, Judge Irwin committed suicide, and Jack soon learned the judge was his biological father. He also learned the girl he loved, Ann Stanton, was having an affair with Gov. Willie Stark. So Jack headed out. He fled from the discovery that the people he loved and the profession he cherished had been discovered as false.

I shared some of Jack's pain. Reality destroyed his innocence. Mine too, but not so deeply. Some flaws in my support system had been discovered. The election results destroyed my naive belief that, if I did a good job, I would be easily reelected. But maybe I hadn't done such a good job. After all, I didn't haul in Lawrence. The election loss also left me jobless. And worse: towards the end of my political campaign, I learned that Barbara was having an affair with my best friend. Truth be told, I didn't greatly mind losing Barbara. It was clear from the day we married that our relationship was doomed, but I did mind losing my best friend. Since Barb and I had not been having intimate relations, and I, too, had discretely sought other companionships—and neither of us questioned the other about any of this—I had no right to moral outrage. But when the truth about ourselves had to be faced, I became unmoored. My self-esteem took a major blow.

Barb and I had been long stoking hope to avoid what was obvious, believing that if we had children of our own, we wouldn't feel the pain we'd each felt in giving up our first child for adoption. So we'd had the kids—and now I greatly feared losing contact with my two daughters, Alison age twelve, and Margreta, ten, to whom I had directed all the love missing from my marriage. They were happy kids. In school, they engaged with friends, were curious about the world, and appeared to relish growing up. I spent much time with them, hiking, skiing, being with their friends, and encouraging them to excel. Barb and I, united in our love for them, concealed as best we could our own estrangement from each other. Added to this was my

Alison and I in sorrow over separation
of her parents

own painful anxiety about the girl I'd fathered fifteen years before. What was she like? How was she now?

Barb had been genuinely unhappy about the election results, and the kids certainly knew it was not a happy time. When, in January 1975, the legislature finally declared Diamond the winner, I was on the outs both at home and in the community, and found it tough to hold my head up, be convivial, and go job hunting. It was time to head out.

I decided to visit my older brother, Eric, and his family of four kids and a dynamic wife, in Seattle, and my younger brother, Peter, in San Francisco. Eric had earned a Ph.D. in geology at Yale while I was in law school, and was now a professor of geology at Washington State. He was prominent in showing that a proposed nuclear power plant in Skagit, Washington, was a bad plan, given the likelihood that it was to be sited on a dangerous fault, and persuaded the Nuclear Regulatory Commission to reject it. As a result of opposing the U.S. Geological Survey and the utility lobby, he lost all his government contracts and was denied promotion. Not long after, an earthquake struck right where he'd predicted. Although I awarded him the "I TOLD YOU SO" award, none of his punishments were rescinded. Pete, a contractor, was divorced, and as far as I could tell was living a semi-hippie life. I knew less about what I could expect when visiting him, but that would make a stay with him all the more intriguing.

I decided a cross-Canada trip would help me with my thinking, and considered taking the train from Montreal to Vancouver. Barb encouraged the trip, probably because she had some heading out to do on her own, at least figuratively speaking. My trip across Canada would be the reverse of the trip across Canada I'd made with her after I completed my Navy active duty in 1960. So, in a way, this reversal in directions seemed appropriately, but unhappily, consistent.

I planned to take a bus from Vancouver to Seattle, then to San Francisco. There was no return schedule or ticket, just an idea that I would return to Montpelier in a few weeks or months. It would take as long as it took. The promise of being in motion in a direction over which I had no control was most comforting, and I welcomed the anonymity and the chance to assess my life on my own terms. Perhaps a long rail voyage advertised as a scenic wonder would assuage the sense of loss and put me on the right track. So, in early February, Barb and the kids drove me to Montreal to see me off. I took some cash—not a lot—and carried a small backpack with my belongings.

The cross-Canada train left on time for its five-day journey through snow and bitter cold. My ticket included a small compartment, with a toilet and a bunk, that was comfortable enough but hardly luxurious; during the day I could sit in the dome car which offered views of the scenery and chances to chat with fellow passengers, read, or meditate about my life. And the train had an excellent dining car.

As I sat gazing out the dome car's windows, the world flashed by to a sound track of clicking wheels against rails, with occasional interruptions of the dirge-like wails of the train's horn. We passed through Ottawa, and then Sudbury—a city where years of burning coal left the land looking dead and blackened with coal ash. This detritus of civilization matched my mood. We passed through the city of Thunder Bay, in northwestern Ontario, then headed north of Lake Superior until finally reaching Canada's great plains that, covered with snow, reflected a bleakness that matched my thoughts.

At times, the deism of my youth was revived by the stunning scenery. But such wonderment and optimism died at night, during periods of self-absorption. I was not mourning lost love. By the time we reached Winnipeg I realized I was mourning the fact I'd never found a love to lose. This was not a happy thought. Both Tolstoy and Dostoevsky, keen observers of human suffering, observed that "Hell is the inability to love." I realized that, in marrying Barbara, I'd followed a code of honor I thought applied to all men and their relationships with women, who I (archaically) thought were weak and needed protection. I'd married, in part, because I felt guilty for how I'd treated Rose, and was unable to reject Barb, whose entreaties led me to propose marriage, only to find on our honeymoon that she was pregnant by another man. Love is a complicated emotion.

At stops along the way, I was able to step outside into the icy wind on station platforms, to watch people in their winter-clothing cocoons shuffle along, trying to keep from freezing. Perhaps they were symbols of life itself, I thought, organisms wrapped in layers of protection from a hostile world and their own personality impediments.

As the train left Winnipeg and eventually rolled into the mountains at Calgary, I drifted into thoughts of career and what might lay ahead after this adventure. The cultural world I grew up in was based on the idea that dads in a family earn the money, and moms manage the house and the family's emotions. I embraced this notion to justify spending long hours building a career and avoiding much self-reflection. An archaic strategy, indeed, with the result that I'd developed only primitive skills in understanding how I felt about people, and how people and events affected my moods, my life in general, and others around me. My near-decade of involvement in politics had led me into a fascinating world I'd previously only read about. A world where everyone judged everyone else's behavior or motives in terms of objective goals that usually were not obscure: advancement, siding with winners rather than losers, career self-interest. A world where influence and ambition rule. I managed a quiet, sardonic laugh as I wondered, Was the whole world a stage? Was the stage the objective world of politics, or an internal psychic world accessible only to psychiatrists? Were we all mere actors playing parts in a play? Or were some of us destined to make changes that actually would improve the world, if only by a little? And, of course, I had been judged, and I didn't like the verdict. Still, I was gaining insight into my own ambitions and behavior.

I began realizing that, as state's attorney, I probably prosecuted numerous people who, like me, were caught in a web of their own upbringing, only they had far fewer resources and, for whatever other reasons, had committed a crime. If they'd broken the law, it was probably for a reason rooted in some unfortunate tangle in their past. I was pretty sure, if they'd had my own experience, with attentive parents, a fine education, and good economic prospects, they probably would not have ended up in criminal court.

Though defeated at the polls, I was consoled by the knowledge that politics is not a career that promises longevity. My single term as attorney general and quick exit from politics at age forty, with more than fifteen minutes of fame in a small state, was perhaps political accomplishment enough. Perhaps I shouldn't be so disappointed at leaving the public stage. I settled on the fact that I would probably never be a U.S. congressman or senator. Those are the only jobs in politics with both longevity and a paying career.

As the train climbed out of Calgary, emerging from the mountains and heading down to Vancouver through Kamloops, I began seeking explanations, or even vindications, for many of the choices I'd made that brought me to his trip. I had a brush with fatalism—a thought that my life, indeed everyone's, was determined by birth and parental, social, economic, and cultural forces beyond our control. Still, I began looking for a way forward. In fact, this is what the trip was all about.

We stopped in Vancouver, a refreshing, busy city. I stayed a day, purchased my bus ticket to Seattle, and found Eric, one year older than I, and his family, living in a comfortable suburban-type home with a view overlooking Lake

Washington, and an easy walk to the university. He had three busy young girls, a son, and his wife, Olga, who had a prominent position in city government as aide to a councilman. She was the politician of the family. She was beautiful, had energy, was articulate, and had a quick mind. They put me up in their guest room, fed me Olga's home cooking, and talked with animation about their careers and kids. It was comforting to spend a few days in a functioning, happy family, while the mental clatter of the clutter of my psychic mess was drowned out.

Then I caught the bus and headed out to Larkspur, California, just north of the Golden Gate Bridge, where Peter, six years younger than I, lived. Peter's world was different. His "family," I judged, was a collection of like-minded hippies, males and females of the same age who lived together in a large, mildly deteriorating house in an arrangement I could not quite understand. I stayed about three days, and they were kind and generous. The more interesting thing to me was that everyone seemed to smoke pot—a lot of it. One evening, I was happily included in a pot party. About ten people, dressed as though they'd just come in from a day of gardening, hauling lumber, or doing other outdoor work, squatted on the floor around a large table, passing around joints, laughing, and talking. After years of being involved with cops trying to bust people doing just what I was doing, I felt a bit anxious if not a bit hypocritical. What if there was a raid?

Peter and another guy went to the kitchen, where I overheard some earnest mysterious talk about cutting lines that I deduced were not telephone or survey lines and decided to ignore. Indeed, I felt more secure pretending to be a stupid newcomer in case the men in blue showed up. I smoked weed for the first time, and either it was too weak or I was too used to alcohol, as I didn't get particularly high, and felt groggy and logy the next morning, like I had a hangover. I decided this weed stuff was not my drug of choice.

After staying with Pete a few days, I was feeling broke. Money was going out and none was coming in. I had some savings, but with no source of future income, was feeling in jeopardy. I asked Peter if he knew of a way I could earn a little cash. "There's a house construction site near here that has debris that needs to be trucked to the dump. You can take my truck for the day." I thanked him, feeling hope was on the way.

I climbed into the pickup, had a brief lesson in its idiosyncrasies followed Pete's directions to the job site, and before long, was on top of a hillside with panoramic views of San Francisco Bay. The Golden Gate Bridge could be seen far below, with billows of clouds moving from the ocean to the eastern shore of the bay. I drove up to the house site. The frame for a rather large house was completed; concrete had been poured for the floor of a two-car garage, and building debris—bits of lumber, scraps of paper, nails, drywall, and lunch leavings—were scattered over the garage floor. I backed the truck up to the garage, got out, and called out to two carpenters who were working on the frame just above the garage.

"Hello, guys! I'm Pete's brother; he said you had some stuff to clean out."

"Over there—you can't miss it," one shouted.

"By the way, whose house is this?" I asked. "It's going to be beautiful. What a great view!"

"Oh, I don't know for sure who owns it," one carpenter said. "Some hotshot lawyer from San Francisco—you know, them lawyers got all the money!"

"Yeah, I know what you mean," I said agreeably. Picking up a shovel from the truck, I began loading the trash. In about thirty minutes the truck was full. I got in the truck, telling the guys I'd be back soon for more, then drove down to the bay and followed the road past San Quentin Prison, allowing visions of the old Vermont Windsor Prison to flash through my mind. I found the dump, thanks to Peter's good directions, unloaded, turned around, and headed back up the hill to the lawyer's house. When I returned, both carpenters approached to talk. "Hey, man" one said, eyeing my khaki pants and polo shirt. "You don't look like you're from around here. Whatcha doing? You going to be working here much?"

"I'm just passing through," I said. "I need a little money to move on. Pete was just letting me do a little work."

"Well, where you going?" one asked. "What brought you here?" I paused, thought about giving some acceptable, boring story they would expect, then figured, Oh, what the hell! "I was the attorney general in Vermont and I lost an election. I'm just bumming around for a while."

"Geez," he said, putting down his tools. Both guys stared at me. We were all quiet for about thirty seconds. One of them broke the silence, saying what we were all thinking, "Geez man, you've come a long way!"

"I guess I have," I replied, probably looking a little sheepish. I turned back to my work as the two looked on, filled another truckload of junk, waved goodbye, and set off for the dump. Indeed, I had come a long way. I avoided thinking about how much further and in what directions I had to go.

The next day, I grabbed my backpack, Pete took me to the bus station, and paid me $40. I set off for Montpelier, via El Paso, Texas, expecting to take about ten days, bumming around whatever city or town I landed in and sleeping at night on the bus. I was going to Texas for two reasons: first to gain more time for reflection by being in motion through time and space with no personal agenda, and second to learn something of my great-grandfather, Svante Magnus Swenson, and his history in Texas. He'd immigrated from Sweden in 1848, landed in New York, and made his way to Austin to work for a distant relative who ran a dry goods store. My great-grandfather's first job was to go out into the plains to visit settlers' ranches and sell home-making items—everything from cooking pots to soap. It was "Indian Country," and potentially dangerous.

He survived, though, and got to know the population well. In a stroke of good fortune, one of his customers was the widow of the owner of a large cattle ranch, who Svante married. When she died not long after, he married her sister, who'd been living in Tennessee. They acquired more land and wealth by shrewd trading in cattle and commodities. By the time of the Civil War, he was a wealthy man.

My great-grandfather detested slavery. He corresponded with the Lincoln Administration to help raise and arm a group whose mission was to keep Texas in the Union. Not a popular choice. He faced threats to his life, and his brigade defected to the Confederacy. He found it prudent to relocate to Mexico in the dead of night. At war's end, he returned to the United States, eventually acquiring the second-largest cattle landholding in Texas, a sugar plantation in Louisiana, and a bank in New York. Svante's career involving penury to riches is a great family story, but also a great story of America. His acumen and hard work sent me to college and law school, via my mother.

I went to Texas to see where it all began, and perhaps to find some inspiration for re-starting my own career. In the end, I managed to fill in a few blanks in family history but the trip did little to trigger the entrepreneurial spirit. I was destined to be a lawyer.

The bus trip, on the other hand, helped me focus my thinking on what coming home, as opposed to "heading out," would mean. The bus pass I'd purchased allowed me to go wherever I wanted, I think, for a month, thereby releasing me from any temporal constraints. I did go mostly in a straight line from California to Texas, then to Vermont. I enjoyed the anonymous travel and often wondered about the lives of fellow passengers, though I seldom interacted with them. There was comfort in settling into a comfortable seat on a large piece of machinery hurtling through the night on unknown roads to unfamiliar destinations. But I did know the final destination, and ruminated on what awaited. I would have to end my marriage, hopefully in a way that wouldn't separate me from my daughters, find a way to earn a living as a lawyer, and find a new home.

Barb, the children, and Hector were glad to see me when I stepped off the bus. To be more specific: Barb was cordial, the children were ecstatic, and Hector could not stop wagging his tail. These were all signs that life could go as any well-navigated ship should in the fog.

Family with Dorothy and Ben

Margreta's Wedding Picture

CHAPTER 20

"The first thing we do, let's kill all the lawyers."
William Shakespeare, *Henry VI Part II*, Act IV, Scene 2

A LAWYER'S LIFE IN PRIVATE PRACTICE

When I stepped off the bus in Montpelier, I had a whole lot more to learn about being a lawyer. It seemed I was entering the second act of my life. Some of life's hardest tasks, like finding true love, earning a living at work worth doing, loving those you care for, and living a creative life, would remain. But there would be one big change. At age forty, I would now have a new aspect of my profession to learn, and I would learn it by doing what I'd never done before. As a private attorney, I would use the law to influence others to give to my clients what they legally and morally deserved. I came to understand why malevolent characters, in real life and in literature, like Shakespeare's Dick the Butcher, might want to "kill all the lawyers." We stood in their way.

My first task, however, was to reorganize the nuclear family. Barb and I, realizing our marriage wouldn't last, assured the children we would remain attentive parents who would continue to love, guide, and support them. Barb then generously announced she would help support me as I set out to recover financially; and finally, in 1975, after I opened a law office, we divorced. I took responsibility for the children, and she moved to New York State with her lover. I knew I wanted to stay in Montpelier; Alison and Margreta were in school there. Barbara and I decided to sell the home we'd purchased with the proceeds of the house we sold in a rising market in New Haven ten years earlier, split the money, and start over independently. This we did with a minimum of conflict, with both of us grateful we'd raised two girls to love deeply. I had no income or capital, but some small savings and the half-share of the house.

Looking for work, I approached lawyers I knew in the few larger firms of five or more lawyers in both Barre and Montpelier, but had no offers. They foresaw no profit in paying a lawyer, with no clients and no private law experience, the kind of salary a former attorney general might expect. My desire to do trial work was also an impediment. Only one firm in the area specialized in that field, and it didn't need help. Established lawyers were polite, offering advice and guidance, but no job.

Thus, I decided to hang out my own shingle. I rented a one-room office on the second floor of a building on State Street, across from the intersection of State and Elm Streets, furnishing it with the same low-priced, low-quality steel furniture I'd purchased while state's attorney: a desk, four chairs, a filing cabinet, dictating equipment, and a typewriter. I was a handy woodworker, so I built a secretarial desk with a typewriter table, hoping to soon afford a secretary. I hung framed copies of my law school degree and the Vermont certificate of admission to the bar. Without an entrepreneurial bone in my body, I expected the phone would ring; I was hopeful, if not convinced, that my public life would draw clients.

One thing I can say—I had an attractive shingle. My contacts in the state Forest and Park Department, adept at such things, made one as a favor, with my name in prominent, capital letters. It was a one-foot by three-foot horizontal sign carved from a beautiful piece of American chestnut, left over from construction of pews at Christ Episcopal Church. I hung it proudly outside the building, and was officially open for business.

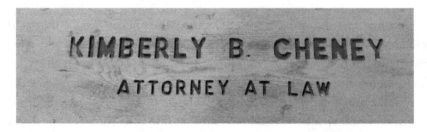

I was forced to learn that I didn't know anything about running a business—including a law practice. The challenge of any business is getting paid, either on time or at all, especially when starting out. There is temptation to take clients simply because you need something to do—usually a poor economic and reputational strategy. But frequently, the case you don't want to take, because it stands on flimsy legal grounds or to save yourself from highly unpleasant personality clashes, could turn out to be your best case. Knowing the difference is a learned skill for any lawyer.

Notoriety did bring in many clients over time, but it didn't help much at the start. One of the first clients to walk in, after saying hello, sat in the chair across from me at my desk, settled down, pulled himself together, and said earnestly in his Northeast Vermont accent, "I need a liar." I was about to tell him indignantly that he had come to the wrong place (though later some clients would come in with precisely that objective in mind), until I realized he was simply saying he needed my honest services and was pronouncing the word "lawyer" in an accent unfamiliar to me. He hired me, and I helped him obtain his worker's compensation benefits.

In late 1976 the difficulty in getting paid had substantial personal repercussions. One client, for whom I set up a business running a motel and tennis camp in the Mad River Valley, was slow to pay. In exchange for a check for full services rendered, I requested the business provide me with one week of tennis camp, including food and lodging. While there on a July day, I ran into Dorothy Tod, a thirty-five-year-old, single, blond filmmaker, who had produced Patrick Leahy's highly effective election television commercials, and who lived nearby. She was at the town of Warren recreation field, helping to celebrate a Fourth of July penny pitch to raise money for the school. I remember her wearing a long dress that dragged in the dust but didn't cover her bare feet.

Richard Snelling, then a candidate for governor, came by shaking hands. I introduced him to Dorothy. Snelling showed a politician's learned pleasure in meeting a potential voter, but immediately prepared to move on. Then I mentioned the work that Dorothy had done for Leahy's campaign, and he instantly showed interest. "I want you to do my campaign!" he blurted without giving the matter more than a moment's thought. Surprisingly, she impolitely declined, bluntly explaining she was tired of politicians promising the moon and not delivering. An interesting conversation, I thought. And perhaps more surprising, Snelling later followed up, she relented, and took the job.

Well, somehow, not long afterwards, I managed to invite myself to her place for dinner. I had slow-paying clients nearby, so I visited one, a grocer, and picked up a couple of lobsters, then another to buy wine for dinner. One thing led to another, and not many days after the lobster dinner Dorothy told me she was pregnant. Having another child at that time in my life was certainly not my intention, although it was clearly hers. In her mid-thirties, she felt her biological clock winding down. I, on the other hand, didn't want to bring into this world another child whom I would have no part in rearing. I was haunted by thoughts of the infant girl I'd released for adoption in 1960, and was always wondering what had become of her. Oddly, I also assumed that someday she would find me.

Dorothy and I decided to marry—for the second time in my life, a wife-to-be was pregnant when we took our vows. Dorothy agreed to move to Montpelier where we bought a house, a large colonial with enough space for her office, me, my two girls, and our son Ben, who was born in April 1977.

Before long, I and another lawyer, Richard Brock, who specialized in real estate, decided to form a firm. Then along came Richard Saudek, who was looking for a landing strip after serving as chairperson of the state Public Service Board until the governorship changed. He joined us, and we formed the firm of Cheney, Brock & Saudek, with offices in downtown Montpelier. The firm provided a reasonable income, lasting about thirty years. We were able to buy a colonial building just out of town, on State Street, to serve as our offices for about twenty of those years. We changed partners from time to time, becoming Cheney, Brock, Saudek & Mullett, and, later still, Cheney, Saudek & Grayck. To impress my out-of-state lawyer friends, I'd tell them the world headquarters of the firm was centrally located in the Capital City, five minutes from the financial district by public transit. If asked for details, I'd simply respond by saying I could walk to the bank downtown in five minutes.

One aspect of the private practice of law is, you never know who will come in the door and how he or she will make the day interesting and help pay the bills. In a small town, it's always someone with a conflict about relationships or money with a spouse, a boss, an employee, an unpaid debt, a police summons, a serious injury in an auto accident, or a fatality. One peculiar case involved an ugly dispute over life insurance proceeds in which a business partner, whose negligent driving had caused the death of his partner, got all the proceeds, while my client, the widow of the deceased partner, got none. The true meaning of the documents was only resolved when the widow enticed "her

cousin Vinny" (known to be in the big-city trash business) to come to negotiations at my office in his stretch limo decorated with fender flags, and driven by a large man with suspicious bulges in his clothing. Vinny privately explained the true meaning of the legal documents to the surviving partner, who'd had difficulty understanding them. With such guidance, the partner transferred the benefits to the deserving widow. In Vermont, a farming state, especially years ago, cows could be an issue. I had a client come in to complain about a neighbor who let his cows wander into the river running through my client's property, urinating and defecating just above my client's favorite swimming hole. Each new client offers a new story of living in a complex society. And each new story demands that a lawyer understand the world as his client sees it, and validate that view before a judge if possible. It is a pulsating, fascinating world.

The fact that there is conflict is not surprising. It is the nature of all living things. Fortunately, in America we have the rule of law to help resolve most disputes. People expect lawyers to determine what that rule of law is in individual cases, and a client expects a lawyer to be clever enough to make others understand that the answer to any question is the answer the client wants. In the best of circumstances, the answer will also conform in some way to what will benefit society.

It is also the lawyer's job to control, as best he can, the client's risk in any conflict, whether it be with others or with economic forces. Assessing risk in making choices is at the heart of human experience, and it's at the heart of legal maneuvering. People must evaluate the chances of winning or losing in litigation, appealing a bureaucratic action, making a business deal, or taking a position in a divorce. Risk evaluation includes taking into account the expenditure of resources needed to get a satisfactory decision. A lawyer is hired to tell the client "when to hold 'em and when to fold 'em." On the lawyer's side of the equation is the economic and reputational risk of the representation, measured by the estimated amount of time necessary to get to the outcome. Advice is often fashioned after a trip to the law library, hunting through the forest of laws hoping to find gold. A trip to the law library is always an intellectually enticing treasure hunt.

In the practice of law, especially when it comes to court proceedings, the character of each client as presented, and even manipulated, by the attorneys is almost always an influence to the outcome. That's because the "facts" of any dispute are those recited by admittedly biased clients who have a stake in the outcome; so who is telling the truth or how deep is anyone's mendacity is usually a determinative but unstated factor governing the outcome of a dispute. Even though everyone has lied at one time or another, it is oddly true that few people admire a liar. A lawyer serves his client best by not allowing the client to be caught in an obvious lie, by counseling how a particular story seems improbable, or why some facts should be emphasized while others are discarded.

Consequently, my first rule of engagement, whether with my client or an opponent, is to begin with the expectation that the stated reason for a particular act is never the real reason. Instead, I would regard the stated reason as something designed to appear acceptable to the hypothetical jury we all carry in our heads. Woe to the lawyer who does not cross-examine his own client to find the real reason for an act. Only then, if necessary, can a questionable act be truthfully explained and perhaps justified. And shame on the lawyer who fails to expose the opponent's evasion.

These lawyerly skills, important as they were for me, were not helpful in molding my marriage with Dorothy into a truly loving relationship. We had not been well-enough acquainted when we'd wed, and soon discovered we had vastly different and conflicting personalities. Dorothy continued making excellent documentary films in a space in our new house, including a film about the difficulties spouses or girlfriends faced as they coped with returning Vietnam veterans with various degrees of PTSD. She did another film—a warm one—featuring me with Ben on short hiking and fishing trips in beautiful sylvan settings. The films reminded viewers of the works she'd produced for Sesame Street, before moving to Vermont. Managing a so-called "blended family" (as post-divorce families were called then) produced its stresses, but generally we did well in this regard. Ben, one could say, had three attentive mothers—Dorothy and his two older sisters—which helped, and a dad who loved watching and helping his son grow up. Dorothy, an artistic person with the mindset of a new-age astrologer, and I, a rational lawyer trying to establish and grow a business, had vastly different ideas of cause and effect, a phenomenon that permeates religion, politics, science, and most relationships. We found this difference an insurmountable obstacle in problem solving and negotiating life's vicissitudes. I would point to some of the nastiness of human beings as the cause of certain difficulties, while she was apt to blame the alignment of the stars and look for answers from astrologers. But despite being such opposites, and despite our decision to break up, I will always be truly grateful to Dorothy for Ben's presence in my life. He has been among my greatest blessings.

I continued helping clients in my office or representing them in court. While my relationship with Dorothy didn't measurably improve, my law practice did, enabling me to broaden my life objectives. I regarded the private practice of law as an opportunity to make a living, but also as a way to promote my intensely subjective concept of justice (Is there any other?). I wanted to continue to pursue the goals I'd espoused in my political life: to comfort the afflicted and afflict the comfortable. German Chancellor Otto von Bismarck once said: "diplomacy is war carried on by other means." It's a quote that stuck in my head over the years, probably because I think the same can be said of the practice of law—it's a form of political warfare carried out "by other means," often on behalf of those who are getting screwed by the system, or by their fellow man.

The profession offers important political opportunities. Lawyers seeking to attract clients, and who know how the laws impact people, are frequently relied upon to serve as leaders in their communities. At that time, I lacked a handy soap box, but I could still express myself by positions taken in court or through my participation on various state boards and committees, such as serving on the Vermont Advisory Committee to the U.S. Civil Rights Commission and serving as chairman of the Vermont Labor Relations Board. To maneuver effectively in this milieu required all the political or persuasive powers and judgment I'd learned in statewide politics.

Vermont Labor Relations Board

In 1978 Governor Snelling, probably in gratitude to Dorothy for helping get him elected, appointed me chairman of the Vermont Labor Relations Board. The pay was $50 for each day worked. Not a lot, and usually I worked in half-day stints, but the experience was helpful in a startup law practice. I had the opportunity to learn about and interact with a sizable part of the population with which I'd had no previous acquaintance. The board had an office and hearing room in Montpelier, staffed by a part-time clerk. When I arrived for my first day, I expected to find a list of pending cases, perhaps some hearing schedules, a library of past decisions that would provide guidance, and labor law treatises. There were no files. The clerk said the chairman, former Lieutenant Governor John S. Burgess, had them in his office in Brattleboro at the far south end of the state. I'd known Burgess for years, but John was busy. I couldn't get him to send the files, and had no idea how bulky they were. I called the governor to request that the state police pick them up, and he agreed. Soon a trooper arrived in Montpelier with a small box of files. I figured I was in business until I opened the box and found the files contained no prior opinions, no docket to schedule new cases, and few clues as to how the board functioned.

By law, the Vermont Labor Relations Board is a quasi-judicial agency with jurisdiction over unfair-labor complaints involving teachers and other public employees. Unique among the states, Vermont's labor board also has jurisdiction over all unionized state employee grievance disputes, including dismissal and discipline. Typically in other jurisdictions, such disputes are resolved by private arbitration using the American Arbitration Association, or, in New York, by arbitrators enrolled with the New York Public Employment Relations Board (PERB), rather than by a state agency or court. Proponents of private grievance arbitration felt it avoided the risk of harm to employer and employee alike from decision makers influenced by state politics. Vermont, as it often does, chose a different course to avoid that contamination, by creating the Labor Relations Board. It had three members—one representing labor, another representing management, and the third, a neutral chairperson—who heard cases as a panel. Fairness would be achieved by having the "neutral" negotiate with at least one of the two sides (and often both) to get a decision. In addition, both unions and the state would save money, using the three volunteer board members instead of paying arbitrators per diem costs. Having no prior experience, my total ignorance on the subject of labor law matters made me a reasonable choice; I had no bias in labor relations matters, or indeed any opinion whatsoever on grievance procedures or issues.

I soon realized the board was dysfunctional. Cases were not heard promptly and were frequently decided by cursory opinions without much explanation of the reasoning supporting the outcome. Like trial court opinions, they were not systematically reported, so each opinion had no precedential value. In practice, the Vermont Supreme Court, on appeal from the board, resolved some of the most ordinary grievances. That was perhaps a fair process, but was also time consuming and expensive. Unfortunately, the high court justices had no special expertise in labor matters or first-hand experience in labor relations matters. It was a poor way to manage the risk of sour or destructive labor relationships and dealing with labor disagreements.

Labor disputes are totally different from most other legal disputes. In most disputes, a decision for one side or the other ends relations between the parties. Not so in labor matters. A decision involving labor and management cannot result in a divorce from the relationship. The state remains the employer and the state employees union continues to represent workers. The employer, the union, and frequently the worker must continue with each other. For this reason the board must also take into consideration what disposition might be best, not only for the individuals in the dispute, but also for the large interested constituencies supporting each individual in the dispute.

For about ten years, while building my law practice and learning some of the skills needed to be a labor arbitrator—which I later became, I immersed myself in labor issues, seeking guidance from out-of-state leaders in New York and attending national conferences where I could learn from a broad spectrum of people experienced in labor relations. During that period, as chairman of the Vermont board, I wrote at least one hundred opinions, which included detailed reasoning for our board's decisions. Many of these opinions cited federal law or academic commentary. The practice helped bolster credibility in the quality of our work and acceptance by involved parties. Appeals to the supreme court decreased. I began publishing our opinions in annual volumes with a thorough and reliable index. These opinions attained precedential value that helped both sides in later conflicts assess the risks involved in their actions, narrow their disputes, and get along with each other.

In addition, with the governor's support, I persuaded the legislature to add two more members to the board, allowing us to designate a variety of three-person hearing panels to decide cases. This prevented parties from knowing beforehand exactly who would rule on their cases, which helped foster settlements because of the risk each party faced with an unknown panel. The new arrangement permitted a sort of appeal in the form of a review by all five members. The board became central to resolution of labor issues. The supreme court even began deferring to the "expertise" of the administrative agency.

One critical education collective bargaining issue that came before the board was the question of whether teachers were allowed to strike. I found that the statutes on the subject seemed to be purposely ambiguous, as though the legislature at one point in the past had put together conflicting language just to pass a bill that no one could fully embrace. I puzzled over the law's various provisions and tried to understand the state's actual policy on this controversial subject. I analyzed the statutory texts, even wondering if such matters as placement of commas or certain modifying words were intended to guide interpretation. In short, I dug deeply into the wording, drafting choices, and other nitty-gritty aspects of construing the existing legislation.

Key to resolving this conundrum was William Kemsley, the labor representative on our board. He'd been an organizer for the United Auto Workers, education director of Michigan's Congress of Industrial Organizations, served with the Marshall Plan in Paris as head of the labor training section, and worked with the United Nations Confederation of Free Trade Unions. He was a passionate advocate for "the working man," tempered by knowledge that the world was a complex place. I asked what he thought about the confusing tangle of words in the legislation, and he replied as he often did, with a short, simple, pungent statement avoiding legalisms and getting to the point: "I think every man or woman has the right to refuse their own labor."

"You are right," I thought. "And that's what we will conclude." With the skilled editorial help of a clerk I'd hired, Amy Davenport, and our management representative, I drafted an opinion that gave teachers the right to strike, but where clarity is hard to find, procedure may be imposed to resolve dispute. A strike was only permitted if collective bargaining had been thorough and done in good faith; and if a strike did occur, the local school boards could impose a contract if all dispute resolution procedures, such as mediation and "fact finding," had taken place during the strike. Unexpectedly, the opinion was not appealed. The legislature did not get involved. The opinion has been followed ever since, having survived several legislative rumbles to change it.

Davenport, by the way, became so interested in law through this process that she "read law," as it is said in Vermont, to become a lawyer. That is, she took advantage of a Vermont process by which a person with a good legal mentor, without going to law school, can study the law, take the bar exam, and become a lawyer. She became an attorney and went on to become an excellent trial court judge. As for Kemsley, I always admired him for his background and good sense, and was privileged to give the eulogy at his funeral.

Like my work in education, I created a functioning system for the labor relations board and enjoyed doing so. The board has grown in recent years and is now under the guidance of attorney Timothy Noonan, whom I hired as counsel. The board now has six members with two neutrals, and it hears cases by three-member panels designated randomly by the Chair. It is a unique system in national labor grievance resolution. The American Arbitration Association awarded me the Whitney North Seymour Arbitration Medal for 1985. "In recognition of outstanding contributions to responsible use of arbitration," said the inscription. (Past recipients included Warren Burger, former Chief Justice of the U.S. Supreme Court; and Eleanor Holmes Norton, former chair of the Equal Employment Opportunity Commission, and a law school classmate of mine.)

Criminal Law Practice

It was not hard transitioning to the "dark side." Defending rather than prosecuting suspects, even those I believed might well be guilty, has its own social utility. Defense of such unfortunates is also a defense of the basic right of everyone to be governed by the laws as articulated in the Constitution and explained by the Supreme Court. Those sources and our history require fairness in the judicial process based on the starting point that a person is innocent unless (not "until") proven guilty. For lawyers, this often means that, when they defend a person charged with even a heinous crime, they are, just as importantly, defending everyone's constitutional rights. In addition to these noble sentiments, there is real pleasure to be derived in occasionally puncturing the hot-air balloon pumped up with the gas of public outcries and released by an overzealous prosecutor or police officer.

There is also satisfaction to be found in defending someone who may have committed a crime due to a momentary error of judgment, or someone who never had a chance in life. Even in cases where defendants are found to be—and manifestly are—guilty, a lawyer can fight for justice by arguing for a fair sentence based on the need for public protection, but also based on humanitarian considerations rather than the uninformed demands of a scornful public. Lawyers in such cases practice their craft under an added burden—the realization that a client is still a human being; and in this particular circumstance, the attorney may be the only friend they have.

Conflicts in a courtroom often involve some of the deepest questions of what it means to be human. They call up beliefs we all have—whether we be judges, jurors, corrections officers, police, or lawyers—about our fundamental nature. Are we essentially good or essentially evil? Forcing such questions on people not used to dealing with such matters, especially jurors, can be a challenge. For the trial lawyer, raising the question and getting the desired answers or verdicts requires legal knowledge but also talents in oratory and acting. Truth be told, some of the best lawyers are performers at heart. I often think I would've been a better lawyer had I spent time in a drama school or had the benefit early in my career of a first-rate thespian mentor.

Liberating an innocent man from an unjust prison sentence is most satisfying. I defended several murder cases. Some were puzzles in which there were no witnesses (other than the accused) to the actual events leading to the victim's death. In such cases, the forensic skills of the doctors who perform the autopsy, or interpret it, provide the foundations of proof as to the cause and manner of death that in turn lead to a finding of guilt or innocence, or reasonable doubt. I discussed a couple of my cases of that nature with attorneys in the state's Defender Generals' Office. I was given helpful advice and referrals to competent defense medical examiners who helped me get good results. Both the legal and medical professions are incubators for argument. A trial lawyer, whether for the defense or the prosecution, can almost always find some expert medical witness to question the testimony of another expert medical witness. The lesson for any trial lawyer is to challenge proclaimed truth, search for alternatives, ask hard questions, in short—be a good detective and then a good advocate.

Tom Olsen's case was of that kind. He'd been convicted in a "shaken baby" case in 1994, resulting in a prison sentence of thirty years to life. The victim was his girlfriend's two-year-old daughter, Melissa Stephens, who died in 1992. In 2006, Olsen's then-lawyer, Jan Dembinski from Woodstock, asked if I would be an expert witness to establish that the lawyers who defended Tom had provided an ineffective defense, which would establish a constitutional right to a new trial. The defender general was willing to pay my fee. Tom had served almost fifteen years by the time I became involved. I learned much later, before I did any work, that Dembinski's request was prompted by an obsessive belief by Tom's landlord, Chris Coughlin of Springfield, Vermont, that Tom was innocent. Over the fifteen years of Tom's incarceration, Coughlin pursued research into the medical contradictions in the state's case, as well as evidence of self-serving motives by police and prosecutors. Coughlin was convinced that Melissa's death was caused by being kicked by caregivers at a local daycare center, and that the center had been improperly supervised by the State Department of Children and Families, which knew of abuses there but had found the accusation by Coughlin to be unsubstantiated. His theory was that state authorities, including the prosecutor, were determined to find a scapegoat for their own negligence in Melissa's case—conspiracy speculations I had not heard until informed of them, years after completing my work. Before becoming involved in the case, I was given only the trial transcript, access to medical records, and defense attorney's files.

The non-medical facts were simple. On the day of her death, Melissa and her five-year-old sister, Ashley, had been cared for from 7:30 a.m. until approximately 4:30 p.m. at a Springfield daycare center run by a Lucile Snide. Melissa's mother, Debbie, a refugee from an abusive husband, was living with Tom and his two daughters in a two-story apartment. Debbie picked up Melissa and Ashley at the center between 4:15 and 4:30, when it closed. She took them home so Tom could care for them, as he frequently did, while she went to an appointment. She arrived home about five minutes after leaving the daycare facility. Ashely walked in the house, but because Melissa was not feeling well, Debbie carried her from her car and handed her to Tom. Within about fifteen minutes, Tom's brother, who'd been planning to move in with Tom, arrived at the house to plan his move. Tom, who was upstairs and who evidently heard his brother enter, called to his brother for help, saying Melissa had fallen down the stairs and was not well. The brother came upstairs to see Melissa virtually comatose on a couch; the two brothers left the other three girls and immediately took Melissa to the Springfield hospital emergency room, arriving about 5 p.m. She had a pulse but soon died.

The medical facts were far more complicated. The deputy state medical examiner, Stephen Adams, performed the autopsy and reviewed the findings of the emergency room physicians. He found Melissa had a constellation of injuries which could cause immediate death: rapidly lethal head injuries with subdural bleeding, potentially lethal injuries to internal organs, lacerations of the liver, hemorrhaging of the pancreas—some of which could have been two days old, a subdural hematoma, and a torn brainstem tear. Most injuries were said to be "minutes to hours old," measured from the time of her death. The abdominal injuries, he said, could only have been caused by forceful kicks or blows with a blunt object. The totality of injuries could be catastrophic, leading to rapid swelling of the brain, which could cause Melissa to lose consciousness and fall down the stairs.

I had also had for review the trial testimony of Randall Alexander, MD, an expert medical witness on "shaken baby syndrome." Dr. Alexander had what appeared to be a lucrative business of being a frequent prosecution witness, having appeared in several states to explain the syndrome. He testified that Melissa was a "shaken baby" victim, who'd been shaken violently with force equivalent to that of a motorcycle hitting a parked truck at ninety miles per hour. How Tom might have created such lethal forces by shaking a baby so hard in frustration to stop her from crying was not explained or questioned, which was all the more unusual since there were no external cranial wounds evidencing such force. Conventional wisdom then, and popular today, although now thoroughly disproved, was that death would be caused by shaking the child, causing the brain to slam against the cranium, thus causing bleeding and the brain to swell, suffocating the child. His testimony was supplemented by Dr. Adams and the emergency room physicians, who agreed Melissa's injuries would have occurred before she fell down the stairs and not because of that fall.

Tom's initial trial attorney, Michael Kainen, from Vermont, engaged pathologist Edward Sussman, MD to review the case. After three consultations with Dr. Sussman, a pathologist for thirty years, Kainen learned (1) Sussman needed color photos taken at autopsy to be certain; (2) a torn brainstem would be immediately lethal; (3) it could not be caused by a fall down stairs; (4) it could have been caused by the autopsy and not be a real injury; (5) some injuries were months old and others recent; and (6) retinal hemorrhages are indicative of shaken baby, but without photos and expert analysis, he couldn't tell their age. With this information, Kainen took the deposition of Dr. Adams, the state medical examiner. Adams testified that the abdominal injuries alone could have caused death and were not due to a fall down stairs. They were old, would have been caused by blunt force of the abdomen, and could have a later manifestation, causing Melissa to be drowsy and fall down the stairs. The brainstem tear was significant and would lead to instant death. He himself did not remove the brain, his assistant did, so he did not know if ineptness during the autopsy tore the brainstem. Brainstem tears are indicators of "shaken baby," and would require a lot of force by extension of the neck.[2] The injuries could not have been caused by a fall down stairs. Kainen apparently could not communicate effectively with Tom, and at his request was allowed to withdraw from the case.

Kainen was replaced by Claude Buttrey and George Ostler, both Vermont lawyers. By agreement, Osler was assigned to the medical aspects of the case. Unfortunately for Tom, he did not spend enough time with Dr. Sussman to understand the complex medical information. He had short telephone calls with him, but only one face-to-face interview, on the day of jury selection. Instead, Buttrey and Ostler constructed a defense on the theory that Melissa had a cold the day she died, was woozy when she came home, was taken by Tom upstairs to rest, but got up, went to the top of the stairs, tripped, and fell down the stairs, suffering the injuries noted by Dr. Adams. None of the testifying doctors supported this theory because the injuries were too severe to have been caused that way, and many of them were old. Although Melissa's injuries could have been hours old, and her sister Ashley told the attorneys that Lucile Snide had violently kicked both her and Melissa at least five times at the daycare facility that day, they chose not to present such evidence. Tom's daughters, aged about nine and eleven, also said he had not shaken Melissa. Buttrey and Ostler reasoned that Ashley or other children would not be believed; any denials from the head of the daycare center would be, and Tom would appear to be a constant abuser over several days, accounting for the older injuries if the jury were told about all of them. That approach left the spontaneous stair fall as the only defense.

But there were several glaring problems with this approach. None of the involved doctors (including Dr. Sussman, who did not testify) believed Melissa's injuries could have been caused by a stair fall. Worse, the defense lawyers intended to prove this theory by cross-examination of prosecution doctors, an extremely difficult task in the best of cases and virtually impossible without a medical expert who would support it. The strategy also excluded the possibility that there was a reasonable doubt as to where and by whom the abdominal injuries were inflicted.

I needed to understand the medical issues, which meant talking with Dr. Sussman. He was retired by then, but agreed to meet with me at his home on Martha's Vineyard. Jan Dembinski came along, and we met for more than four hours to review all the medical evidence, including the autopsy report

---

2 Goldsmith & Plunkett, 25 The American Journal of Forensic Medicine and Pathology, Number 2, June 2004

and trial testimony. After thoroughly examining and cross-examining Dr. Sussman, I became convinced there was ample evidence, because of the age and nature of the abdominal injuries, that a daycare assault could reasonably have been found to have caused death. In addition, Dr. Sussman disputed that vigorous shaking could not have caused the subdural hematomas unless accompanied by a severe external blow to the head. Dr. Sussman also gave a convincing explanation, based on his thirty years of experience, of why the brain stem tear was more likely a result of an error in doing the autopsy itself, rather than being an immediate cause of death. He explained that autopsy work is a rather grim business involving carefully cutting up bodies. Removing the brain requires removing the scalp, grasping a gelatinous brain with both hands and pulling it upwards, a process that could result in tearing the brainstem. Since Melissa had a pulse in the emergency room, the brainstem was intact at that time and could not have been caused by Tom or a stair fall. Adams had taken no photographs of the area (a violation of standard autopsy procedures published in 1987,which he provided to me), which would have been necessary for him to determine the age of the injuries, in particular the age of any retinal hemorrhages. Dembinski wrote me much later, after the case was concluded: "We all have you to thank for coming on board. Our trip to Dr. Sussman was wonderful—a chance for me to witness a couple of old pros trying to sift out the truth through all the details."

What I learned from Dr. Sussman was that Tom's lawyers missed the opportunity of putting together a winning defense based on a reasonable doubt, by conceding that the injuries probably happened the day Melissa died. The emergency room physicians would have supported the conclusion that Melissa had been injured before she got home, resulting in edema to her brain and rapid fatal swelling, which could have explained why she fell down the stairs. The failure of Tom's lawyers to understand these medical issues and present them as evidence showed they had been ineffective. I prepared an affidavit of my proposed testimony outlining my opinion as to why Buttrey and Ostler had been ineffective.[3] I analyzed the prosecution's medical testimony and showed how Dr. Sussman would have been able to cast reasonable doubt on Dr. Alexander's conclusions, both through his own testimony and cross-examination. I also emphasized that Ashley would confirm she'd been kicked in the stomach at the daycare, one more basis for reasonable doubt. I gave my

---

3. Of course, this information was not available at time of trial, so Buttrey and Olsen were not implicated. Dr. Sussman referred me to it.

affidavit to Dembinski, who filed it in support of a motion for a new trial in September 2007.

But the motion had a serious obstacle. Dr. Sussman, who'd retired, was unwilling to be a witness. Still, neither the incumbent state's attorney, Robert Sand, nor Dembinski was enthusiastic about having a new trial sixteen years after Melissa's death. The factual basis outlined in my proposed testimony did cause Sand some concerns—enough so that, in 2009, he came to an agreement with Tom's lawyer and with Tom personally, that the conviction would stand but that Tom should be resentenced to a jail term of the amount of time already served. After a judge agreed, Tom was released from prison in 2009.

I cannot imagine Tom's suffering caused by fifteen years in jail for a crime he almost certainly did not commit. Since death could not have been caused solely by shaking Melissa, the medical evidence was equally strong to support lethal injuries occurring at Tom's home or at the daycare facility. He was charged with murder because he was the last person to see her alive, even though the injuries that killed her were, in greater probability, inflicted by someone else.

Divorce and Family Practice

As my practice evolved I took on more divorce cases, because criminal law and labor law did not provide enough income. Unlike many lawyers who avoid divorce cases because of their distaste for nasty arguments between spouses and the lack of any intriguing legal issues, I found satisfaction in them. I found in divorce cases an opportunity to relate deeply and meaningfully with people in a defining moment in their lives, when future happiness or economic security were at risk. Divorce cases can also raise evolving cultural issues regarding relations between the sexes: is all work done by a spouse, either in or out of the house and particularly where children are involved, of equal worth in money? Is youth a wasting asset, especially for women who lose the ability to choose with whom to have children? Do men and women really have equal economic opportunities? Should anyone, especially a judge, really care why a marriage failed, especially in cases of affairs shortly before the divorce, and measure that opinion in money?

Judges in divorce cases are given wide discretion in how to allocate money and other things of immense value, most notably and often the ex-husband's or ex-wife's relationship with their children. These immensely important decisions by family court judges are rarely overturned by appeals, which means, to be effective, it's really important for a divorce attorney to know the idiosyncrasies of the various judges, either through experience or conversations with other attorneys.

One mystery of human experience is how people in authority actually make their decisions. Our present culture puts a premium on amassing data and devising a computer-driven algorithm to help with decision making. Some people, for example, will buy a $100 lottery ticket to win a $300 prize, and a computer can calculate how many will do so. With divorces, though, in the end it seems more likely the judge's personal life experiences and impressions of the character of the parties will determine outcomes. One judge actually awarded child custody to men because he believed women were responsible for maintaining the marriage, and if they failed, Dad should have the kids. Numerous appeals and legislative reviews corrected this problem. I certainly can't explain how judges make decisions, and often believe they can't either. My own working principle is that judgment is based essentially on unarticulated values resulting from one's parental, sibling, or spousal relationships, and economic and social circumstances during formative years. When this can't be assessed, or when dealing with a totally unfamiliar judge, I've figured it's best to act as respectful as possible to everyone involved, present my case as though facts mattered greatly—even if they may not, and hope for the best.

Over time, I became deeply dissatisfied with how custody disputes over children were resolved. The conventional criteria for a judge's decision was said to be "what are the best interests of the child?" In my experience, contestants too often took this criterion to mean that what was best for the child was— you guessed it—what was best for them. Worse, judges appeared to me a bag of biases uninformed by any social science knowledge of critical factors in child mental health.

I began thinking about this problem while at Yale Law School. One of the school's pedagogical goals has been to develop curricula combining law with other disciplines. One such enterprise was to study how legal theories regarding what was best for children in a divorce compared with what scholars in social sciences had learned regarding childhood development. When I was in law school, Joseph Goldstein, Anna Freud, and Albert J. Solnit, all leading scholars in law and children's development, were working on their book *Beyond the Best Interest of the Child*. Their thesis rested, among other things, on the

222

proposition that a child in a divorce would have a more positive development if one parent were dead than if both parents were alive and having bitter arguments over custody. I wrote and published a paper (in *Children* 13, No. 3 [May 1966], an interdisciplinary journal of professions serving children published by the U.S. Government) on the criteria to be used in child neglect cases, to determine whether a child should be removed from his or her parents and placed in foster care. Then, long after law school, as I did more custody cases, I was concerned that judges had little understanding of scholarly social theory of childhood development.

As my concerns grew, I found that other divorce attorneys agreed with me. In 1982 or 1983, a particularly articulate and energetic attorney, Trina Bech, who worked in Windsor County and who agreed with me on these matters, decided it was time to act. We formed a group of enlightened souls who set out to make a change. We managed to persuade the Vermont General Assembly to create a committee with a mandate to report back on how to improve child custody decisions. The committee, known as The Family Proceedings Advisory Committee (FPAC), was charged with developing new criteria for judges to apply in determining which parent should receive custody, and defined the best interests of the child in light of research findings by social scientists. The committee, composed of legislators, a judge, both male and female attorneys and mental-health workers, elected Trina and me as co-chairs.

In 1985, after many discussions with psychiatrists, social workers, judges, and lawyers, we presented our work to the House Judiciary Committee to work into a bill. The committee accepted most of our proposals and drafted a bill that became law, resulting in a complete revision of state law regarding how child custody in divorce cases would be determined. The law created ten criteria a judge must consider in making a custody decision. In condensed form, they required a judge to compare the parents' ability and disposition to parent their children, and award custody based on these listed criteria:

> Love, affection, and guidance
> Food, shelter, health care, and safety
> Meet the child's developmental needs
> Adjustment to home, school, and community
> Foster a positive relationship with other parent
> Relationship to primary care provider
> Relationship with other important people
> Parents' ability to communicate with each other

Any prior abusive conduct

No preference to one sex, with regard to siblings of opposite sex

As an example of how the first criterion was to be applied, Trina and I wrote that the word love in "love, affection, and guidance" for the child in this context was not simply an emotion to be satisfied by a parent saying "I love my kids." Rather, it was meant to be evidentiary-based behavior. The essence of "love" is essentially subordinating one's own needs to those of the loved person. It would mean, for example, not denigrating the character of the other parent, because hearing such complaints or uncomplimentary words might cause a child to lose a parent. Another example is in the use of the word "affection," which can be different than "love." I created my own test relating to this criterion, and would ask a client simply, "Please describe your kid." If he (commonly) said matter-of-factly, "Oh, he's about five-foot tall, blue eyes, weighs about 110 pounds, and has an athletic build," I would likely evaluate it as a disqualifying answer. If he said, with a smile on his face, "Oh, he loves to play cards with his sister; and you should see him getting dressed up for Halloween—it's a riot," I might be more likely to conclude he really liked his boy. The other criteria were also to be applied on the basis of factual findings, that is, based on "show me" don't "tell me" what you did.

In addition to the custody criteria, I drafted a separate measure based on a law in Colorado, creating a formula for computing the amount of child support that would be paid and creating a state Office of Child Support to monitor and enforce such awards. Without such clear standards on support, judicial decisions had produced a wide disparity in awards that could not rationally be explained. Essentially, the formula required a computation of joint income to determine the standard of living the child would have prior to the divorce, a percentage of such income that would usually be expended on child rearing, and an allocation of support to be paid by the higher earner to the lower earner.

Adoption

As I was completing my work on child custody criteria, a new drama exploded in my life. On Ben's ninth birthday, in 1986, Dorothy and I and the children were at our Montpelier home celebrating, when the phone rang. Dorothy answered and reported that some woman wanted to talk to me. I took the phone, and because I frequently got calls from troubled clients whose confidentiality had to be respected, I moved out of Dorothy's hearing. The conversation that ensued went something like this: A young woman who did not identify herself asked if she had reached Kimberly Cheney, who'd been in the Navy in San Diego and gone to Yale? I acknowledged those facts to be so, and she went on to say something like, "Oh, I was born on December 15th and wonder if I'm related to you." The thought flitted through my mind that the person calling may be my daughter. "I don't know," I answered. "What year and where were you born?"

"In California, in 1960," she answered, removing any lingering doubts.

"Hmm, well, you could be related," I ventured.

"Were you in the Navy in San Diego about then?" she asked again.

"Yes," I acknowledged.

"Did you release a child for adoption in 1960?" she asked.

"Yes, I did. How did you know?"

"This is Amy, your daughter!" the happy woman blurted.

"Amazing you're calling today!" I said. "It's my son's birthday. I've always wondered about you on that day." The conversation went on from there. I was stunned. I had stored deeply in my subconscious the idea that one day, my daughter would find me and end my sorrow at having a child I thought I would never know. I told her I had hoped for years that she would find me. We exchanged expressions of our mutual happiness in finding one another. Amy said she'd been searching for me for years and had finally obtained my phone number from the Yale Alumni Association. We talked for maybe half an hour, in a disjointed way, about where we lived, how we could connect in person, and what we were doing with our lives. Before hanging up, we made plans to talk again soon.

About six months later, I flew to San Francisco to meet her. It was the only purpose of my trip. We met at Baker Beach under the Golden Gate Bridge. She was attending college (My mother later flew by herself to attend Amy's graduation ceremony, sitting alone in the hot sun as penance for urging me to marry Barbara despite my guilty feelings about Amy's pending birth). At Baker Beach I met a fit, athletic-looking young woman with brown hair, blue eyes, a large, roundish face, and what appeared to be a Cheney nose—no doubt, she was my child. We hugged and talked in a somewhat guarded way about our lives, took some pictures, and agreed to meet again after we got to know each other. I returned to San Francisco a couple of times, so we did, indeed, become better acquainted.

On my second trip, we met in the small house of one of her friends. We took seats on a couch, and suddenly she flung herself into my arms, hugging and crying with joy. I was embarrassed to be hugged so completely by a young woman I didn't know. I expect she, too, was anxious and agitated. We began discussing our feelings about this reunion, and I told her I felt sorrow over what had happened, but did not feel guilty about having her adopted, given the circumstances at the time. She said something like, "Cheer up; you will."

As we continued talking, I felt a sneeze coming on and let it out with my characteristic explosiveness. Amy again burst into sobs, leaving me confused and worried. "Kim," she said, "it's impossible to explain how that sneeze made me feel. I sneeze like that, too—loud and uncontrollable. My mother would criticize me, telling me to sneeze quietly, like a good little girl. It would humiliate me. If I'd grown up with you, I would have felt right at home, as part of the family."

This was my first exposure to what adoptees call genetic bewilderment, because no one in the family they grew up in looks like them, talks like them, moves like them, sneezes like them—which can lead to feelings of profound rejection. Then she described a "Cinderella-sweep-the-halls" kind of childhood, saying her adoptive parents had two boys of their own, to whom she was subordinated. She reported other unhappy experiences, and she'd been right—I did feel guilty. Soon I, too, was in tears. From that day forward, serious discussions about adoption can bring me to tears.

I learned much later that she found me through her adoptive mother's doctor, who coincidentally had been consulted by Amy's mother, Mary Jane, seeking an abortion. Amy went to Sacramento, where she'd been born, and by mistake a clerk handed over her original birth certificate. She was recorded as "Baby Jane Doe." Jane was Mary Jane's middle name. With the information on the original birth certificate, which would have been a treasure for many adoptees, she was able to find me and, later, Mary Jane. Sometime later, she changed her name to Amy Jane Cheney, taking a first name from her adoptive family and one from each of her other families.

After Amy found me, I became deeply involved in adoption issues. Frequently, each person in the triad of birth parents, adoptive parents, and adoptees experiences mental-health consequences. There's the platitude that adoption is "A Happy Ending for All," but it seldom is when it's the result of unwanted pregnancy. Birth parents often struggle with life-long feelings of loss; adoptive parents often fear their child would leave them for the birth parent if the chance presented itself, and adoptees can suffer from profound rejection. Reunions of birth parents and their adopted children are often fraught with pain and futile attempts at deep reconciliation. These relationships, which result in what I call "discrete mental-health issues" can be extraordinarily complex. The subject is fully explored in the book, *Birth Bond*, by Gediman and Brown, New Horizons Press, Far Hills, New Jersey (1989).

Beginning in 1985 or so, during my own struggle and attempts to understand the spectrum of intense feelings that birth parents, adoptive parents, and adoptees have, I attended several local and national conferences on the subject. At one American Adoption Conference, at question time, I took the microphone and said I was interested in opening all sealed records on adoption, and asked if any Vermonters were present. Marjorie Garfield of Calais, a town just north of Montpelier, came over to introduce herself and to say she was an adoptee interested in open adoption records.

We discussed my feelings about being a birth father and hers about being adopted. When we returned to Vermont, we met a few times to discuss these personal issues, how the existing laws and practices impacted each member of the triad, and what could or should be done about it. Marge, about ten years younger than I and a freelance photographer, was a passionate advocate for the adoptee's right to know her birth parents' identities, a subject Amy had schooled me on. Marge was active in various local Vermont adoptee and birth parent support groups, to which she introduced me. I began to immerse myself in what was becoming a movement. We became determined to lift the secrecy that enshrouded adoptions, so that adoptees could find their biological parents.

The problem is, unwanted pregnancies were regarded as shameful experiences, especially for women, and many wanted their secrets to be kept. Sometimes, birth fathers, men unlike me, also wanted a lid on records. As for the adoptees, the unwitting product of the birth parents' decisions, we felt they should have the choice to find or not find their biological parents. The biological parents had a choice when they risked unwanted pregnancy, but they should not also have the choice to punish their child with life-long ignorance of his or her origin.

There are other problems with adoption. To name a few: back in the day, birth fathers were not contacted and asked for consent to relinquish their child; occasionally, adoptive parents seek to undo an adoption when the child has an undisclosed or unknown disability; birth parents may want visiting rights with their discovered child; and same-sex adoptions may be anathema to some. Drawing on my legislative experience with FPAC, sometime around 1990, we successfully pushed the legislature to create the Adoption Reform Task Force, composed of legislators, judges, triad members, and advocates in the social services field whose purpose was to propose a complete revision of the Vermont adoption law. I was designated the chairperson.

Many years before, lawyers across the country advocating for consistent national laws relating to adoption helped form what was known as the Commission on Uniform Laws. The commission held conferences to which states sent delegates who worked to propose uniform laws to be enacted by each state. Marge and I read a recent uniform law proposal for a comprehensive adoption law which appeared to address most of the matters that concerned us, so we used the uniform proposal as a template for legislative adjustments here in Vermont.

I gained some notoriety in this effort, and at one point was quoted on the front page of the *Burlington Free Press* as saying adoption amounted to a system of lies designed to shield members of the triad from awareness of potential serious emotional issues arising out of adoption. I urged full disclosure of these potential problems. I and other members of the reform commission went to legislative hearings, gave press interviews, and consulted with affected agencies to promote our proposed law. We tried to persuade the legislature to remove all secrecy surrounding the identity of birth parents, but were opposed in that effort by, among others, the Vermont Commission on Women, a state agency promoting women's rights and opportunities.

Though we didn't get everything we hoped for, the legislature in 1996—almost ten years after I started work on this issue—came through with a 125-page law that corrected many problems in the patchwork system of previous band-aid measures. Significant changes, all of which were controversial, included allowing same-sex couples to adopt, even if unmarried. For adoptions prior to July of 1986 a provision was made for either adoptees or birth parents to petition the probate court to inquire of the other if they wanted to be identified, and if so, to make it possible. For later adoptions, disclosure would be ordered unless there was an affirmative objection, or if the court later found, after hearing, that disclosure would be likely to cause harm to a person. Adoptee siblings were also included in the disclosure provision. In addition, a state registry would be created of all adoptions, making identification possible if ordered by the court. Opposition to disclosure was principally motivated by a feminist perspective that the privacy rights of birthmothers outweighed any needs of the adoptee. On the other hand, father's rights were significantly expanded. The bill was a start, and produced many improvements in the law.

I was rewarded with many expressions of gratitude, especially from birth mothers, for acknowledging their emotional pain. The one from adoptee Marge was truly wonderful, expressing how hard this work was. She wrote: I feel privileged that I was close enough to witness how you moved with grace and artistry, through the rocks and hard places of the process. You were indeed an inspiration to me, and you were what kept me going, kept me able to pull myself through the impossibly difficult times, when I thought all hope was lost and felt my spirit being crushed. You always knew what to do . . . The 'death march' was a good metaphor for this; you tirelessly leading the charge; I draggin' my weary ass up the mountain—pushing, ever pushing—until it was done.

One day, during a break in a court hearing, a teary-eyed court reporter called me to her work table to pour out her thanks to me for expressing how it felt to give up a child for adoption. And to my surprise, a secretary I'd had for a short time while doing adoption work, who'd left for another job, wrote me a letter telling how empowering it was for her to be in the office at the time changes were coming. She said my work gave her freedom to open up about her sadness and shame for giving away a child.

Ben with Brother Eric and me

Family Developments

Around this time, Ben, who is dyslexic, was failing badly in Montpelier public schools. He needed help. Dorothy and I obtained an excellent diagnosis of his educational challenges, and in 1986 enrolled him in The Greenwood School in Putney, Vermont, the premier private school for dyslexic boys. This experience virtually saved his life. In public school, he'd felt stupid, alone, and worthless, but at Greenwood, he learned he was smart, creative, and could master his disability.

With Ben away at school for two years, Dorothy and I decided to divorce, without rancor. We agreed that I would be the primary caretaker for Ben, who would live with me after he graduated from Greenwood School, entered Montpelier High School, or went on to college. My two girls, Alison and Margreta, had already gone off to college. Dorothy, a positive helpmate in their early adolescence, returned to live in her house in Warren. We were grateful to each other for making Ben possible and for helping to make his life meaningful. I was grateful to both of my ex-wives for agreeing that I would be the primary caretaker for my children. And we all strove to remain connected.

In 1995, at the celebration following my daughter Alison's second wedding, at a party held in New Jersey, my two ex-wives danced enthusiastically with each other as they shared their joy at Alison's good fortune. All my children, including Amy, came. So did Barbara's relinquished daughter, Deena. Everyone applauded what amounted to still another new beginning. It was a remarkable celebration indeed, of hope and understanding, that took a lot of work and insight on everyone's part to make possible.

When I invited my secretary to a party at my office celebrating passage of the Adoption Reform Act, I got a surprise. She'd helped format and prepare many documents for that effort, and after the party, sent me an emotional note of thanks. She began by saying that, when she'd come to work for the firm, she'd been struggling to come to terms with having been a birth mother, and had been corresponding inconclusively with her daughter about having a personal meeting. To her surprise, she wrote, what she found was ". . . adoption reform swirling around me at work. I only half-listened. I only half-wanted to know." She went on to write: "In February, I found I was *almost* there, *just* about ready to meet my daughter. But it was after telling my story to you, you sharing yours, and hearing you say, 'You've got to meet her! What are you waiting for?' that gave me the final push to set a date—and it was done. And meeting Susan (Kimberly Ann) was truly one of the most rewarding days of my life. Seeing, touching, hugging her . . . seeing her smile, and hearing her own voice tell me she understood meant the world to me. It was a dream—knowing. I can only imagine what you've done for all the people at the party tonight, not to mention those you don't know but who *are* and *will be* touched in the future through your tireless devotion—I applaud you."

I was surprised! And, of course, I was pleased that she'd begun to come to an understanding of her life which I had helped to initiate.

A decade later, my friends and Barbara Smith's friends conspired to bring us together. It was subtle. My friends would say things like, "Kim you look kinda lonely; we know someone you ought to meet, and we've told her so." Her friends, who'd given her loving support after her second husband died of pancreatic cancer, said, "Barb, you look kinda lonely; we know someone you really ought to meet, and we've told him so." Barb and I met for lunch one day, to get acquainted. I found a woman slightly younger than me, who'd had her share of life's challenges and experiences. She'd been married twice and had two grown children. Most importantly, she had a deep understanding that a compassionate life is happier than a judgmental one.

Soon, without the help of lobsters or similar aphrodisiac, we decided to live together as an experiment for the future. One of my non-lawyer projects

during this period was to build a kayak suitable for carrying my dog and me along the surface of Vermont's ponds.

On the day of its scheduled launching in 2007, I proposed to Barbara that I have a ceremony of some sort marking my year's work and that she should be a witness and maybe break a champagne bottle over the bow. She agreed. But it was a setup. Unbeknown to her, I'd decided to make a double-launching: of a boat and of a new life for both of us. I got the boat onto Molly's Pond in Marshfield with my dog, Mombassa, aboard, paddled a short distance and then to shore, where Barb was waiting. Making sure I had her attention, I raised my sign. She accepted and we were married on the lawn of the Big House in Keene Valley, on July 11, 2007.

I enjoyed attending reunions to hang out and share memories with my old roommates, friends, and their spouses. At my thirtieth college reunion, the Yale Alumni Association wanted to impress on us that Yale remained a vital institution devoted to molding leaders in many fields for the future, and so assembled a group of bright undergraduates to tell us about their experiences at Yale and their hopes for the future. About 150 of us met at the principal lecture hall in the medical school to hear what they had to say. The audience was mostly elderly graduates. At age fifty-two, I was on the young side. Perhaps ten students from various majors, such as physics, literature, art, biology, and engineering were given the stage for about five minutes each, to introduce themselves and talk about their work and interests.

One student, who was in his senior year and had earned honors as a biology major, talked passionately about his college experience. He'd graduated from a Midwestern high school with honors in biology, which helped him get into Yale where he found exciting professors and challenges. He concluded by saying, "I'm doing real research with some of the most renowned faculty in the world. I'm amazed at how much I've learned and how helpful the professors are. We may discover and isolate the genes that cause Downs Syndrome. It is an inspiration to be here."

Questions from the alumni were invited. Flushed by the excitement of the student's presentation, one old grad commented, "Wow, that was a wonderful statement! I'm impressed by what the college has done for you. What are you going to do next?"

The student was ready for that question and said immediately, "I'm going to law school." The crowd initially sat in stunned silence, then spontaneously let out a groan of disappointment, if not disgust, that filled the room. The idea that a student with such a promising mind would abandon a career developing social progress to become, of all things, a lawyer—champion of all things petty and corrupt—was preposterous. Silence descended upon the stricken crowd until one greybeard graduate yelled, "Why?" The question was anticipated, so the answer came quickly.

"Because I've learned that all science is merely an argument," the student announced, evidently proud of himself for sharing what he considered profound insight.

The audience's and the student's responses frequently come to mind. The groan expressed a common view of the public toward lawyers, fostered by lawyer jokes. It also revealed a collective and understandable concern that a great young mind was ruling out a profession in which he might make amazing discoveries for the good of many. Yet, it would be easy to find some truth in the student's view. Much of the history of science demonstrates that discovery is only validated after long and tedious arguments overcoming biases, world view, economic interests, and in some cases religion. Galileo's argument that the earth revolves around the sun is one example. Charles Darwin's theory of evolution is another. Climate change is still another, today.

At least in theory, scientific discovery is made by analyzing evidence free of any biases that might be rooted in a conventionally accepted world view of what the evidence should prove. The results of scientific discoveries are scientific "facts" that scientists must consider in making still new scientific discoveries.

The legal system in America also places a premium on facts. Law schools teach the need for rigorous mastery of complex facts held together by compelling storylines that resist easy dismissal by contradiction or additional, countervailing facts. A lawyer confronts an opposing argument by showing the argument is based on a suspect world view, or faulty or weak judicial precedent, or faulty analysis, or "facts" that are not really facts at all. A lawyer making a case in court is much like the scientist making a discovery, then pushing for its acceptance.

So, perhaps the student was right. Perhaps science depends more on argument than we might guess. Both science and the field of law exist in a world of conflict and debate. Both scientists and lawyers live or die by force of marshalled facts, artfully presented and strongly advocated.

But the alumni groaned. Their groan grew out of stereotypical thinking that contentious bickering is the hallmark of lawyering—a sentiment that admittedly has some truth, but ignores the larger truth that such "bickering" or arguing mirrors the very fabric of our political and social world. The practice of law at least attempts to resolve these struggles by reason and peaceful means—a nice alternative to a swing of the sword.

I was encouraged by hearing the young Yale student voice his insight. A restless focused mind is an asset in any profession, and I would welcome that student into the law profession. Or I would applaud his decision if he were to return to his scientific studies. Either way, he would be well-armed with critical thinking.

I took one road—I happened to choose the legal profession, which has done much to foster life, liberty, and the pursuit of happiness. It requires absorption of facts, demands concrete thinking, and provides opportunity for mental combat. I have been privileged to be part of an amazing band of brothers and sisters.

Epilogue:

Vermont State Police – The Undoing

"As far as the events leading up to this [Lawrence Affair], I know for a lot of people this could be described as a tragedy and nothing less than that. I would have to say, in my opinion, all of it was avoidable and was avoidable right from the outset. As far as I could tell there was a very substantial question at the outset that the Vermont State Police were seriously in cahoots with Lawrence or their lab, which enabled Lawrence to operate in the fashion that he did."

Robert Gensburg, Giroux Report to Governor Salmon, 1976

The Lawrence Affair oppressed me both personally and professionally for several years. On a professional level, I was appalled that so many innocent people had been convicted of crimes. On a personal level, I'd known what had to be done to prevent or lessen the impact of Paul Lawrence's crimes, gave orders to do so, but was misled into thinking the plan was operational. What needed to be done was to arrange for an undercover police officer to investigate the integrity of his methods and the truth of his claims. When Lawrence was finally arrested, I regretted not having pushed State Police Commissioner Edward Corcoran harder to investigate him, and I blamed myself for being naive. Why had I believed the state police would do what they'd agreed to, in a timely fashion? Had I pushed harder and been more aware, perhaps fewer people would have suffered; and possibly, I might even have been reelected attorney general.

But then came the investigations into the Lawrence Affair and repercussions for the Vermont State Police. After six investigations—one coming after a despairing state police officer shot and killed himself at the statehouse entrance, and another completed even after the assistant attorney general doing the investigation was told by the incoming attorney general he would be fired if he released his report—it was evident that nothing I could have done would have moved the state police, under Corcoran, to expose Lawrence prior to his arrest.

The first investigation occurred in 1975. That year, in the wake of Lawrence's arrest, the legislature's House Appropriations Committee held a hearing to determine what went wrong. Its conclusion was that the management structure of the state police organization shared much blame for Lawrence's crimes, writing:

> The major problem of the Department of Public Safety (state police) lies in the area of personnel management. Those now running the department are imbued with an outdated philosophy of police management (as they view) troopers as enlistees subject to their unchecked command and having few personal rights. *This philosophy ends to incline the department's leadership to act in secrecy with continual hints of retribution to those expressing discontent* [emphasis mine].

A more specific description of the command attitude is that state police would allow no outside scrutiny. Manifestation of this policy were evident in personnel management: if the top brass (commissioner, deputy, and division heads) determined there was conduct by subordinates contrary to internal management protocols, even criminal misconduct whose public exposure would discredit "The Force," discipline would be administered out of public view to protect the image of the force. The degree and form of punishment would be determined at the whim of the commissioner, without public hearings or witnesses. Punishment typically involved reassigning an offender to unwelcome duty far from his present work site, forcing the trooper to leave home, possibly move family, and undertake unwelcome duty. Offenders usually would resign rather than suffer such inconvenience. This outcome was fortunate for the offender and the image of the state police, because this "voluntary" action meant there was nothing derogatory in the personnel files. The committee did not examine the etiology of this practice. My personal view is that police work brings criticism from so many aspects of society—criminals, conservatives, liberals, judges, legislators, and political activists—that it's a self-protective reflex. This problem of unaccountability was exacerbated by instability of state police leadership during a six-year period, from 1975-1981, when the department was headed by five different commissioners.

The next investigation, in 1976, was conducted by a commission appointed by Governor Thomas Salmon to help determine who and whether to pardon people convicted of crimes by Lawrence's testimony. The Rev. Raymond Giroux, a Catholic priest who was chair of the State Parole Board, headed the commission which came to be called the Giroux Commission. Salmon personally appointed attorney Robert Gensburg (whom I met when he resigned as Caledonia State's Attorney, after seeing the horrors of Windsor prison in 1968) as lead investigator, who in turn was assisted by a dogged state police investigator, Robert Army. Army had a reputation as a passionate searcher for the truth, regardless of who might be embarrassed. The Giroux investigation proved that Corcoran had ample reason to fire Lawrence for his conduct when Lawrence was a state trooper; and if he had done so, it's unlikely Lawrence would have been hired by any other police agency.

The Giroux Report documented two good reasons why Corcoran should have fired Lawrence and made record of doing so. In 1970, M. Jerome Diamond, then Windham County State's Attorney, told state police he would not prosecute any cases brought by Lawrence, who at the time had been working as an undercover narcotics officer. The reason for that action by Diamond, cited in the Giroux Report as case 201, was that Lawrence had once given sworn statements placing himself at two different locations, making two different drug buys simultaneously. The Giroux Report also revealed that, in September 1971, Lawrence was "accused of assaulting a manacled prisoner, by beating him on the head with a flashlight as well as by beating him while two other officers were attempting to subdue him." The reporting officer said Lawrence was "unnecessarily rough." Lawrence's behavior in firing shots into a building to simulate a gun battle with burglars, as detailed by the Champlain Security Report, was also noted.

But Lawrence was permitted to resign. He was never charged with a crime or violation of any police protocols. He received an "outstanding" rating in his final performance evaluation, dated December 7, 1971. True to the culture of the state police, Commissioner Corcoran signed off on this evaluation, even though there was dissent. One police captain, who was

Lawrence's supervisor, recommended Lawrence be fired. Neither incident appeared in Lawrence's private personnel file or any public document, and the Giroux Report concluded that these omissions permitted Lawrence's later employment in St. Albans, and the debacle that followed.

The report detailed Lawrence's criminal behavior during his stint with the St. Albans Police Department, and recommended pardons in seventy-one of the eighty-three convictions involving Lawrence. Since Lawrence had not been a state police officer at the time he worked in St Albans, the state police had no operational authority over him or his conduct. Nevertheless, state police Corporal Stanley Merriam had been assigned to the St. Albans area during that time—which was consistent with department policy of having officers present at operations of public interest so as to establish the state police, not local authorities, as the leaders in law enforcement.

The Giroux Commission's investigator, Gensburg, spread the blame even further, having found "a hundred examples of poor St. Albans police practices," including the fact that there were "no written reports, telephone logs and radio logs" to help track citizens' complaints and police conduct. Gensburg also reported "[n]either George Hebert, chief of St. Albans Police Department, nor State's Attorney Ronald Kilburn, nor former State's Attorney E. Michael McGinn, nor Assistant Attorney General William Keefe had sufficient knowledge about the substance and procedure of police undercover drug law enforcement to properly supervise Lawrence's activities."

Gensburg specifically noted that Keefe "had sufficient information about the questionable nature of Lawrence's personal history and police activities for careful inquiry into these matters, which was never carried out." Merriam had been assigned to St. Albans supposedly to monitor any such shortcomings. There is no record of Commissioner Corcoran ever asking for such information or that any report was ever submitted.

As to Lawrence himself, the Giroux Commission found many cases in which Lawrence simply lied about buying drugs from the suspects whom he'd never met. Gensburg concluded that many of the drugs Lawrence said he confiscated actually came from drug samples he received from the New York State Police laboratory when he was police chief in Vergennes, Vermont. Such samples, in kits, were prepared to help train other officers in identifying certain illegal drugs. Vergennes officers said they never saw such a kit. Lawrence then would obtain "buy money" from local police departments, and used the drugs and money to frame young people in St. Albans and elsewhere. On at least seven occasions, charges were filed against people with whom he had no contact whatsoever.

Gensburg's comments in the Giroux Report went so far as to say he suspected the Vermont State Police were "in cahoots" with Lawrence, implying that perhaps Vermont's own state police lab assisted Lawrence in some improper way. Gensburg's separate report did not contain any rigorous investigation into this possible aspect of the case. But Gensburg clearly stated that Merriam had reason to know Lawrence was crooked. On May 21, 1974, a Franklin County part-time deputy sheriff, James King, told Merriam he'd searched a drawer in a suspect's house, turned the drawers over on a bed, found nothing, and returned the drawers to the nightstand from which they'd been removed. Lawrence entered the room, looked in the same drawer, and found drugs. But Merriam told King not to tell anyone about this. Merriam insisted he was a state trooper and knew what to do. King did as he was told. Merriam was certainly "in cahoots" with Lawrence. Army uncovered documents validating my request, that Corcoran agreed to, to have an undercover investigation of Lawrence, which he then failed to do. Given the close relationship between Gensburg and Army, I conclude Gensburg knew of this dereliction of duty.

Lawrence's arrest, and state police inaction concerning Merriam, became the basis for further investigations into state police misconduct. Immediately after Lawrence's arrest in July 1974, I directed Assistant Attorney General Bill Keefe to conduct an inquest and interrogate both Merriam and King concerning King's account of discovering Lawrence's criminal behavior and being told to "shut up" by Merriam. King maintained his accusation, which Merriam denied. I then ordered Keefe to coordinate with the state police to give polygraph exams to the men. Both agreed to be tested and were polygraphed by an operator from the Maine State Police, selected by Corcoran. King was found to be truthful; Merriam's denial was determined to be deceitful. The test outcome, when correlated with seven known Lawrence operations of complete fabrication, would appear to remove any doubt that Merriam had lied under oath at the inquest.

Polygraphs are based on operator judgment regarding the graphic tracing of bodily functions of a tested person. The theoretical basis is that mendacity in answering an incriminating question, when compared with answers to control questions where facts are known, such as the subject's home address and birthday, will cause alterations in heartbeat, sweat, breathing, and other functions that are recorded on a graph. Variations can mean lying. In theory, trained operators will come to similar conclusions from reading the graphs alone. Standard polygraph technique requires the operator to question the subject for an explanation as to why certain graphs showed possible deception. This process is called "verification of the instrument." Often, skilled interrogation by the polygraph operator of already-apprehensive subjects about questionable graph findings can result in admissions of deceit. Merriam refused to submit to the "verification" process. A reasonable deduction is that he did not want to further incriminate himself; not participating fully in the test was better than invoking the protections of the Fifth Amendment. Even though polygraph tests are not admissible in court, they are an important tool frequently relied upon by police agencies in investigations.

The Vermont State Police took no disciplinary action against Merriam. Instead, he was promoted. The polygraph results, however, became the "damned spot" state police command could not wash out. The Merriam polygraph results were placed in a file drawer in the office of the second-in-command of the state police, Maj. Glenn Davis, in a plain, unmarked envelope. But the standard practice at the department at the time was to maintain any polygraphs in a secure dedicated file for later review. The results of any test given to or by state police would then be available for review when an officer is considered for promotion or sensitive reassignment. Davis contended the report was flawed because Merriam did not submit to "verification," yet he drew no inference from Merriam's refusal. Corcoran did know of Merriam's polygraph result. Indeed, he sent me a copy of it while I was attorney general.

Corcoran resigned as commissioner as a result of public concern over the Lawrence Affair. But before doing so, in 1977, he assigned Merriam to be the "outpost officer" in Lamoille County. "Outpost officer" was the title given to the state trooper assigned to be the state's lead law-enforcement officer in a particular county. He was expected to bring high-quality police help and guidance to local police and sheriffs' departments. Merriam brought just the opposite.

In December 1977 the Hardwick police chief, Michael Lauzon, was involved in a traffic accident. State Trooper Kenneth Strong, a subordinate of Merriam, determined the chief was driving drunk, but decided not to press charges. Merriam supported this action even though, during the investigation, Lauzon admitted to drinking at least six beers before getting into his car. Merriam gave the state's attorney, Scott McGee, his reasons for failing to charge Lauzon. Chief among them was his claim there was no evidence of intoxication. But McGee became suspicious, believing Merriam had not told the truth about what happened. Instead, McGee figured Merriam was concealing favorable treatment of a fellow police officer.

McGee had heard comments about Merriam's part in the Lawrence Affair, prompting him to ask Gensburg about Merriam's integrity. Gensburg told him of the polygraph report and where it was located. McGee obtained a copy of it from the Franklin District Court in St Albans, where it had been filed under seal and could only be obtained by permission of the presiding judge. Once he saw the report, McGee was even more concerned about Merriam's honesty in the Lauzon DWI case. McGee followed up by informing the new commissioner, Francis Lynch, that he would not prosecute any cases originated by Merriam, or any cases in which Merriam had participated. McGee's action threatened both to scuttle the outpost program and to further denigrate the Vermont State Police.

Lynch's response was to initiate his own probes. He assigned detectives to investigate whether the Hardwick chief was, in fact, guilty of drunk driving, but he also engaged two investigators from the Connecticut State Police to investigate McGee, to determine if he had improper motives for attacking Merriam. Incensed, McGee again consulted Gensburg, and then-Caledonia State's Attorney Dale Gray, to determine how to meet this threat. They decided to bring the conflict to the attention of Governor Richard Snelling.

On May 1, 1978, Snelling's counsel, William Gilbert, met with Commissioner Lynch, Attorney General M. Jerome Diamond, and State's Attorneys McGee and Gray. The Merriam polygraph report was distributed at the meeting. As a result of the meeting, Snelling ordered that all state police files relating to Merriam be impounded, copied, and inspected by his counsel, William Gilbert. None of the files gathered contained any record or copy of Merriam's polygraph in the Lawrence case. The governor also ordered Lynch to submit to an investigation by the attorney general into the entire controversy, including why the Merriam polygraph results were concealed. Lynch said he had no prior knowledge of the polygraph, and, in any event, did not believe in polygraphs.

In the course of his investigation, Diamond asked Lynch for various documents, which were not forthcoming. Gilbert forcefully reminded Lynch he was obligated to cooperate. In May 1979, Lynch, although familiar with the polygraph reports and delinquent in his own reports, wrote Snelling that he found no basis to take action against Merriam. Moreover, he said he would allow Merriam to take the exam for promotion to state police lieutenant.

Diamond continued his investigation. His report to the governor, issued the following month, raised questions about why the Merriam polygraph was hidden, suggesting intentional wrongdoing by Lynch for not taking action against Merriam and being hostile to investigations conducted by state police officers. Diamond also noted where other responsible officers unconvincingly denied knowledge of the polygraph report. He said state police commanders were hostile to any outside investigations of police officers and would likely conceal any known wrongdoing.

The catastrophic results of this "outdated management philosophy" became publicly apparent the following month. On July 24, 1979, Snelling fired Lynch, saying he'd lost confidence in him. He felt Lynch had lied about his knowledge of the Merriam polygraph and that he had stonewalled the investigation in other ways. Six days later, a state police corporal, Howard Gould, shot and killed himself in the entrance to the statehouse. He had been a good, honest cop (found to be so by subsequent investigation). Gould left a suicide note, saying, "I hope you all sleep well tonight." Gould's family did not release the full text of Gould's suicide note, so it is unknown to whom Gould's note referred. The family, however, quickly reported that the comment did not refer to Governor Snelling's firing of Lynch. The public was left to speculate as to what exactly drove Gould to suicide.

Though fired, Lynch, in a display of arrogance, donned his uniform and marched into his office for work, announcing that he would sue Snelling to keep his job, asserting the governor didn't have the authority to fire him. His argument: although he was appointed by the governor, he was confirmed by the state Senate, so only the Senate could fire him. Diamond swiftly obtained a court order removing Lynch from office.

Snelling then named Warren Cone, a Woodstock, Vermont, native and U.S. Navy Rear Admiral, as the interim commissioner. Cone began an investigation, parallel with Diamond's, into the Lamoille County imbroglio. Then, in an attempt to get to the bottom of things and end the state police scandal once and for all, Snelling ordered still another investigation, this one by a "blue ribbon" committee, headed by the highly regarded former Supreme Court Justice F. Ray Keyser, Sr. The Keyser Commission was tasked to determine if Diamond's and Cone's investigations were both accurate. The Keyser Report, filed in April 1980, concluded that the attorney general's report (and Cone's separate investigation) condemning Lynch's handling of the missing Merriam polygraph and the Police Chief Lauzon coverup by Merriam were substantially accurate. The report also concurred that McGee had legitimate concerns about Merriam's integrity and that various senior state police officers had ignored Merriam's unacceptable actions, failing to discipline him.

The Keyser Report urged sensible and long overdue reforms in state police management and internal investigation protocol, as the Giroux Report and the 1975 House Committee had done before. The report called for more sensible and transparent disciplinary measures than the punitive reassignment of duties. It said the state police had a bias against investigating wrongdoing among its officers, and that it was inclined to distort or cover up any reports of misconduct for fear of bad publicity. Following the Keyser Report, Merriam agreed to a disciplinary reduction in rank to corporal, although many officers believed he should have been fired. The Keyser Report also recommended these reforms, which the legislature eventually passed laws to implement:

1. Regulations be written to establish what actions by officers are subject to discipline in order to end personal vendettas.

2. Due-process hearings regarding disciplinary actions be available to the accused, including use of subpoenas for witnesses at disciplinary hearings.

3. An independent office for internal investigations be created.

4. Records be kept of all disciplinary complaints and outcomes.

5. A civilian review board be created to periodically review such records.

6. Actions be taken to prevent bickering and competition among different police agencies.

Cpl. Gould's suicide, painful as it was for his family and shocking as it was for the state, immediately raised new questions about state police competency and the department's standards of behavior. Caledonia County State's Attorney Gray and Attorney General Diamond soon learned that Gould's suicide was an outgrowth of what came to be called the "Router Bit Affair." This affair involved the theft of router bits (small, precision-woodworking tools) by a deputy sheriff trainee, Nelson Charron, whom Gould supervised. Charron, when he wasn't policing, worked in a Caledonia County factory that manufactured the tools, and was permitted to take defective bits, known as "seconds," for his own use.

Charron frequently passed some of them on to state troopers as gifts, which was legal and fine, until he soon began taking "firsts," that is, quality bits, and passing them on to troopers as gifts as well. In theory, some officers would have been guilty of receiving stolen property had they known Charron stole them, although there was never conclusive evidence they knew this. Still, the very possibility that state police officers had received stolen property was troubling.

Another blow to the integrity of the state police occurred when state police top command falsely blamed subordinates for failure to investigate the thefts and punish the guilty. News and rumors travel quickly in a small rural community, like St. Johnsbury, especially those of misbehavior by state police. Sergeant David Reed, the senior officer in the area and Gould's supervisor, without direction by superior officers, began an investigation into the circumstances surrounding the thefts and the gifting. For unexplained reasons, during this process Reed falsely told a state senator from Caledonia County, Gerald Morse, that the FBI was also looking into the matter. Morse passed this information to Snelling, who asked Commissioner Cone for details. Meanwhile, Caledonia State's Attorney Dale Gray, on his own, initiated an inquest to interrogate troopers about their possible knowledge of receiving "firsts." This inquest was the apparent trigger for Gould's suicide. He didn't testify, but being summoned to appear and possibly being observed at the courthouse may have created concerns that he'd done something wrong. Anxiety would certainly have increased when details of the inquest were leaked, certainly not by Gould, to the press, including accounts indicating some of Gould's subordinates may have been thieves.

Why did Gould kill himself? It is a fair assumption that he feared being accused of either theft or a coverup, or of inaction that allowed further tarnishing of the reputation of the state police, an organization he admired greatly and was proud to serve.

Gray's inquest was an "outside investigation," as the state police called such probes other than their own, and was disturbing to state police command. Commissioner Cone's response (a throwback to prior management behavior) was twofold: he brought disciplinary charges against Reed for discussing the investigation with Senator Morse, for not swiftly investigating and punishing delinquent officers, and for creating bad publicity for the state police; and he launched an investigation into Gray to determine if the county prosecutor was having an affair with a female trooper assigned as investigator to Gray's office. Meanwhile, only one person was criminally charged in the Router Bit Affair: Charron, who pleaded guilty to theft.

These responses enraged, rather than satisfied Diamond and Gray. They did not think the possible culpability and punishment of officers who'd had no, or even peripheral, involvement in the Router Bit Affair had been fairly evaluated. In addition, I suspect Diamond believed, because of his electoral rivalry with Snelling, the Republican incumbent wanted to suppress any further state police investigations that might give Diamond favorable publicity while also riling top state police management. Diamond pressed on, appointing Assistant Attorney General David S. Putter to do a full investigation in criminal culpability, and to assess whether the disciplinary measures meted out by the top commanders were actually warranted or were made simply to improve the image of the state police. This "outside investigation" took the usual prosecutorial course, convening another inquest which involved subpoenaing many police officers to testify under oath.

Putter, as usual, had trouble getting information from the state police. He subpoenaed ten of the involved officers—all along the chain of command— to testify. His aim was to examine the various troopers' possible liability for criminal conduct, or, if there were no criminal violations, to determine whether department regulations prohibiting officers from accepting gifts had been violated, and finally, whether disciplinary actions imposed were justified. It took Putter the remainder of 1979, and until the end of 1980, to complete his 200-page report. He and Diamond concluded that no charges should be brought against troopers, because there was no proof they knew "firsts" were stolen, or even that they knew "firsts" were distinguishable from "seconds." They also concluded that Sgt. Reed, who'd been punished by the commissioner for failing to carry out orders to properly investigate possible criminality in the transfer of the router bits, had never actually been ordered to do so. They recommended he be given a full due process hearing to determine his culpability, or whether it was a cover-up by "top brass" to excuse their own inaction. (A hearing was later held, in which Reed was exonerated.)

Meanwhile, Diamond's term as attorney general was to expire in January 1981. He lost the November 1980 election to Snelling, and a Republican, John Easton, was to replace him as attorney general. Soon, both Snelling and Easton attempted to suppress Putter's (and Diamond's) report, Easton going so far as to let Putter know he would be fired if the report were released. Nevertheless, Putter and Diamond worked hard to complete the report while Diamond still had a few weeks in office. Then, on January 7, 1981, the last day of Diamond's term, the report was publicly released. As promised, Putter was fired on the first day of John Easton's tenure.

The complete report was printed in the *Burlington Free Press*, over several days. It detailed many instances of officers being wrongfully punished for failure to investigate, when in fact, management had set a policy of silence and cover-up.

Among officers exonerated of neglect-of-duty in failing to investigate were Nelson Lay and Edward Fish, both of whom I'd worked with as state's attorney and came to respect. Lay, who was the area barracks commander, was improperly punished for not ordering a prompt investigation into the gifting of the router bits. He was transferred from Lamoille County to work in traffic control in Washington County, which required he make a 130-mile daily drive to work. He was also compelled to take early retirement in lieu of being dismissed without recourse, thereby losing his pension. Putter found no culpability on Lay's part. Lt. Fish was also unfairly punished.

The Putter Report, ordered by Diamond, was a superb factual and precise chronicle of corruption and incompetence in state police management. Soon after taking office, Easton reconsidered his opposition to the report and supported its conclusion, although he didn't rehire Putter. Finally, on February 4, 1981, another new state police commissioner, Paul Philbrook, sent a note to all members of the Vermont State Police in which he noted that both Diamond and Easton concluded certain actions on Philbrook's part were required. Philbrook, however, failed to state, publicly at least, what changes were required, what charges should be brought, or what specific regulations had been violated. Philbrook did announce that the department would retain attorney Robert D. Rachlin to review the Putter-Diamond reports and make recommendations for action; the outcome of that effort was never made public. However, the overall result of the Router Bit Affair was that, in the future, police disciplinary actions were to be made public and officers would be allowed to appeal their discipline to the Vermont Labor Relations Board.

Thus, six years after the Lawrence Affair, and many investigations later, the corruption that created it was exposed and a process set in motion to prevent such things from happening again. The investigations helped explain why Corcoran lied to me and never attempted to unmask Lawrence. Long-overdue changes in state police culture that brought about the Lawrence Affair were finally implemented because of the persistence of many Vermont prosecutors and determined governors of both parties. A welcome event, indeed.

Former Attorneys General (first row, left to right):
Kimberly Cheney (R), 1973-1975; M. Jerome Diamond (D), 1975-1980;
William Sorrell (D), 1998-2017; Jeffrey Amestoy (R), 1985-1997.
Not shown: John Easton (R), 1981-1985; T. J. Donovan (D), 2016-present.

ABOUT THE AUTHOR

In 1964, Kimberly Cheney, after four years of active duty in the U. S. Navy, graduated from Yale Law School and began work in a law firm in New Haven, Conn. In 1967, with his wife Barbara and two children, Alison and Margreta, the family moved to Montpelier, Vermont, where Cheney began eight years of state government service as counsel to the Department of Education, State's Attorney of Washington County, and Attorney General during a time of social turmoil, and rapid political change. Cheney has forty three years of private practice law in Montpelier including criminal law, personal injury, and divorce, while serving on several boards and commissions leading to establishment of a functioning Public Employees Labor Relations board, helping author a complete revision of criteria for judges to determine which parent divorcing should have custody of the children, and a revision of state laws pertaining to adoption. His career of public and private practice of law illustrates a professional dedication to creative innovation for public benefit.

Also Available from Rootstock Publishing:

The Atomic Bomb on My Back
Taniguchi Sumiteru

Blue Desert
Celia Jeffries

China in Another Time: A Personal Story
Claire Malcolm Lintilhac

Fly with A Murder of Crows: A Memoir
Tuvia Feldman

The Inland Sea: A Mystery
Sam Clark

Junkyard at No Town
J.C. Myers

The Language of Liberty:
A Citizen's Vocabulary
Edwin C. Hagenstein

The Lost Grip: Poems
Eva Zimet

Lucy Dancer
Story and Illustrations by Eva Zimet

Nobody Hitchhikes Anymore
Ed Griffin-Nolan

Preaching Happiness:
Creating a Just and Joyful World
Ginny Sassaman

Red Scare in the Green Mountains:
Vermont in the McCarthy Era
1946-1960
Rick Winston

Safe as Lightning: Poems
Scudder H. Parker

Street of Storytellers
Doug Wilhelm

Tales of Bialystok: A Jewish Journey
from Czarist Russia to America
Charles Zachariah Goldberg

To the Man in the Red Suit: Poems
Christina Fulton

Uncivil Liberties: A Novel
Bernie Lambek

The Violin Family
Melissa Perley;
Illustrated by Fiona Lee Maclean

Wave of the Day: Collected Poems
Mary Elizabeth Winn

Whole Worlds Could Pass Away:
Collected Stories
Rickey Gard Diamond